TECHNOLOGY AND SOCIETY

TECHNOLOGY AND SOCIETY

Advisory Editor
DANIEL J. BOORSTIN, author of
The Americans and Director of
The National Museum of History
and Technology, Smithsonian Institution

The Story
of
Public Utilities

By
Edward Hungerford

ARNO PRESS
A NEW YORK TIMES COMPANY
New York · 1972

Reprint Edition 1972 by Arno Press Inc.

Reprinted from a copy in The Columbia
University Library

Technology and Society
ISBN for complete set: 0-405-04680-4
See last pages of this volume for titles.

Manufactured in the United States of America

––––––––––––

Library of Congress Cataloging in Publication Data

Hungerford, Edward, 1875-1948.
    The story of public utilities.

    (Technology and society)
    Reprint of the 1928 ed.
    1. Public utilites--United States. I. Title.
II. Series.
HD2766.H85 1972   363.6'0973   72-5053
ISBN 0-405-04705-3

THE UPPER FALLS OF THE GENESEE RIVER AT ROCHESTER, N. Y.

The Story
of
Public Utilities

By
Edward Hungerford

With 81 Illustrations

G. P. Putnam's Sons
New York — London
The Knickerbocker Press
1928

Made in the United States of America

FOREWORD

The Story of Public Utilities aims to give in as simple a way as possible a picture of the origin, the development, the general organization and the practical workings of the utilities which serve our cities and our country. It is written in the belief that the increasing importance of public utilities in home, industrial and civic life justifies the inclusion of such a study as a part of the supplementary work in the social studies and the science classes of our public school system.

Public utilities are natural developments and in recent years under governmental regulation have grown in this country to enormous proportions. They are business institutions which have been successful chiefly because they have been conducted on business principles. Our modern civilization has made it impossible to do without them, as today nearly every human enterprise and endeavor is in some form or other dependent upon the utilities. All rely upon them for heat, light, power, communication, transportation, water supply, etc.

This book has been prepared by Edward Hungerford, formerly a resident of Rochester and a well-known writer on travel and transportation, to supply the fundamental facts concerning public·utilities as they exist in our communities at the present time. It is intended

to supplement textbooks in science and social studies
by bringing together interesting and helpful information
that is now obtainable only in scattered articles and
small pamphlets. In this way it will add to the
effectiveness of the work now being carried on in
progressive schools.

Our future citizens should be well informed with regard to the growth and importance of these activities.
They should be familiar with the factors and forces
that have made possible our present industrial development, and they should be prepared for intelligent
participation in all those activities which are so essential
to progress. Communication and transportation furnish the means by which the people participate in the
co-operative activities of civilized society, thus leading
to the development of large communities.

Our large cities would be impossible without adequate
water supply and effective means of heating and lighting. New power developments have made possible
great manufacturing plants in our cities. Much credit
is due to the far sighted business men who have made
the plans and raised the funds for many of the great
enterprises without which modern civilization could not
exist. State and federal laws protect the interests of
the people and regulate these enterprises for the good
of all concerned.

If this book assists the youth of our city and country
in a clearer understanding of the fundamental economic,
scientific and business problems underlying the financing, operation, regulation and control of the public
utilities of this and other communities, it will have
served its purpose.

The publication of the work is in no sense a commercial venture. For this reason the copyright has been vested in the Children's Memorial Scholarship Fund, Inc., and royalties accruing from the sale of the book will be devoted to the purposes of the fund. The Children's Memorial Scholarship Fund was founded on the first anniversary of the Armistice to perpetuate the memory of Rochester heroes of the World War. It enables pupils to continue in school who would otherwise be obliged to withdraw from financial necessity.

Acknowledgment is due the various public utilities, public authorities and school officials of Rochester whose co-operation has made possible *The Story of Public Utilities*.

Mrs. Henry G. Danforth,
President, Board of Education,
Rochester, New York.

CONTENTS

CHAPTER   PAGE

I.—THE BEGINNINGS OF THE AMERICAN CITY   3

II.—PATHWAYS OF COMMUNITY TRANSPORT   .   12

III.—AMERICAN RAILROAD DEVELOPMENT—I .   24

IV.—AMERICAN RAILROAD DEVELOPMENT—II .   50

V.—OUR RAILROADS OF TODAY   .   .   .   65

VI.—THE COMING OF THE TROLLEY CAR   .   84

VII.—THE STREET RAILWAY OF TODAY   .   .   94

VIII.—THE DEVELOPMENT OF CITY LIGHTING—
ARTIFICIAL GAS   113

IX.—MANUFACTURED GAS TODAY   .   .   .   127

X.—THE DEVELOPMENT OF LIGHTING—ELEC-
TRICITY   146

XI.—MODERN ELECTRIC LIGHT AND POWER   .   164

XII.—THE STORY OF THE TELEGRAPH   .   .   187

XIII.—THE COMING OF THE TELEPHONE   .   .   217

XIV.—THE TELEPHONE TODAY .   .   .   236

XV.—MUNICIPAL UTILITIES—STREETS AND
BRIDGES   275

CONTENTS

CHAPTER   PAGE

XVI.—Municipal Utilities—Water, Sewerage
    and Parks 291

XVII.—Service Organization and Policy . 319

XVIII.—Financing and Regulating the Utilities 325

XIX.—The Future of the American City . 357

Index 365

ILLUSTRATIONS

FACING
PAGE

THE UPPER FALLS OF THE GENESEE RIVER AT
ROCHESTER, N. Y. . . . *Frontispiece*

ALBANY, FROM AN OLD FRENCH WOOD-CUT . . 4

FORT PITT, NOW THE CITY OF PITTSBURGH . . 6

PITTSBURGH IS LOCATED AT THE CONFLUENCE OF
THE ALLEGHANY AND MONONGAHELA RIVERS . 8

THE LOWER FALLS OF THE GENESEE RIVER AT
ROCHESTER, 1820 10

EARLY WOOD-CUT OF THE PORT OF ROCHESTER, NEW
YORK 12

CANALS WERE ONCE A CHIEF MEANS OF TRANSPOR-
TATION 14

THE ROCHESTER-CANANDAIGUA STAGE, 1815 . . 20

THE "COVERED WAGON," BY F. C. DARLEY . . 22

THE DE WITT CLINTON TRAIN 26

PETER COOPER'S *Tom Thumb*, THE FIRST LOCOMO-
TIVE BUILT IN AMERICA 28

ONE OF THE FIRST TRAINS TO CROSS THE ALLEGHANY
MOUNTAINS 30

FACING
PAGE

PASSENGER CAR ON THE BALTIMORE AND OHIO RAIL-
ROAD, 1830 48

THE *Pioneer*, AN EARLY LOCOMOTIVE ON THE UNION
PACIFIC SYSTEM 60

BUILDING THE TRANSCONTINENTAL RAILROAD SYSTEM 62

THE GOLDEN SPIKE CEREMONY AT PROMONTORY,
UTAH, MAY 10, 1869 64

TRANSPORTATION OF COAL ON THE BUFFALO, ROCHES-
TER, AND PITTSBURGH RAILROAD . . . 68

ORE YARDS AND DOCKS, PENNSYLVANIA RAILROAD,
ASHTABULA, OHIO 70

THE TWENTIETH CENTURY LIMITED OF THE NEW
YORK CENTRAL RAILROAD 72

TRAIN CONTROL BOARD AND OPERATOR, GRAND CEN-
TRAL TERMINAL, NEW YORK 78

THE LEHIGH VALLEY FREIGHT TRANSFER STATION
AT MANCHESTER, NEW YORK 80

JERSEY CITY PIER OF THE ERIE RAILROAD . . 82

HORSE-DRAWN STREET CAR, 1885 . . . 86

EDISON'S FIRST EXPERIMENTAL ELECTRIC TRAIN,
MENLO PARK, NEW JERSEY 88

EARLY TYPE OF ELECTRIC TROLLEY CARS USED IN
ROCHESTER, NEW YORK 90

THE "SUBMARINE" TYPE STREET CAR, LATE MODEL 96

MODERN INTERURBAN TROLLEY CAR. ROCHESTER,
LOCKPORT, AND BUFFALO RAILROAD COMPANY . 98

MODERN ELECTRIC TROLLEY CARS, ROCHESTER, NEW
YORK, 1927 106

FACING
PAGE

INTERURBAN BUSSES, A NEW FACTOR IN TRANSPORTA-
TION 110

A TRACKLESS TROLLEY 112

MURDOCH DEMONSTRATING HIS DISCOVERY . . 116

THE LAMP LIGHTER OF YESTERDAY . . . 122

THE GAS RANGE AS USED BY DOMESTIC SCIENCE
PUPILS AT JEFFERSON JUNIOR HIGH SCHOOL,
ROCHESTER, NEW YORK 126

MODERN GAS-FIRED GLASS MELTING FURNACE . 128

NEW SECTION OF THE WEST STATION GAS MANUFAC-
TURING PLANT OF THE ROCHESTER GAS AND
ELECTRIC CORPORATION 130

SIZING, STORAGE, AND LOADING BINS FOR COKE,
ROCHESTER GAS AND ELECTRIC CORPORATION . 134

CROSS SECTION OF A PORTION OF A GAS MANUFAC-
TURING PLANT 136

A MODERN GAS HOLDER 140

STATE INSPECTOR PUTTING HIS SEAL OF APPROVAL
ON GAS METERS 144

THOMAS EDISON AND STAFF IN HIS LABORATORY AT
MENLO PARK, 1880 148

ILLUMINATION OF ADMINISTRATION BUILDING, CHICAGO
WORLD'S FAIR, 1893 156

ELECTRIC TOWER AND TEMPLE OF MUSIC, PAN-AMER-
ICAN EXPOSITION, BUFFALO, 1901 . . . 158

INTERIOR OF THE OLD PEARL STREET STATION,
EDISON ELECTRIC ILLUMINATING COMPANY . 160

FACING
PAGE

MODERN HYDRAULIC POWER STATION . . . 168

A STEAM "STAND-BY" STATION 170

INTERIOR VIEW OF A CENTRAL POWER STATION . 176

WHERE POWER FROM NIAGARA FALLS IS RECEIVED
AND TRANSFORMED AT ROCHESTER, N. Y. . . 184

PROFESSOR MORSE SENDING THE FIRST TELEGRAM,
WASHINGTON, MAY 24, 1844 192

WHERE TELEGRAPHIC COMMUNICATIONS IN MORSE
CODE ARE TRANSLATED 194

WESTERN UNION TELEGRAPH OFFICE, TOLEDO, OHIO 196

A PONY EXPRESS RIDER, FROM A MOTION PICTURE
ADAPTATION 198

THE *Colonia*, THE LARGEST SHIP ENGAGED IN CABLE
LAYING 208

BELL'S ORIGINAL CENTENNIAL TELEPHONE RECEIVER 220

PROFESSOR BELL DEMONSTRATING THE TELEPHONE
AT SALEM, MASS., 1877 222

PYRAMID TYPE SWITCHBOARD, 1882 . . . 224

THE FIRST TELEPHONE EXCHANGE IN NEW YORK
CITY 226

INTERIOR OF A MODERN TELEPHONE EXCHANGE . 250

THE CABLE RUNS OF A MODERN TELEPHONE EX-
CHANGE 252

CENTRAL, INFORMATION DESK, MAIN EXCHANGE,
ROCHESTER TELEPHONE CORPORATION, RO-
CHESTER, NEW YORK 254

ILLUSTRATIONS xiii

FACING
PAGE

PRESIDENT W. S. GIFFORD OPENS THE NEW YORK-
LONDON TELEPHONE LINE, JANUARY 7, 1927 . 262

TRANSATLANTIC RADIO TELEPHONE CIRCUITS . . 264

TELEVISION TRANSMITTING APPARATUS . . . 270

WHILE TALKING TO A NEW YORK AUDIENCE SECRE-
TARY HOOVER IS SEEN BY MEANS OF TELEVISION 272

THE EXPERIMENTAL RADIO STATION OF BELL TELE-
PHONE LABORATORIES FROM WHICH TELEVISION BY
RADIO WAS DEMONSTRATED ON APRIL 7TH, 1927 . 274

VIEW OF THE STORM KING HIGHWAY, ALONG THE
PALISADES OF THE HUDSON RIVER . . . 280

PAVEMENT LAYING SIMPLIFIED BY USE OF MODERN
EQUIPMENT 282

PLUSHMILL'S MEMORIAL BRIDGE, NEAR PHILADEL-
PHIA 286

OLD SUSPENSION BRIDGE AT LEWISTON, BELOW
NIAGARA FALLS 288

BROOKLYN BRIDGE VIEWED FROM THE MANHATTAN
SIDE 290

ASHOKAN RESERVOIR, CATSKILL MOUNTAINS. ONE
OF THE RESERVOIRS OF THE WATER SUPPLY
SYSTEM OF THE CITY OF NEW YORK . . . 298

A METHOD OF AERATING A CITY'S WATER SUPPLY . 304

TRICKLING FILTERS OF ONE OF ROCHESTER'S SEWAGE
DISPOSAL PLANTS 314

FACING
PAGE

SCENE IN HIGHLAND PARK, ROCHESTER, N. Y.   . 316

PUBLIC UTILITY SERVICE INSPECTOR ON DUTY   . 320

OFFICE OF A MODERN UTILITY   322

TYPICAL STOCK CERTIFICATE AND DIVIDEND CHECK
    OF A PUBLIC UTILITY CORPORATION   .   .   . 330

A PUBLIC UTILITY BOND   332

NEW YORK STATE UTILITIES ARE REGULATED BY THE
    STATE GOVERNMENT, STATE CAPITOL, ALBANY,
    NEW YORK   344

POPULATION GRAPH OF A TYPICAL AMERICAN CITY 358

THE IMPOSING MUNICIPAL GROUP OF SPRINGFIELD,
    MASS.   360

VIEW OF HARTFORD, FROM THE CONNECTICUT RIVER 362

The Story of Public Utilities

The Story of Public Utilities

CHAPTER I

THE BEGINNINGS OF THE AMERICAN CITY

A GROUP of pioneers, whose interests may or may not be more or less common, gather gradually at some site. They may have a definite idea of creating a community at that place, or, as frequently happens, their coming together may be more or less accidental. The former is more likely to be the case. Such a settlement forms the beginning, not only of any one American community, but of practically every city and village and town within the borders of the United States.

Communities generally are created in certain definite places because there are definite reasons for their establishment there. There is a good harbor. There is water power for mills. There are immediate mineral resources of great value. Possibly there is a surrounding agricultural country which demands a center for its trading, its banking, and repairs to its farming equipment. Few cities are accidents. Almost all of them have had very definite reasons indeed for their location.

3

When the Romans occupied Paris, nearly two thousand years ago, they did so because it was the point where practicable navigation of the Seine from the sea ceased. The two small islands which now form the heart of the French capital were an ideal site for a town where men and goods could change from large boats to small boats capable of being propelled through the shallow rough reaches of the upper Seine and of the Marne, which had their confluence nearby. It was a natural townsite.

In the same way, London was a natural location, a breaking point in transit at the head of navigation upon the Thames. It was a logical point for the upbuilding of a city, which soon grew to greater size than its founders could possibly have dreamed, and in the course of a few centuries, came to be the very largest of all the large cities of the world.

Crossing the Atlantic to North America, Albany in the state of New York, for the selfsame reason, was an early city of some importance. It stood at the head of navigation upon the Hudson, near the confluence of the Mohawk, which, in certain seasons of the year, was partly navigable. It, too, was a breaking point in transport. Men might ascend the Hudson in sailboats with comparative ease, but at Albany they disembarked for the little known interior portions of the North American continent.

There were no railroads. The highroads were few and far between and unspeakably bad; but by crossing to Schenectady, seventeen miles west of Albany, small boats, hand-poled, might ascend the Mohawk, sometimes shallow and sometimes swift-running, to a point near Rome, New York, where there was a short "carry," or portage, to the waters of Oneida Lake.

ALBANY, FROM AN OLD FRENCH WOOD-CUT.

This in turn led through the Oswego River, to Lake Ontario, the lowest and most easterly of the Great Lakes, which were destined in a future generation to become the largest carriers of water-borne commerce in the world.

Speedily this became recognized as a definite route, so much so that hardly had the exciting days of the American Revolution ended, before a company had been organized to construct locks in the narrowest and swiftest portion of the Mohawk River. In the narrow defile at Little Falls, portions of these locks still remain. They were the first attempts in this country to aid inland navigation artificially.

For the same reason that Albany became an important town, Oswego also became one. A few years later, Buffalo, at the east end of Lake Erie, and the lowest lake port for unimpeded navigation through to the very head of the Great Lakes, attained importance. Until the completion of the first Welland Canal in 1827, the falls and the rapids of Niagara formed a very serious obstruction to communication between Lakes Erie and Ontario.

Looking outside the state of New York, one finds Hartford, at the head of navigation upon the Connecticut, and Georgetown (today a part of the city of Washington), at a similar point upon the Potomac, early towns of importance for the selfsame reason as was Albany. And so also were Richmond, Virginia; and Augusta, Georgia; and in Canada, the great city of Montreal at the head of tidewater navigation upon the St. Lawrence River.

A confluence of important rivers was almost certain to bring about the building of a town. This was particularly true after the coming of the steamboat, a little less than a century and a quarter ago. For this reason we had Pittsburgh, Pennsylvania; and St. Louis, Missouri. Louisville, Kentucky, came into existence because, as at Little Falls, New York, there was the necessity of cutting artificial canals or locks to aid navigation upon an important river.

Waterpower made important American industrial cities. First in New England it created towns like Lowell and Lawrence, Massachusetts; Manchester, New Hampshire; and, at a later day, Holyoke, Massachusetts. So came Paterson, New Jersey, and Rochester, New York, and still later Minneapolis, Minnesota. Almost always is there definite reasons for the founding of a town.

A group of people has begun to gather, perhaps almost unconsciously, at some site which has seemed to them to be attractive for home building, as well as for the location of the various enterprises by which they hope to earn their livelihood.

Gradually, out of what may have been mere circumstance, something vaguely resembling a community creeps into existence. To facilitate getting from one house to another, a path is cleared. This, presently made wide enough for the passage of wagons, becomes a crude form of street. The street, even the footpath which in all probability preceded it, is a community convenience; it is the very beginning of what today we call a public utility.

Soon there may be another street, perhaps leading to the mill, or the store, or the schoolhouse, or the church. A third street, and a fourth, may follow in due course. An American village, possibly a city, is being born.

FORT PITT, NOW THE CITY OF PITTSBURGH.

Folk begin to find it difficult at night, stumbling along those rough first streets after dark. It is not always convenient to have a lantern handy and presently the young community sets up a lamp at the corner of two streets, atop of a short, wooden post. It flickers and sends out its kindly glow for all. It is the beginning of street lighting. Another utility has been created.

People cannot live well or happily in groups without good water and provision for the proper disposal of their refuse. There comes a town pump, therefore, which is another community help and another utility, even though of a crude sort.

When the town becomes big enough so that the walk to the pump is an inconvenience for its housewives, it will begin looking for a steady source of pure water, a nearby brook or river or small lake, and it will then place pipes under the streets to bring this water to each of the other houses. Under the streets will be laid still other pipes, water-flushed, for the disposal of the refuse. These pipes will be called sewers. Here are two more utilities.

After a while they may be laying a third set of pipes in those streets. By this time there are sure to be many more than two or three or four or five thorough-fares. In these last pipes they will be bringing from the common point of its production, the manufactured gas that will be burned in the streets, in the houses, in the stores, in the factories, in the schools and in the churches, to drive the darkness out. A real utility has begun to grow and to expand.

Presently the community, now becoming a very siz-able one, finds itself suffering from growing pains.

It is becoming quite a walk, perhaps quite a drive, from one end of the town to the other, or even straight across it. Yet the town continues its steady growth, maybe a rapid one as well as a steady one. It is possible that a railroad already has found its way to it to give it swift communication with the outer world; far better, far swifter than either highway or waterway might possibly give. Some one takes the idea of the railroad upon which the steam locomotive with its train operates, and places an imitation of it in the principal streets of the town, which already is coming to be known as a considerable city. Upon these tracks, smoothly imbedded in the center of the more important streets, there appear small passenger cars drawn by horses, for we still are in the early years of American progress. This is a street railway. It, too, is ranked as a utility, and a most important one.

Next comes the telegraph, in these early days known, quite formally, as the Magnetic Telegraph, and almost in the mere twinkling of an eye our town can communicate with its fellows one hundred or five hundred miles away. For a long time we have had the post office, the local station of the extensive national institution of the mails. But this has been, from the outset, so recognized and so distinct a federal government service that we shall not regard it at this time as a utility, although in many ways it might properly be classed as such.

Presently word comes that a telegraph, known as the cable, has reached its copper strand all the way under the broad Atlantic, and upon the very heels of this, the tidings that one at last may send a message by telegraph all the way across the continent to distant San Francisco.

PITTSBURGH IS LOCATED AT THE CONFLUENCE OF THE ALLEGHANY AND MONONGAHELA RIVERS.

Yet even the fanciful wonder of the telegraph is presently eclipsed. No longer is it a mysterious sort of communication, being tapped by a code series of metallic sounds that ride upon the growing web of copper wires. Now it is the human voice itself that goes, clearly and distinctly, across the land and the thing that carries it they call the telephone.

As the telegraph gradually has expanded its area, so in turn does the telephone, until the day arrives when, by means of it, one may hear a voice that one loves, speak from far across the United States or Canada, or even from distant Cuba or Mexico.

Great is electricity! Many are its wonders! Now they are putting wires suspended over the centers of the tracks of the horse railway in the street and queer broomlike looking things that they call "trolleys" on the tops of the horse cars. These trolleys run the street cars more swiftly and more easily than before and the horses are saved for other purposes. The trolley cars grow bigger and longer. They reach further out toward the edge of the town, which presently itself begins to expand radically, and for long distances away from its original center.

Great is electricity! Many are its wonders! New lamps, much stronger than those which burned gas or kerosene, and giving forth a powerful white light, appear in the city streets and after a time these are ranged along the sides of the more important thorough-fares in great frequency and with some real desire for ornamentation. Small lights, also made radiant by electricity, and giving forth a steady yellowish glow, are installed in the houses, in the stores and in the factories, which have become more numerous by this time.

Moreover, the electric current that goes toward lighting the modern city has many other important uses. It becomes the most effective servant of the housewife. It cleans her carpet, cooks her meals, washes her dishes, even operates her sewing machine. On hot days it keeps mechanical fans revolving at a swift rate so that there may be a steady stream of cool, refreshing air. Because of it man may work at higher efficiency in the summer days than before the coming of electricity.

Great is electricity! Many are its wonders! The human voice and the telegraph code speak through the ether and today we also know the wireless. The concert from the theater or from the public hall comes by the magic of the radio into the most isolated house within the community, or into the loneliest farmhouse of the entire countryside. The lecture or the sermon follows in its train. The skillful facility of the motion picture is, in this way, supplemented. The community begins to ask, "What invention shall we see next? To all of these great utilities what is the next that is to be added?"

Public utilities, as we think of them in this day and age, are apt to be rather definite units, such as railroads, steam or electric, devoted to the transportation of the general public, the telegraph, the telephone, the gas and electric lighting services, water supply, sewage disposal and the like, all requiring a large and highly specialized organization and supervision as compared with the more ordinary community needs, such as country highways, city streets, bridges or even canals. It is hard to draw a precise line. Schools, and even churches, ofttimes have large and highly specialized

The Lower Falls of the Genesee in 1820

organizations, but these are not, in any ordinarily recognized sense, public utilities.

Common practice has come to designate as public utilities the large organisms that have just been set down here as such. It might well have called them public necessities. The modern city not only comes to utilize them, but in a very true sense to lean upon them. If the average sizable American city were to be deprived of its telephone or telegraph service for merely twenty-four hours, genuine public inconvenience would result. Despite the all but universal prevalence of the automobile today, a suspension of railroad service and of the street railway service for a like period of time would fairly paralyze business for all save the smallest cities. Cessation of light and water and sewage disposal would result quickly in appalling public disaster. These things are, indeed, more than mere utilities; they are, each of them, tremendous civic necessities. One by one, we shall investigate all of them. Without preference or prejudice we shall endeavor to consider them in something of the chronological order of their development.

CHAPTER II

PATHWAYS OF COMMUNITY TRANSPORT

THE first pathways of commerce in America were the waterways. The navigable rivers, reaching their way inland from the Atlantic seaboard, were seized upon eagerly by the pioneers as a means of transporting their household effects and themselves from salt water to the hinterland of unknown promise. The bigger the river, the larger was the opportunity of penetrating the interior. Such splendid streams as the Hudson, the Delaware or the Potomac, affording, for more than a hundred miles in from the sea, a fairway for ocean craft drawing a considerable depth of water, were hailed as real gifts; while the St. Lawrence, navigable for more than nine hundred miles, up to the base of Mount Royal, which presently became Montreal, was a rare treasure-trove to the earliest explorers and the settlers who came upon their heels.

Yet the smaller rivers were not to be scorned. Streams like the Connecticut, the Penobscot, the Kennebec and the Susquehanna also had their possibilities, while by transferring goods and humans to smaller boats or *bateaux*, as the French explorers called them, the possibilities of the smaller streams went much further. The shallow reaches of the Mississippi, the Ohio, the Missouri, the Illinois and all

EARLY WOOD-CUT OF THE PORT OF ROCHESTER, NEW YORK.

their tributaries, then became accessible; while if the *bateaux* were small enough to admit of being carried for short distances overland on the shoulders of one or more men, the possibilities of river travel became vastly greater. Then it was that falls or rapids no longer were absolute barriers to the ascent of a river. A great part of the interior of the North American continent immediately became accessible to exploration and settlement, for many of the large rivers of the interior fed directly into the Great Lakes. Of the connection between those Lakes and the waters of the upper Hudson across the central and western portions of the state of New York, we have just read.

The invention of the first practicable steamboat revolutionized the possibilities of these inland waterways. Other early inventors had tinkered with the device. John Fitch had a quite remarkable craft upon the Delaware at an earlier date, but Robert Fulton's *Clermont*, which made its first appearance upon the Hudson in the summer of 1807, is generally adjudged to be the first practical vessel to use steam as a motive power.

So practical and so successful was it, that it was followed quickly by others, both upon the Hudson and the Delaware. Early steamboats were built upon Lake Champlain, and in the summer of 1816, the steamer *Ontario* was begun at Sackett's Harbor, New York. This was the first steamer ever built on water subject to a swell, and it demonstrated immediately the fitness of the steamboat principle for open waters as well as for sheltered rivers. The first steamer to operate on the upper Lakes was the *Walk-on-the-Water*, which was built and launched at Buffalo.

Through the first half of the last century, the steamboat idea spread like wildfire. By the late 'thirties, deep-hulled vessels were ploughing their way across the Atlantic, while flat-bottomed ones went poking their noses up the narrow reaches of the inland streams of the United States.

All these things had a distinct bearing upon the development of the American city. As we have seen in the preceding chapter, the break from land to water or vice versa almost invariably created a town, frequently a good-sized one. Buffalo came into existence because of the swift increase of traffic upon the upper Lakes, and Pittsburgh because of that upon the Ohio. Lake traffic fostered Cleveland and Detroit and Milwaukee and Chicago; and that of the inland rivers, Cincinnati, Louisville, St. Louis and St. Paul. It was said of St. Louis at the time immediately preceding the Civil War, that so many steamboats came to her levee it was quite impossible to place them lengthwise against the several miles of wharfage there; they could only place their bows against the shore, as today we sometimes park automobiles in crowded but fairly wide streets.

The steamboat had its limitations, and they were very great ones. The greatest was the fact that it could not go overland. Men dug canals, for a time in increasing numbers, to connect stretches of water naturally navigable; but these artificial waterways were not only expensive, but difficult to build and to maintain. With the exception of comparatively short-stretch-canals, such as the Welland connecting Lakes Erie and Ontario, the canals and locks around the rapids of the upper stretches of the St. Lawrence, the Ohio and the Mississippi, and the Sault Ste. Marie

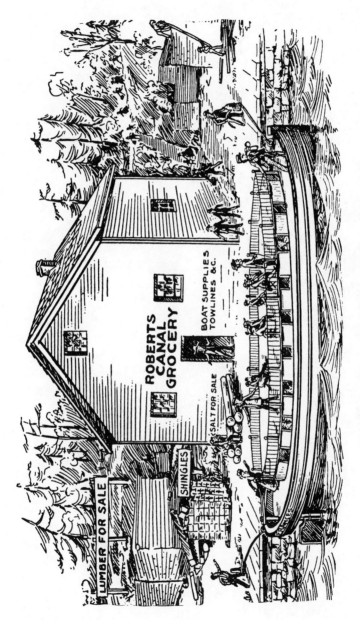

Canals Were Once a Chief Means of Transportation.

connecting Lakes Huron and Superior, most of these canals are today considered fairly obsolete.

An exception might possibly be made in favor of the New York Barge Canal, an extremely elaborate enterprise begun in recent years, not only to connect the waters of the Hudson near Albany with those of Lake Ontario at Oswego and of Lake Erie near Buffalo, but also the upper Hudson with Lake Champlain and so, in turn, with the St. Lawrence River. But even this important waterway system has not yet developed a traffic to justify the vast amount of money expended upon it.

Because the steamboat could not go overland, the highway came early into existence. It existed at first here in America in a fairly crude form, even though on the other side of the Atlantic good roads had been known for two thousand years. The Romans were the first roadbuilders of note. When they laid down the Appian Way, originally running all the way from Rome to Brundisium, 350 miles, they opened the first of the world's great streets. Most of the original Appian Way disappeared long ago. A much newer road, built by Pope Pius VI in 1789, has become quite widely known by that name.

A road only slightly less famous than the Appian Way was that which the Romans built up and down Great Britain, which became known in history as Watling Street. This very ancient thoroughfare once ran from Dover upon the English Channel to and through London, and by separate branches, on to Chester and Carlisle and York and the Roman Wall near Newcastle. Except in places, it has disappeared. But the English roads of after years, the South Road from London to Brighton, and the North, from the British capital to York and beyond, are still efficient and in these days of the motor vehicle very, very busy highways.

For many years sparsely settled America could do but little toward gaining real roads. Mountains and rivers intervened and even when the first settlers finally mastered the highly practical art of bridge-building, they could build their pathways only over the smaller streams. The larger ones still were obstacles, to be crossed by man and beast and vehicle only on cumbersome and slow-moving ferryboats. Thus it came to pass that the first important highways in North America were those of Mexico, a land comparatively free from large rivers, where Enrico Cortez four centuries ago built roads so well and so thoroughly that they continue in use today, in many cases with the original pavements.

Yet, as grew the thirteen colonies upon the Atlantic Coast, later destined to become the United States of America, there also grew the demand for better communication between them. Coasting sloops from port town to port town, dependent always upon the vagaries of wind and weather, were hardly to be counted upon as reliable. The highroad, became the accepted means of transportation. As the bridge builders bettered their profession, the range of these roads increased until about the beginning of the eighteenth century, when there came to be a continuous road all the way from Boston to New York. A few years later this was to receive the generally applied name of the Boston Post Road, a name which endures to this day. That name tells its own story.

Just as today our federal post office department endeavors to improve communication—the type of communication we know as the mails—by every form of aid, even to aviation, so in that earlier day, two hundred years ago, the postal authorities of the struggling colonies endeavored to improve the through roads.

For it need not be imagined that these were at the outset even remotely comparable with those splendid paved thoroughfares that the Romans built so many centuries before, or even with those of Cortez in Mexico. Our earliest roads were, in a large sense, a development of Indian trails, existing for no one knows how many years. Where softly moccasined feet had pattered there came the heavy boots of the white man and also his horses and his carts. All the while more trails had been opened to them. Men with their great axes had cut down the trees and opened ways to a decent width. Afterwards they had made crude attempts at grading. Finally they came to the building of the bridges that connected one road with the other.

First came the pioneer with heavy pack upon his shoulders; then this burden was transferred to a horse; and finally the horse was fastened in the traces of a car or wagon. The cars and wagons were becoming more frequent and more regular in their comings and their goings, until the day the great wagons that carried passengers, their luggage and the mail, came to be known, quite officially, as stage-coaches.

These coaches ran, with a deal of regularity, upon well-established routes and with no little speed in their going. Until the coming of the railroad, they afforded the most dependable inland mode of communication.

The Boston Post Road, east of New Haven, really

was three distinct roads, running more or less parallel:
the Upper or northern one, running west from Boston,
passing through Sudbury, Marlboro, Worcester, Brook-
field and Springfield, Massachusetts, and Windsor,
Hartford and Middletown, Connecticut; the Middle
Road, coming out from Boston, via Roxbury, Milford
and Uxbridge, Massachusetts, and Pomfret, Connecticut, to Hartford, where it joined the Upper Road;
the Lower Road threading Dedham, Wrentham and
Attleboro, Massachusetts, Providence, Bristol and
Newport, Rhode Island, and New London, Saybrook,
Guilford and Branford, Connecticut, before coming to
New Haven.   Even these main routes were subject to
slight variations from time to time.

Ranking with the Boston road in name and in importance was the Albany Post Road, which only a few
years later was opened up along the eastern shore of the
Hudson to the old town of Rensselaer, just across the
river from Albany and connected with it by ferry.
This highway passed through the sleepy Dutch settle-
ments of Yonkers, Tarrytown, Peekskill, Fishkill,
Poughkeepsie, Rhinebeck, Claverack and Kinderhook,
as it wended its picturesque way north from the city
of New York.

Yet nowhere was it more picturesque than at its very
beginnings, at the south tip of the wonderful island of
Manhattan generally known as the Battery.   Here, as
Broadway, one of the notable streets of the world, it
began, and here it still begins its course.   In the various
historical eras of the city of New York it was called
De Heere Wagh Wegh, the Broad Wagon Way, the
Common Highway and the Great Public Road.
Eventually the second of these designations, slightly

shortened, became the accepted and the permanent name of the street which, as the city of New York continued to grow in size and in importance, itself became greater and far more important, until Broadway became known the world over.

Frequently main highroads have become, in this fashion, important city streets. The Boston Post Road is not only a main thoroughfare in many of the cities and the towns that it threads, but in New York City it is itself a real highway, extending to a junction with Broadway at the old City Hall and hardly a mile distant from the Battery. On the island of Manhattan it is today, in its several links, Park Row, the Bowery and Third Avenue. Some of its ancient mileposts still remain in place, in the heart of the city and under the rumblings of the elevated railway.

From Albany, the capital of the state of New York, another important road extended due west. This was generally known as the Genesee Road, although the first link of it, from Albany to Cherry Valley, had been built in 1802 as the Great Western Turnpike. Gradually it was extended, first westward, to Richfield Springs, Morrisville, and Cazenovia, then to Auburn, Geneva, Canandaigua, Avon and Batavia on its way to Buffalo. This road, which presently became the artery of traffic of a vast migration of people and their beasts and goods toward the little known West, ran considerably south of the path eventually chosen for the Erie Canal and, at a still later day, followed by the main line of the New York Central Railroad. Despite the early settlement of the Mohawk valley and the founding of such towns in it as Schenectady and Palatine and Utica, it was felt, because of the frequent floodings of the stream, that it formed a dangerous place in which to build an important and a dependable road.

To the south were many other roads, both across the Southern Tier counties and also across Pennsylvania. Although the term was used elsewhere, it was in Pennsylvania that the through roads invariably were called turnpikes. This came from their numerous tollgates which continued in use until a few years ago. The dictionary says that a turnpike is a gate that turns. The connotation is a simple one indeed.

One of the most famous of these early Pennsylvania pikes was the Lancaster, which today takes the rider on the Lincoln Highway directly west from Philadelphia. From a very bad road, it came quickly to be a very good one. At one time it was considered the best in the United States. A gentleman who rode over it in 1796, afterwards wrote:

There is but one turnpike road on the continent which is between Lancaster and Philadelphia, a distance of sixty-six miles, and it is a masterpiece of its kind; it is paved with stone the whole way and overlaid with gravel so that it is never obstructed during the most severe season. . . .

It is further related that on many of these turnpike roads the owners of wagons were encouraged to use very broad tires for their wheels. For such the tolls were reduced materially.

While roads of this sort were the exception a hundred years or more ago, rather than the rule, all of them steadily continued to grow better, until, in 1808, a definite measure was passed by Congress establishing the National Road. This was a pet project of Thomas Jefferson, although George Washington had conceived

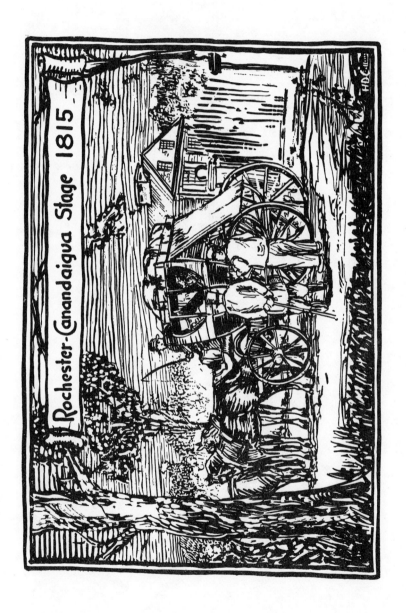

Rochester-Canandaigua Stage 1815

its possibilities long before while surveying the valleys of the Potomac and the Monongahela. Jefferson continued to watch its progress almost until the day of his death.

The legal beginning of the National Road was at Cumberland, Maryland, even though the fine pike extending east from that point through Hagerstown and Frederick to Baltimore, in its actual use, always was considered an integral part of it. From Cumberland it ran west over the stiff slopes of the Alleghanies through Brownsville and Washington (Pennsylvania) and down to the Ohio at the little Virginia city of Wheeling. To bring it over the yellow Ohio, John A. Roebling was to construct for it, a few years later, the first of the remarkable suspension bridges that made his name famous the world over—a structure which still stands as a monument to his genius.

From Wheeling the National Road ran west through Zanesville and Newark to Columbus, the capital of Ohio; and from Columbus to Indianapolis, the capital of Indiana. The original scheme was to continue it on across Illinois to St. Louis, where it could connect with the Booneville Road which led to Independence, Missouri, where there branched those two remarkable pathways of early romance, the Santa Fe and the Oregon Trails.

Into St. Louis the National Road was never finished; not officially, at least. It took until 1851 to build it as far west as Vandalia, Illinois. By that time the railroad was well established across the land. The era of the motor car and the motor truck was long decades ahead. The need for improved highways was greatly lessened. At Vandalia the National Road connected with good ordinary Illinois roads—north, south and west. For its traffic, which already had dwindled to nothingness, these would more than amply suffice as connections.

Yet, in at least the first two decades of its existence, the National Road was a highway worthy of the name. Over it there journeyed, day and night in a stream almost unending, a vast migration of the peoples who were to upbuild the central and the western portions of these United States. Sometimes they only went over it as far as Wheeling and there took passage in flat boats down the Ohio, which leads into more than ten thousand miles of other navigable rivers. Wheeling early attained a relative importance among the cities of America that it has not held in recent years. For a time it was a boom town, because the junction of a highway and a waterway almost always makes much business and, in turn, a city or a town.

This, then, is the idea worth remembering: it is in its direct relationship to the city that the highway becomes of largest interest here and now, as a means for the transport of produce for consumption or of people to barter and trade.

Today, the highway in America is again coming into general use. Neglected for many years, since the amplification of our railroad systems, its new birth has come through the advent of the motor car. Roads, little known, half forgotten, have sprung into a vast new importance. You cannot place more than 25,000,000 motor vehicles upon the highways of the United States without producing some rather definite effects upon those highways themselves. This the motor car already has done.

Nowhere is the rebirth of the American highway more

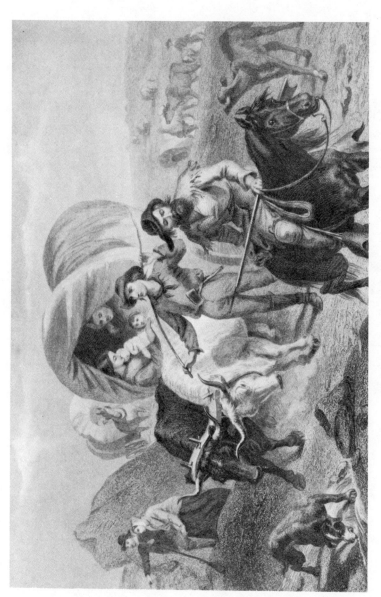

The "Covered Wagon," by F. C. Darley.

dramatic or more vital than in its direct relationship to the American city. Greatly has it enlarged the radius of the city. Spreading out in every direction from it to the open country, it has broadened the field of opportunity, both for residential and industrial purposes. It is still very new. The transformation it has wrought is by no means completed.

Yet the public highway, even the highway adjacent to the city, is not a utility—not at least in the sense in which we are regarding the utilities in the pages of this book. It is as a back-ground to the utilities that it has been given this place here. It forms a setting for many utilities,—for street lightings, for street railways, for the pipes, the wires, the conduits, of many utility services. It is in this way that it has earned its own place in this picture.

CHAPTER III

AMERICAN RAILROAD DEVELOPMENT—I

WITH the invention of the steam locomotive, the entire commercial map of the United States was changed radically. Up to that time, the development of this country had been limited very largely to the building of towns and of villages along water routes— either along the rim of the North Atlantic or the great estuaries that lead into it, or along the navigable rivers and lakes. There were, of course, many highways. Travel upon some of these at the beginning of the last century already had reached to sizable proportions. But most of these highroads were bad. At the best, travel upon them was slow, tedious and uncomfortable. Men rode in stagecoaches and wagons and chaises, but in the course of a very long day could not accomplish many miles of travel. It was considered quite a thing when, right at the close of the Revolution, it was announced that "flying wagons" had been developed, in which one might go from New York to Philadelphia, ninety miles, within two days. Today this is a trip of but two hours by fast express, upon the railroad.

Josiah Quincy, president of Harvard University, wrote graphically in his diary, of riding by highway from Boston to New York, at the end of the eighteenth century. He says:

24

. . . The carriages were old and the shackling and much of the harness made of ropes.   One pair of horses carried us eighteen miles.   We generally reached our resting place for the night, if no accident intervened, at ten o'clock, and after a frugal supper, went to bed, with a notice that we should be called at three next morning, which generally proved to be half past two, and then, whether it snowed or rained, the traveler must rise and make ready by the help of a horn lantern and a farthing candle, and proceed on his way over bad roads, sometimes getting out to help the coachman out of a quagmire or rut, and arrived in New York after a week's hard traveling, wondering at the ease as well as the expedition with which our journey was effected. . . .

THE FIRST USE OF THE LOCOMOTIVE IN THE UNITED STATES

In 1825, George Stephenson built, in England, the *Rocket*, the first successful steam locomotive to be operated anywhere in the world.   Four years later, a locomotive of the Stephenson type, the *Stourbridge Lion*, was brought in a sailing ship from England to the United States, up the Hudson by packet-sloop and by canal barge to Honesdale, in the north-eastern corner of Pennsylvania.   There, upon August 8, 1829, it turned its wheels under its own power for the first time, and a vast new era in the industrial and social development of America was begun.

The *Stourbridge Lion* was purchased by the Delaware & Hudson Canal Company for use upon its short rail lines, running from its mines in the mountains, down to the head of its canal at Honesdale.   There were, at that time, a number of railroads in the United States, all of them short and most of them connecting coal mines with water transport of one form or another. The first railroad was the line, three miles in length, that Gridley Bryant built in 1826 from the quarries just west of Quincy, Massachusetts, down to a tidewater dock, to assist in getting out the great stones for the Bunker Hill monument, which was just being built.

It will be noticed that these were not railroads in the sense that we speak of a railroad today. They were, in truth, but industrial devices to aid in the work of other industries. They were private railroads rather than public.

The Mohawk & Hudson, chartered on April 17, 1826, to build a line from Albany to Schenectady was, in all probability, the first public railroad to be organized within the United States. Other roads were chartered that year but never were built. On August 9, 1831, this small road, the progenitor of the present great New York Central system, operated its first train, hauled by the locomotive *DeWitt Clinton*, which was not imported, but was an American product, having been built by the West Point Foundry, in the city of New York. The engine weighed but 6,758½ pounds. Often a modern locomotive will weigh from 300 to 400 tons.

The *Clinton* hauled in her train a tender and two or three cars—these last modeled after stage-coaches,, but with wheels of iron, with a flange upon the rim of the tires to hold them to the rail. Yet one should hold no illusions about the comforts of riding on that first New York Central train. The altered stage-coaches rocked and rolled terribly; the passengers were nearly jolted out of their seats and the cinders made the trip upon it a

THE DE WITT CLINTON TRAIN.

sort of human misery. There was no device on the locomotive by which these could be deflected, as is done today. Instead, they showered the passengers, in two or three cases setting fire to the umbrellas which were raised as a somewhat ineffectual device to ward them off.

Even before this first New York Central train moved, another railroad had been chartered and placed in operation for passengers and for freight. This was the Baltimore & Ohio Railroad, which was incorporated on April 24, 1827, and which, on May 24, 1830, began the regular movement of trains between Baltimore and Ellicotts Mills, thirteen miles distant. This road, for the first few years of its life, was operated exclusively by horse power. In fact the idea was entertained for a time by its promoters that horses would be used to haul its cars all the way to the Ohio, more than 350 miles from Baltimore.

To reach the inland waterways of the country was the great hope and ambition of most of these early railroad projects. In the middle of the United States, there were, and still are, two great systems of natural water routes. One of these consists of the Great Lakes and their tributary rivers; the other is the Mississippi with the important streams that flow into it, the Missouri and the Ohio chief amongst these.

The far visioned men who lived along the Atlantic seaboard one hundred years ago realized that if they could establish easy communication with these inland waterway systems, colonization and trade would begin upon a mighty scale within the heart of the United States. Up to the year 1825, nearly half a century after the establishment of our government, with the proclamation of the Declaration of Independence, there had been practically no development of the nation more than one hundred miles inland from the coast. In that year the completion of the Erie Canal marked a tremendous change, however. Not only was the city of New York to benefit vastly by this water route from the navigable Hudson River, at Albany, to Lake Erie, at Buffalo, but, through the center of New York State, a chain of important cities—Utica, Syracuse, Rochester—was to spring up quickly.

The rival seaports along the Atlantic soon saw what the new Erie Canal was doing for New York. Alarmed, they sought methods of commercial reprisal. They, too, must have routes to the interior. Philadelphia began to urge the remarkable combination of railroad and canal that many years afterwards, was to become the all-rail Pennsylvania system. The city of Washington sought federal aid for the Chesapeake and Ohio Canal, a water route projected through the valley of the Potomac and over the Alleghanies to Pittsburgh, at the head of navigation upon the Ohio River.

Baltimore was in a quandary. No such natural route to the hinterland, as was nature's great gift to New York, awaited her. She saw quickly the utter absurdity of the Chesapeake and Ohio project. To attempt even to carry a canal over the top of a mountain range more than 2,000 feet above tidewater, was visionary. The compromise combination of canal and railroad, such as was already in construction across Pennsylvania did not appeal to her.

But these rumors of the railroad, which was already beginning to conquer England by storm, interested her. She despatched agents to Great Britain to see for them-

PETER COOPER'S "TOM THUMB," THE FIRST LOCOMOTIVE BUILT IN AMERICA

selves and to report. When they came back, enthusiastic over what they had seen in the United Kingdom, Baltimore no longer hesitated. She prepared to build a railroad of her own of some sort or other, all the way to the Ohio, and so keep herself on a commercial equality with both Philadelphia and New York.

The third one of these early railroad projects deserves at least a paragraph of attention. In those days, Charleston, South Carolina, was a keen business rival of New York, Boston, Philadelphia and Baltimore. She, too, decided she would have her own route to the interior country, and that it should be a rail route. So was born the South Carolina Railroad, which was slowly put down, from the harbor of Charleston to Augusta, Georgia, 126 miles away. Upon this road the early American built locomotive, the *Best Friend*, also built by the West Point Foundry, was successfully operated, on December 14, 1830.

For various reasons, chiefly financial, this through route from Charleston did not come quickly into being. The South Carolina Railroad eventually was merged with other lines, and Charleston lost her distinctive system, with the result that she fell far behind in the race for supremacy with the seaport cities of the North.

In New England, Boston and Salem, a century ago, were keen commercial rivals. Boston saw the necessity of a through rail route to the West, and in the 'thirties began building the Boston & Worcester, which a very few years later, in combination with the Western Railroad, became known as the Boston & Albany, the present connecting arm of the New York Central Railroad into the heart of New England. Salem dillydallied. Her interests, she said, were of the sea and the

ships that sail upon it, not in such new-fangled con-
traptions as railroads. She hesitated, and sank to a
commercial nothingness.

THE CRUDENESS OF EARLY RAILROAD CONSTRUCTION

It should be remembered all this while, that these
very early rail lines were of the simplest possible
construction. Literally they were highroads, with
rails laid upon them. They were no better planned, in
regard to curvature or grades, than the highways.
Hills, which today would be regarded as mere nothings,
ofttimes represented a serious problem to the engineers
of the early railroads. When they came to one of them
which could not be easily avoided by going around it,
they would lay a double line of rails straight up the
slope and at the top place a stationary engine with a
cable for hauling up the cars, or letting them down.
This was called an inclined plane and it was a crude
and expensive thing to operate. Yet so sure were some
of the railroad planners of the second decade of the last
century that the steam locomotive could only be made
to operate upon level or very nearly level track, that
they built many of these devices. The Mohawk &
Hudson, which we have just seen as the mother of the
New York Central family of railroads, used one just
west of Albany and another east of Schenectady. The
promoters of the Baltimore & Ohio seriously proposed
to cross the high Alleghanies with a series of inclined
planes. There were two on the main line of what is
today the Pennsylvania system.
Some of these old planes still are in existence in the
coal districts of Pennsylvania. One of them, at
Mauch Chunk, in the valley of the Lehigh, now owned

One of the First Trains to Cross the Alleghany Mountains.

by the Jersey Central Railroad and used only for passenger excursionists, has for almost a century been the delight of travelers and tourists. On it, the cars are hauled to the top of the road by a stationary engine and cables and then descend by gravity, nearly eighteen miles. Other planes still in use are at Ashley and at Mahoning, Pennsylvania.

William Norris, of Philadelphia, was one of the first to show that the locomotive could be made to go up a steep hill. He was an engine builder and early in 1836 there came from his works a "locomotive machine," as they were often called in those days, which presently was recognized as being the finest thing of its sort yet built. Patriotically, it was named the *George Washington*. It also was the biggest engine that had been put together up to that time. It weighed 14,400 pounds, and it had cylinders ten by eighteen inches, and a single pair of drivers, forty-eight inches in diameter.

On the Philadelphia & Columbia Railroad (a part of the Pennsylvania Railroad of today) the *George Washington*, in July, 1836, performed a feat that became world famed. That railroad also had a plane, located just outside the limits of the Philadelphia of that day. It rose for 2800 feet, at the terrific grade of 360 feet to the mile. Yet up that grade the *Washington* drew, unassisted by cables of any sort, two well-filled passenger cars, which weighed all told nearly sixteen tons, making the ascent in a little less than two minutes and a half.

This was indeed a prodigious performance. It not only brought to Norris much fame, but many orders for his locomotives. Other engines attempted like feats. There were some remarkable tests upon the early planes of the Baltimore & Ohio. But none of these quite equalled the epoch-making achievement of the *George Washington.*

EARLY RAILROAD DEVELOPMENT IN THE STATE OF NEW YORK—THE ERIE

The tremendous traffic that came to the Erie Canal, within the first decade after its completion, stimulated to a still greater growth the fortunate cities and towns that lined it. The villages along the south rim of New York State, the so-called Southern Tier, grew jealous. They decided that they too wanted to be on a through route between the ocean and the Lakes. They moved to such an end. So was chartered, on April 24, 1832, the New York & Erie Railroad, which was to run parallel to, but many miles south of, the Erie Canal.

The charter under which this company was organized provided that its entire capital of $10,000,000 must be subscribed and five percent of the amount actually paid in, before it could incorporate. This, its promoters felt, was a hopeless burden. They anticipated much opposition from the cities and towns along the banks of the Erie Canal. Local ambitions and local jealousies were always to play a large part in the location of our American railroads.

Finally, however, these men succeeded in reducing the subscription requirements for the organization of their new line to an even million dollars. This, despite the newness of the Southern Tier, was raised, and the company finally incorporated on August 9, 1833, just four years, almost to the day, after the first operation of the *Stourbridge Lion*, and two years, actually to the day, after the *DeWitt Clinton* had pulled the first train from Albany to Schenectady.

For many years progress on the building of the New York & Erie, known today as the Erie, was indeed halting. Because of a jealous insistence at first on the part of the New York legislature that the new line be kept entirely within the confines of the Empire State, it was not planned to begin it at New York City, but at a small place on the west bank of the Hudson, called Piermont, and situated twenty-four miles north of the metropolis. Dunkirk, on Lake Erie, was chosen as its western terminus.

On November 7, 1835, ground was first broken for the new road at Deposit, New York, almost equidistant between Piermont and Dunkirk. Then, for some years, the work lingered sadly. The great fire in New York, a month after the breaking of ground, and the terrible financial panics that swept the nation in the succeeding years, were almost fatal to the enterprise. It was only a loan of three million dollars from the state of New York, afterwards turned into a gift outright, that enabled work to go forward once again, with the result that on June 30, 1841, a trainload of passengers was taken through from the bank of the Hudson to Ramapo. Three months later, the line was open to Goshen, 46 miles west of Piermont. Yet it was not until December, 1848, that the first train entered Binghamton.

The road was completed to Corning twelve months later, and after more times of great financial stress, finally through to Dunkirk, May 15, 1851. After the custom of the times, a special train of distinguished

people was operated over the line.   One of the honored
guests on this train was Daniel Webster.   Mr. Webster
wished to have a better view of the New York State
country than the small car-windows afforded and to
meet his wishes, it is related, a rocking chair was
strapped to a flat-car, hauled at the rear end of the
train.

The Erie at that moment was the longest single
railroad in the world.   It reached for four hundred
miles, from Piermont to Dunkirk.   A little later, the
terminal arrangements were changed.   The device of
running a connecting steamboat from New York to
Piermont was found to be a difficult one, particularly
in winter when navigation on the Hudson is apt to be
impeded with floating ice.   Therefore a connecting
railroad was built from Suffern through Paterson,
New Jersey, to Jersey City, and this presently became
a part of the main line of the Erie.

The New York State prejudice against the invasion of
other states by the other road had long since been
overcome.   In the planning of railroads, geographical
necessities generally are greater than those of
legislatures.   In fact, complaining of the taxes that
were being levied upon it at Albany, the Erie, in the late
'forties, had not hesitated to locate its principal shops
at Susquehanna, in Pennsylvania, just across the state
line.

James G. King, the second president of the New York
& Erie, had, with some hesitancy, predicted in 1835,
that the road might earn eventually as much as
$200,000 a year from its freight service.   Yet within
the first six months of its completion through to
Dunkirk, its freight revenues alone amounted to

$1,755,285. No man, no matter how far-sighted, might safely predict the future development of the American railroad, any more than he might safely venture a prophecy of the astounding progress that it was to bring to the cities and towns along its lines.

THE WELDING OF THE FIRST NEW YORK CENTRAL
RAILROAD

At about the same time that the New York & Erie was completed to Dunkirk, two other important trunk-line railroads, so-called, were built from the Atlantic seaboard to the interior country. These were the Pennsylvania, which was finally finished from Philadelphia to Pittsburgh at the headwaters of the Ohio, and the Baltimore & Ohio, which after many years of terrific financial effort, was completed from Baltimore to Wheeling, some seventy miles down the Ohio from Pittsburgh.

Yet an all-rail route from the Atlantic seaboard to the interior country had preceded all three of these railroads, by nearly a decade. We have already seen the opening of the Mohawk & Hudson Railroad, from Albany to Schenectady. It was instantly successful. Upon its heels came a connecting one, to meet with an equal success, the Utica & Schenectady. Railroads from Utica to Syracuse and from Syracuse to Auburn quickly followed. In 1837, the Tonawanda Railroad was opened from Rochester to Batavia, and a few years later, to Attica and Buffalo. One of the last links of this chain to be forged was that between Rochester and Auburn. It was completed in the fall of 1841, and when, two years later, the Tonawanda Railroad was finished one could go from Albany to Buffalo, 300 miles, by railroad; in fact, from Boston to Buffalo, 500 miles, by rail, with only two breaks in the track—at Albany, where both passengers and freight must needs be ferried across the Hudson, and at Rochester, where a gap of a half-mile across the city was not bridged until three years later. There were many changes of cars—at Worcester, at Albany, at Utica, at Auburn and at Rochester. But these, in the minds of travelers of that early day, were regarded as being merely incidental.

This all-rail route from Boston to Buffalo, which actually preceded the indirect through one from New York to Buffalo (by way of the New York & Harlem to Chatham, upon the Western Railroad), came into swift popularity. Early it became a sharp competitor of the Erie Canal. Because of the fact that it was ready at every month of the year for the haulage of freight— the canal generally being blocked by ice for five months out of the twelve—and the fact that it offered pass- engers expedited transport, it swung into almost instant popularity. The proponents of the Erie Canal at Albany were particularly bitter at the instant success of this new railroad enterprise and used their influence in favor of legislative statutes limiting its opportunities for hauling freight. Thus the railroad devoted itself at first to the development of its passenger business.

The first cars for the Auburn & Rochester, for instance, constructed by Mr. Davenport, of Cambridge- port, Massachusetts, were reputed to have been easily the most elegant things of their sort that had ever been built. A contemporary account refers to them as "modern luxuries" and goes on to say:

. . .The size of the cars (28 feet by 8 feet) forms a pleasant room, handsomely painted, with floor matting, with windows secured from jarring and with curtains to shield from the blazing sun.   We should have said *rooms* for in four out of the six cars . . . there is a ladies' apartment, with luxurious sofas for seats, and in recesses may be found a washstand and other conveniences.   The arrangement of the apartment for ladies we consider the greatest improvement. . . . The ladies can now have their choice, either of a sofa in their own apartment, or a seat in the main saloon of the cars, as their health and inclination may require.

There is no warrant, however, for exaggerating the comfort of this rail trip across New York State in the 'forties.   It was, at the best, a tedious affair.   The "modern luxury" cars on the Auburn & Rochester were a decided exception.   Some of the passenger cars were so low that a tall man could hardly stand upright within one of them, and there was an unpleasant possibility always, not only on these, but on some of the other railroads of that early day, that one of the iron "strap" rails would work loose and force its way up through the floor of the cars.   Passengers were known to have been impaled on these "snake-heads," as they were called.   It was a most disagreeable experience.

The freight trains were even less impressive.   The box cars had but four wheels and thirty-four barrels of flour loaded one to its full capacity.   The switching was done by horses which brought the cars in and off the main tracks, where they were handled in trains, as many as fourteen or fifteen cars to the single locomotive.

Nevertheless, the amount of traffic that passed over these separate but correlated railroads of central and western portions of the state of New York was, from the beginning, tremendous. There had been great travel across the state even before the coming of the railroad or of the canal. The reason was that this was the only path from the Atlantic seaboard to the great new interior sections of that land, that was not compelled to cross high and almost impassable mountain ranges. Before the completion of the Erie Canal, in 1825, there were sixteen lines of stagecoaches in operation along the Genesee Turnpike. Through towns like Geneva and Canandaigua and Rochester and Batavia, these coaches passed almost at hourly intervals.

When the Erie Canal was opened, section by section, packet-boats, bright and new and attractive, came, first to supplement and then to supplant the stagecoaches. Along the western section of the canal, prior to the completion of the railroad, there operated each spring, summer and autumn, not less than three or four of these daily packet-boat lines.

The completion of the pioneer railroad across the state, even though by the somewhat roundabout route through Auburn, Geneva and Canandaigua, gave great stimulus to this traffic. Men and their families and goods began pouring over it in an unending stream toward the West, until there came '49 and the gold excitement in California, when this stream became a tidal flood of folk. After this the closer co-ordination of the roads across central and western New York was an ensuing fact that hardly could be avoided.

There came, gradually, a definite tendency toward eliminating the time-taking and aggravating changes of cars in the 300-mile journey across the state. There were also hopes of quickening the train service.

Theoretically, an express train ran from Albany to Buffalo in fourteen hours, though actually the time consumed was apt to be twice as much. Today the distance is covered in a little more than six hours. The fare was $9.75 and there were no parlor cars, although George M. Pullman, a carpenter from Albion, New York, was to find, in the middle of the 'fifties, passenger cars on the New York Central with crude sleeping berths fitted in them. The suggestion he got from riding in one of these cars formed the nucleus for the modern Pullman.

Before the end of the 'forties, some of these through passenger trains were in operation between the ferry and the steamboat docks at the river's edge in Albany, and the lake boat docks in the harbor of Buffalo. Ticketing and baggage arrangements had been adopted; and an express company, to be known for long years to come as the American Express Company, was already in service across the state.

These were the beginnings of the New York Central Railroad, which was incorporated in 1853 out of ten separate railroads reaching all the way across the state. In that same year, it built direct lines from Batavia to Buffalo and the so-called "Direct Road" from Rochester to Syracuse through Lyons, thereby appreciably shortening its main route. At Buffalo it not only connected with lake steamers, but with railroads already being built across Canada and along the south rim of Lake Erie. At Albany, it will be recalled, there was connection by ferry across the Hudson with the Boston and Albany, and, by 1851, with the Hudson River Railroad, which had just been completed from New York, and was even shorter than the river itself.

At Rochester, there diverged a branch to Niagara Falls and the wonderful new suspension bridge that Col. John A. Roebling had just completed across the gorge of the Niagara near that place.

It was not until 1869 that a railroad bridge was built across the Hudson at Albany and then it was that another merger came to pass, this time resulting in the creation of the New York Central & Hudson River Railroad, a single system upon which one might now ride without change of cars from the city of New York all the way to Buffalo. It was not until 1914 that a return was made to the shorter and more historic name of the New York Central Railroad. At that time, the important Lake Shore & Michigan Southern, extending from Buffalo to Chicago, was merged into the parent company and a single New York Central Railroad created between New York and Chicago; while in the more generic term of New York Central Lines were included other important roads, such as the Michigan Central, the Big Four, and the Pittsburgh & Lake Erie.

In the wake of the New York Central and of the Erie across the state of New York, there gradually came other railroads. A line built from New York City across country to the foot of Lake Ontario was known first as the Oswego Midland and then as the New York, Ontario and Western. An important system grew in the northern part of the state, the Rome, Watertown & Ogdensburgh, which at the time of its merger with the Central in March, 1891, stretched, with its main line, all the way from Suspension Bridge, at Niagara Falls, to Massena Springs, close to the north boundary of the state. Coal railroads thrust themselves up from the south. The Delaware & Hudson Company ceased to be

a canal and became a railroad extending all the way
from Wilkes Barre, Pennsylvania, up through the
Albany gateway to Rouses Point, in the extreme
northeastern corner of New York. The Delaware,
Lackawanna & Western, which had merged itself into
the Erie at Great Bend, in 1882 built its own line
through to Buffalo, and developed from it various
branches, to Utica, to Syracuse and Oswego and to
Ithaca. The Lehigh Valley, also reaching out of the
anthracite coal country of northeastern Pennsylvania,
a little later decided no longer to have its terminals
at Geneva and at Auburn. In 1892 the Lehigh built
on through to Rochester and to Buffalo. When the
lines of the Lehigh Valley had been completed in 1869
up to the New York State line at Waverly, they were
connected with the rails of the Erie there. But the
Erie then had a six-foot gauge. To enable the
standard-gauge Lehigh Valley trains to reach Elmira,
a third-rail was laid in the Erie tracks. In 1876 this
additional rail was continued into Buffalo. The Lehigh
Valley continued to use these portions of the Erie track
until its own line was completed into Buffalo, in
September, 1892.

There were other railroad enterprises in the state in
all these years. The West Shore was built from New
York to Buffalo, up the west bank of the Hudson and
paralleling the New York Central all the way from
Albany to Buffalo. Within a year of its completion in
1884, it failed, utterly and completely, and soon after
it too was merged into the New York Central. A road
from Rochester to Salamanca, where it connected with
the Erie and the Atlantic and Great Western Railroad,
was put through in the beginning of the 'seventies,

under the title of the Rochester & State Line. This line, much enlarged and carried both into Buffalo and down into the bituminous regions of Pennsylvania, is now the Buffalo, Rochester & Pittsburgh, a bituminous carrier of great importance. A third road, of some size and importance in western New York, was the Western New York & Pennsylvania, which, about twenty years ago, was merged into the Pennsylvania system, giving that railroad direct access to both Rochester and Buffalo. For many years it has also owned the Northern Central reaching from Baltimore, north across Pennsylvania and western New York, with its northernmost terminals at Sodus and at Canandaigua.

THE PENNSYLVANIA AND THE BALTIMORE & OHIO RAILROADS

Already we have seen the beginnings of each of these important trunk-line systems of today. We have watched the citizens of oldtime Baltimore struggling to build some sort of a railroad over the crest of the Alleghanies to the navigable Ohio, to the Mississippi, and to the vast chain of inland waterways that served the entire central section of the continent; and we have seen William Norris operating the locomotive *George Washington* on an early section of the main rail line across the state of Pennsylvania.

This route across the Keystone State was first planned and put into actual operation as a curious combination of canal, of level railroad and of inclined plane. The Philadelphia & Columbia Railroad, upon which the hill-climbing proclivities of the *George Washington* were displayed, was but the first link in that combination, or chain, of an inland transport route.

Although originally intended to connect Philadelphia, at the confluence of the Delaware and the Schuykill Rivers with Columbia, a port upon the Susquehanna, it was, soon after its completion to that point, extended from Lancaster to Harrisburg, also upon the Susquehanna, and the capital of the state. From this point west, a canal followed the valley of the Juniata to Hollidaysburg, at the foot of the Alleghanies.

From the Hollidaysburg basin of the canal, an inclined plane rose sharply. At the summit of the mountain there was another stretch of level railroad which pierced the first tunnel to be bored in all America, and then connected with a second plane which descended the western slope of the mountains and joined, near Johnstown, a canal that led to Pittsburgh and the navigable waters of the upper Ohio. This railroad over the top of the mountains was known as the Portage Railroad, and Charles Dickens, in his *American Notes*, wrote an amusing account of it, as he saw it in the 'forties.

The Philadelphia & Columbia was opened April 16, 1834, when the locomotive *Black Hawk*, and a passenger train made a trip over the entire length of the line. The road was owned and operated by the state, although not very successfully. The original plan for it was to open it to all comers, on the same principle that any highway is open to the public. Horses were to be used and any man could drive a wagon upon it, provided he had placed the proper sort of flanged wheels upon his vehicle. The line was double-tracked from the outset and it was thought that it would soon become a great public convenience.

As a matter of fact, nothing but confusion resulted.

Some farmers, with their great, fitted Conestoga wagons, could go faster than others. There was no way in which a fast-going wagon could overtake and pass a slow-going one. The coming of the locomotive only added to this confusion. After a very few years of trial, the state of Pennsylvania abandoned the experiment and placed the operation of the Columbia line in the hands of a private company, which ran it in regular steam railroad fashion.

The Alleghany Portage Railroad, as it was called officially, had one track completed in 1833, and the other in the spring of the following year. It was thirty-six miles in length, its summit being 1398 feet above the eastern canal basin at Hollidaysburg and 1171 feet above the western one at Johnstown. It was in its way good, infinitely better, of course, than "packing" freight in horse-drawn wagons over the terrible mountain roads of the Alleghanies, but it had its own distinct limitations. Despite its double track and its neat tunnel it was impossible to pass more than 576 of the small railroad cars of that period over it within twenty-four hours. It is reported that it became so congested that it took the average passenger more than seven hours to make the crossing of the level thirty-six-mile stretch alone.

Supposedly, upon its completion, a traveler could go from Philadelphia to Pittsburgh over these so-called "state works," 118 miles by rail and 277 by canal, in ninety-one hours, or at an average rate of 4.34 miles per hour, hardly more than a good pace for a pedestrian. One can go by train from New York to San Francisco today, 3200 miles, in ninety-two hours and thirty-five minutes of actual elapsed time, although that same run has been made in a special train, as long ago as June, 1876, in eighty-four hours and seventeen minutes, actual elapsed time.

About 1845, a movement began to transfer the rest of the Pennsylvania "state works" to a single private company, which should operate them as well as the Philadelphia & Columbia, with which they were so closely associated. This resulted two years later, in the chartering of the present Pennsylvania Railroad Company, which not only took over the existing combined canal-and-rail route between Philadelphia and Pittsburgh, but prepared to abandon the canals and the Alleghany Portage Railroad between Harrisburg and Pittsburgh, replacing them with a modern double-tracked railroad.

With this in view, ground was broken at Harrisburg for the beginnings of that railroad on July 7, 1848, and a finished connection made by it with the Portage Railroad by November 1, 1850. Work was continued on through to Pittsburgh and, on December 10, 1852, a through train ran for the first time from Philadelphia all the way to Pittsburgh although over the historic Portage road. That line was not completely abandoned until two years later, when a new connecting link over the crest of the Alleghanies, generally parallel, but with much lower grades and easier curves, was completed and put into use.

With the main stem of the Pennsylvania thus completed, there remained the problem of perfecting its connections with the city and harbor of New York. As far back as April 1, 1839, the United Railroads of New Jersey, officially the New Jersey Railroad and Transportation Company, had after vast opposition, political and financial, succeeded in completing an all-rail line from Jersey City to Camden, on the Delaware, just across from Philadelphia. With great glee, it was announced that now one could travel in the steam trains all that ninety miles in six hours. Ten years later, a full sixty minutes had been taken off this running time and this was then regarded as a real accomplishment. At about the same time (1849) a single pair of rails was laid within Theodore Burr's famous wooden bridge over the Delaware at Trenton and rail communication brought down the Pennsylvania side of the river into Philadelphia. It was not until some years afterward, however, that the United Railroads of New Jersey were merged into the Pennsylvania Railroad and the upbuilding of one of the noteworthy railroad systems of America began.

In after years, many other roads, large and small, were to be brought into this system: east of Pittsburgh the most notable of them, the Philadelphia, Wilmington & Baltimore, the Baltimore & Potomac, the Northern Central, the Cumberland Valley and the Western New York & Pennsylvania; west of that important gateway city, the Fort Wayne, the Panhandle, the Vandalia and the Grand Rapids & Indiana.

Of the struggles of the Baltimore & Ohio through the first three decades, it may be said that, in addition to the hard engineering problems such as confronted its immediate neighbor to the north, and the financial ones that were common to most of the railroads of that early day, it had peculiar political ones with which to contend. Its first main stem from Baltimore to the Ohio at Wheeling, which was completed and opened for regular traffic, January 1, 1853, passed through two states, Maryland and Virginia, that had always shown considerable jealousy of one another. The promoters of the railroad were dragged hither and thither between the contentions of these commonwealths. If Maryland gave money, Virginia would not. If Virginia gave money, it was with embarrassing stipulations that Wheeling, which still was within her boundaries, should become the sole western terminus of the road. This was a thrust at the idea in the minds of some of its progenitors that Pittsburgh, already beginning to be recognized as an important key city, be made its chief terminal upon the banks of the Ohio. Virginia sought to prevent such a thing coming to pass, and so also did the friends of the Pennsylvania "state works" within their own state.

In the long run, however, the Baltimore & Ohio managed to reach Pittsburgh in the year 1874. It also reached Parkersburg, on the Ohio, ninety-three miles below Wheeling, early in 1857.

But the Baltimore & Ohio, having finally reached the banks of the Ohio, after a quarter of a century of fearsome struggle, found that it had won a somewhat empty victory. Navigation upon that stream, at its best was not an easy matter. The great era of steamboating upon our American rivers was about to decline. The invasion of the Middle West by the locomotive already had begun. Lines were being hurried through to Cleveland, to Detroit, to Chicago.

Of this invasion, much more will be said in the succeeding chapter. For the present, it need merely be said that the Baltimore & Ohio, having succeeded in completing a line all the way from its chief ocean port to Parkersburg, found other lines opening simultaneously toward the west.   The Marietta & Cincinnati started from a point in the state of Ohio nearly opposite Parkersburg and ran into what was then almost always called the Queen City of the West.   The Ohio & Mississippi connected with it at Cincinnati and continued over the long, flat stretches of southern Indiana and Illinois up to East St. Louis, completing a through route by which a traveler could now go from New York to St. Louis, by changing cars five times and by making two short steamboat voyages, one on the Delaware and one on the Ohio, and three intermediate ferry trips. Cumbersome as this was, however, it was vastly better than anything that had gone before.

From Baltimore east, the connection to New York was over the rails of the Philadelphia, Wilmington & Baltimore and the United Railroads of New Jersey.   In later years, these lines, coming into the hands of the rival Pennsylvania system, were to offer scant interchange facilities to the Baltimore & Ohio, which presently was to retaliate by effecting its own entrance into the harbor of New York, putting down its own rails as far as Philadelphia and east of that city using those of the Reading and the Central Railroad of New Jersey systems.

But the combination of United Railroads, the Philadelphia, Wilmington & Baltimore, and the Baltimore & Ohio, for many, many years made not only a through route to the West but practically the only one along the Atlantic seaboard to the South.   As far back as 1835, the Baltimore & Ohio had put the first pair of rails into the national capital, the so-called Washington Branch, which left the main line of the road just nine miles west of Baltimore.   This came into speedy favor, and for a

Passenger Car on the Baltimore and Ohio Railroad, 1830.

number of years it handled a traffic considerably in excess of that which went up and down the main line of the road.

Below Washington, however, the rail service to the South was rather poor. One could take a steamboat at that city and, by going down the Potomac for about thirty miles, board a train which took one straight to Richmond, and connections leading still further south, while right from Washington itself, a straggling railroad led across Long Bridge, afterwards to become a historic landmark, through Alexandria and Manasses to Orange. Beyond this point railroad service again became much more irregular and uncertain.

CHAPTER IV

AMERICAN RAILROAD DEVELOPMENT—II

THE advance of the railroad across the Middle West was swift and comparatively easy. The long, level stretches of the vast Mississippi basin offered no such engineering difficulties as did the Alleghanies, or the mountainous hills of New England. Moreover, the railroad no longer was an infant in arms. By the middle of the last century, when the rail development of that great section of the United States was begun in real earnest, it was twenty years old. Its season of wild and fantastic experimentation, common to almost every new industry, was past. Of course there would be many new things invented and developed, but the great foundation factors of rail transport had been securely laid. The work next at hand consisted of a development of that form of transportation upon lines already laid down and tested.

While it was not until almost 1850, or at least until well into the fourth decade of the past century, that this rail development of the central portions of the North American continent began in real earnest, one finds that in Ohio a railroad was actually projected and built as early as 1835. This was the Mad River & Lake Erie Railroad which was begun south from Sandusky in that year. A portion of it was opened for traffic in

1838. In connection with the Little Miami road from Springfield to Cincinnati, which was finished in 1846, it formed the first through railroad from Lake Erie to the Ohio River. Five years later, a second line was completed from Lake Erie to the Little Miami Railroad. This road started at Cleveland, which was just beginning to come into its own as an important city, and passed through Columbus, the capital of the state, on its way to Springfield. It was known officially as the Cleveland, Columbus & Cincinnati and today it is one of the main lines of the so-called Big Four Railroad, which is one of the New York Central group.

The Little Miami Railroad in its day was regarded by the Ohio folk with a fervent admiration. From a guide book of it, published in 1854, one gains a slight idea of that affection. The small book goes on to say:

. . . . The Little Miami Railroad did not exist twelve years since—nor any other railway in the Valley of the Ohio—but now it is here, to take you on your journey with all the speed, comfort and convenience of any such road, in any country; and there are now (1854) three thousand miles of railway in this valley! Year after year hundreds of miles are added to the number, and where it once took weeks to accomplish a journey, it now takes only hours! What a revolution! But the revolution is not in gain of time only, nor even money. The great change is in society. Thousands meet now where tens met twenty years since. Look through these cars, and you see around men, women and children going to see friends, or transact business, or seeking pleasure, where they could not have dreamed of going a few years since. Some are only going to the next town; some to the Lakes; some to the Atlantic; some to Europe. . . . The Railroad and the Steamboat have made man almost ubiquitous on this little earth and his fondness for novelty and change is gratified beyond the dreams of fancy.   Where will this stop?

A third line between Lake Erie and the Ohio, was the Cleveland & Pittsburgh, which was opened in 1852, and almost immediately formed a valuable connection for the Pennsylvania and the Baltimore & Ohio systems reaching into Pittsburgh from the East.

Already we have seen the New York Central absorbing the former Lake Shore & Michigan Southern Railway and acquiring by purchase the Michigan Central. Originally these roads were bitter rivals.   In 1850 and '51, they were racing across the southern portions of the Peninsular State, the one from Toledo and the other from Detroit, to reach Chicago which already was recognized as destined to become one of the greatest, if not the very greatest city of the interior United States. The Michigan Central won the race, although only by a few weeks.   It thrust its line across to the new Illinois Central and so gained quick entrance into the city of its destination.   The Michigan Southern came in soon afterward.   This was in 1852.

Later the Michigan Southern was to be combined with the Lake Shore, a merger of railroads connecting Toledo with Cleveland and Buffalo.   The Lake Shore & Michigan Southern, as it soon came to be known, eventually straightened its somewhat roundabout main line by building "cut offs" or direct lines for many miles both east and west of Toledo.

In a similar way the Michigan Central was made, by the acquisition of a very straight stretch of railroad along the north bank of Lake Erie, which had been known as the Canada Southern, into a through route between Buffalo and Chicago. This connected with the old New York Central & Hudson River system by bridges over the Niagara River, both at Buffalo and at Suspension Bridge.

RAILROAD DEVELOPMENT IN ILLINOIS

With these roads and the extensions of the Baltimore & Ohio and the Pennsylvania that were noticed in the last chapter, the states of Ohio and Indiana as well as the southern portions of Michigan, began to be well gridironed with railroads. Illinois followed.

The legislature of that pioneer state as long ago as February, 1837, was induced to appropriate more than $10,000,000 for internal improvements, chiefly railroads. How hard a tax that was on a struggling new country, then without sufficient revenue even to meet its current expenses, may be realized when it is stated that it imposed a debt of $34.10 upon every man, woman and child within the commonwealth. Illinois towns were few and far between. Chicago, today a city of three million folk, had but 1450 population and a garrison to protect it from the Indians. The Illinois prairies stretched for miles, without the slightest evidence of human life or human habitation showing itself. Yet the legislature of that new state not only appropriated $10,000,000 for railroads in 1837, but the following year, an additional $5,000,000.

They had faith in railroads, those pioneers. Sometimes they showed too much faith. There came unscrupulous promoters who traded on that faith and accepted hard earned savings for which no value ever was given. But these cases were exceptions.

Even they were founded upon a growing knowledge of what the "iron horse," as they used to like to call the locomotive, had accomplished for villages and cities further east; upon the transformation it had wrought, all within so short a space of time. No wonder men gave their savings, ofttimes fought for the privilege of investing them in new railroad enterprises. Scores of railroad schemes, some of them frankly of little value, came to the fore.

Of all of these very first railroad plans in the middle west none was ever carried far enough to see the actual laying of rails, save the Northern Cross Railroad, which was to run a main line from Quincy, an important early river port on the Mississippi, east to Indiana. Another line was to cross this at right angles; hence the name, Northern Cross.

Ground for this road was broken August, 1837, but two years after the beginning of the Mad River & Lake Erie Railroad at Sandusky, and but seven years after the first railroad train in the country, on the Baltimore and Ohio, to operate for passengers, had begun its work. Strap rails from the East were carried up the river to Meredosia in the spring of 1838 and track laying was begun before the middle of May. That November the first locomotive in Illinois hauled a highly select party, eight miles out over the prairie and back. During the next two or three years, despite the fearful financial conditions prevailing throughout the land, construction work was pushed on the Northern Cross, with the result that on February 15, 1842, a combined freight and passenger train began a three-times-a-week service between Jacksonville and Springfield, fifty-seven miles apart.

After a time, the locomotive ran off the poorly laid track and was badly damaged. The road had no money to repair it and so a mule was substituted as motive power. This railroad finally was sold (1847). Larger cars and three locomotives were purchased and it went to work again, this time not to cease its operations, but to become, at a later day, a part of the present Wabash system.

THE ILLINOIS CENTRAL—A STATE-OWNED RAILROAD

Even before the breaking of ground for the ill-fated Northern Cross, there was incorporated in Illinois, a railroad company whose name at least was finally to represent a real success, and to carry the good name and fame of the state all over the nation. This was the Illinois Central, which in its very first corporate form, came into existence on January 18, 1836. It was planned to be built north and south the entire length of the state, with state aid and under state supervision.

This first company, however, was doomed to be short-lived. Like a thousand other railroad companies of its day, it became insolvent and soon its affairs were closed, but the idea of the Illinois Central, itself, persisted, and on March 6, 1843, the Great Western Railway Company was incorporated, to take over the original charter and build the road.

It was not more fortunate than its predecessor. Men were beginning to find that it is one thing to plan a railroad and quite another thing to finance and build it. The Great Western's charter was repealed in 1845 and then renewed once again four years later, but still no progress was made in the actual building of the Illinois

Central.   The people of the state fretted greatly under the repeated delays.

The result was that in January, 1850, a law was passed giving a grant of state lands to a railroad to be built from Chicago not only to Cairo, at the extreme southerly tip of the state, but to the seaport of Mobile, upon the Gulf of Mexico.   The author of this law was Stephen A. Douglas, the brilliant attorney and operator, who afterwards was to come to fame as the great, although unsuccessful, opponent of Abraham Lincoln. Lincoln's name was connected with the formation period of the Illinois Central, but only as a local attorney for a short time.

With a land grant as its substantial backing, the much mooted Illinois Central project began at last to attract serious attention in the East.   A group of eastern capitalists decided to support the plan.   The Great Western was induced to surrender its charter and on February 10, 1851 the present Illinois Central company was formally incorporated to replace it.   The charter of the new company expressly provided that it would have to take its grant and complete its line by July 4, 1854.   These conditions were accepted.

Never in all the quarter century of railroad building that had gone forward here in the United States, had so great a task been placed before railroad builders. More than seven hundred miles of line had to be built by one company, within but a little more than three years.   Even with a level state to be traversed, the project was enormous.

It was undertaken, nevertheless, and carried through to a reasonably prompt culmination.   The then main line of the road, from Cairo to La Salle, 301 miles, was

completed, Janury 8, 1855; the Galena Branch, from
La Salle to Dunleith, in June of the same year; and the
one from Chicago to a junction with the old main line,
249 miles south of Lake Michigan, on September 21,
1856. Eventually the state was to profit very greatly
by the aid which it had given this railroad enterprise.
But very wisely it decided to forego the temptation to
take over and operate the road on its own account, as
was urged upon it more than once.

The Illinois Central today is one of the strongest systems in the United States, and the only very important
one running directly north and south. It never reached
Mobile, but for many years its chief southern terminal
has been in the more important port of New Orleans.
It operates a vast network of lines and is all the while in
steady process of expansion.

THE IRON HORSE REACHES THE MISSISSIPPI—AND CROSSES IT

Along the westerly edge of the great state of Illinois,
runs the course of the Mississippi, with its many
tributaries serving by far the largest drainage area in
the world. Upon the Mississippi and the more important streams draining into it, there ran in the middle
of the last century the mightiest fleet of steamboats
that ever had been known. The earliest railroad
promoters were careful to keep away from even the
thought of competition with that armada. Yet,
eventually, almost in the hour of the outbreak of the
Civil War, the river steamboat was suddenly to find
that it had a tremendous antagonist in the iron horse.
He steadily was to increase in strength, while the
steamboat lost ground, until this last mode of transport

was but a shadow of its former mightiness, a wraith that spoke feebly, though eloquently, of past glories.

By 1855 the railroad had reached the east bank of the Father of Waters, and the following year it had thrust its first bridge over the Mississippi, at Rock Island, the pioneer line and one that was to take for itself the name of that small Illinois city. The path of this bridge, some 1,535 feet in length, ran right over Rock Island itself, that island being reserved entirely by the United States government as a military workshop and arsenal.

This bridge was at once the center of much contention. The steamboat men hated it. In the entire length of the Mississippi south of St. Paul, it was the first bridge of any sort with which they had to contend. Moreover, the design of the structure excited their especial ire, and after a blazing steamer had been sent drifting down against it in an ineffectual attempt to destroy it, the case was taken both into the courts and into Congress, and became a *cause celebre*. In it the name of Abraham Lincoln appeared, prominently this time, as a chief attorney for the struggling railroad.

Eventually the case was compromised. The badly planned first bridge was torn down and a far better one, at higher level, was erected, at the joint expense of the federal government and the Rock Island railroad.

The extension of the Chicago & Rock Island to the bank of the Mississippi was followed quickly by the building of the Galena & Chicago Union,—the beginnings of the present Chicago & Northwestern system,—the Chicago & Alton, and the Chicago, Burlington & Quincy—all of these, railroads which have since continued and prospered.

Within three or four years after the completion of the Rock Island bridge the iron horse was at the brink of the Missouri, at the old historic trading post of St. Joseph. Officially, this was the Hannibal & St. Joseph, which in its own day and generation, had no little reputation, and which long since became a part of the Burlington system. This line was finished into St. Joseph in 1859, and it was not until seven years later that another railroad was built to the banks of the distant Missouri, when the Chicago & Northwestern poked its way into Council Bluffs, Iowa, there to connect with the Union Pacific, already under way far off toward the West.

St. Joseph long had been an important starting point for stagecoach routes for California and Oregon. The completion of the Hannibal & St. Joseph Railroad greatly stimulated these activities until there came the time when a four-horse or a six-horse coach started from it on its tedious way across the western part of the continent, each twenty-four hours, or oftener. It was not only a tedious, but ofttimes a highly disagreeable and a hazardous trip. Two thousand weary miles stretched between St. Joe and Sacramento, where the traveler could board a steamboat for a night's run down to San Francisco. With good fortune the coach went through in six weeks; more often it took a far longer time than this.

BRIDGING THE CONTINENT BY RAILROAD

The first transcontinental railroad was only seven or eight years behind the first transcontinental telegraph wire, which was put through in 1862. Even before the Civil War had begun, men were actively engaged in preparing to build the Union Pacific, a thousand miles straight west from Council Bluffs, Iowa, to Ogden, Utah. At Ogden it was to make a connection with the Central Pacific, that remarkable railroad enterprise out of California, which already was poking its nose eastward over the great Sierras.

On May 10, 1869, these two roads, one building toward the West, the other toward the East, met at Promontory, Utah, a short distance west of Ogden, where, with stirring ceremony, the rails were joined. After this a man, with his goods, might travel all the way across the continent by rail,— from New York, from Boston, from a thousand intermediate points, to Sacramento, at Pacific tide-water, and within an easy 90-mile run by steamboat from San Francisco.

Concerning that memorable day of the joining of the two railroads that made America's first transcontinental route, it was to be written:

Until the rails met that day at Promontory, the Union was incomplete. It was but a geographical dogma, a mere political theory, which an attempt to materialize the proposed Pacific Empire, or other contingency, might readily have changed. The driving of that last spike riveted the bonds that made the East and West one grand whole as surely as it held the rail in place. All the magnificent achievements of after years have been possible to the great nation then made a virile fact; whether they would have been possible otherwise may well be doubted.

By the beginning of 1867, the Union Pacific was operating to a point 305 miles west of Omaha. The completion of the Chicago & Northwestern to Council

The "Pioneer," an Early Locomotive on the Union Pacific System.

Bluffs (just across the Missouri from Omaha, and the legal eastern terminus of the Union Pacific) not only was a great stimulus to the construction work, but it opened an efficient line of communication for bringing in heavy supplies of every sort.   The result was that by August, 1868, the Union Pacific already was 698 miles west of Omaha.   Work began to go forward at a great speed.

As has just been stated, work on the first transcontinental railroad was also proceeding eastward from the Pacific Coast.   The story of the organization of the Central Pacific is quite as romantic as that of some of the early systems along the Atlantic seaboard. A hardware store in the brisk capital city of California, Sacramento, bore above its door, a sign which read "Huntington & Hopkins."   In the gold days, these two men had acquired more than a local reputation for shrewdness and for business ability.   Among their cronies was Leland Stanford who ran a grocery store but a few doors away.   Another was Charles Crocker, a local dry-goods merchant.

These four storekeepers of Sacramento, in almost impassioned vision, planned to build a railroad over the Sierras and off toward the East.   In fact, they not only planned such a road, but actually built it, despite difficulties at times seemingly insurmountable.   But their faith, their energy, their co-operation, was almost indomitable.   Back and forth to the East they went across the continent in the plunging stagecoaches or by boat by the Panama route, to Washington, to gain the support of Congress, and to New York and to Boston, to help finance their stupendous project.   Most of these missions were finally successful.   The Central Pacific

Railroad came into existence. Grading was begun upon it at Sacramento, January 1, 1863.

These years of the 'sixties were hard years for the Union. It was plunged into the great Civil War, upon the outcome of which its very existence depended. Even as important and as necessary an improvement as a transcontinental railroad, was compelled to wait the finishing of the war. Therefore it is not to be wondered at that three years and eight months after the first breaking of ground for it, the Central Pacific reached but a brief seventy miles east from Sacramento.

After this, however, things moved more swiftly. In the next two months, twenty-three more miles of rail were laid down and Cisco, at an altitude of 2,286 feet, was reached. The road was now well within the Sierras. To cross them not less than fifteen tunnels must be driven. The task was, indeed, appalling. Yet all that summer of 1867, the Central Pacific was pushed forward, with 10,000 men and 10,300 teams of horses to assist in the work. By December 1, all of the tunnels had been bored and trains were running through to Truckee, at the very top of the Sierras and 140 miles east of Sacramento. The hardest part of the construction work had been completed.

The Spring of 1868 found these two companies of the first transcontinental route almost in equal progress of advancement. Whilst the Central Pacific had been crossing the Sierras, the Union Pacific had been surmounting Evans Pass, in Wyoming, rising to an altitude of 8,242 feet. Both roads at last had ample funds and both were almost at equal distance from the Great Salt Lake, the Union Pacific being 522 miles away and the Central Pacific, 545.

Building the Transcontinental Railroad System.

With the opening of that memorable spring, there began a campaign of railroad construction such as has never been seen elsewhere. From 20,000 to 25,000 men were employed constantly and as much as 600 tons of material were used in the course of twenty-four hours. "A mile of track a day" became the slogan of the workers and even this remarkable figure was at times exceeded. At one time not less than thirty vessels, laden with rail supplies for the Central Pacific, were on their way on the long 19,000-mile journey from New York to San Francisco around the Horn. Up around Truckee, twenty-five saw-mills worked feverishly in cutting timber for its ties, its trestles and its snow-sheds—these last a real necessity in the Sierras.

In 1867, 240 miles of track were laid by the Union Pacific; in 1868, 425 miles; and in 1869, up to May 10, when the tracks were finally joined at Promontory, 125 miles. In the same years, the Central Pacific had laid through the Sierras, 94 miles the first year, 363 miles the second year and 186 miles the third year. In the mind of any railroad engineer these figures speak for themselves.

OTHER TRANSCONTINENTAL RAILROADS

It was not until 1883 that the tremendous enterprise of bridging the country with a railroad was again accomplished. In that year the Northern Pacific, connecting St. Paul, Minnesota, with Tacoma, Washington (afterwards with Portland, Oregon, and Seattle also), just below the northern rim of the country, was first opened and a great new territory stood ready for development. At about the same time a railroad along the southerly edge of the United States—the

Southern Pacific, from San Francisco and Los Angeles to El Paso, Texas, and to New Orleans—was completed, which in due time, absorbed the famous Central Pacific. After this, the railroads in the West came rapidly. The Santa Fé built its connection from Albuquerque, New Mexico, to Los Angeles and became the fourth transcontinental route. It was finished through to Chicago in 1888. A tremendous number of lines interlaced all of these.

In more recent years, railroad extension in the United States has not been so swift. The development of our railroad properties has taken more intensive forms. Important branches and "cut offs" have been built, additional main line tracks put down, great yards and terminals constructed. It is estimated that the traffic upon our American railroads doubles in volume each ten years or thereabouts, which shows that for this steadily growing flood not only locomotives and new cars must be provided in great plenty, but abundant trackage upon which to operate them. This means that the real development of the American railroad never really ceases. As long as its traffic continues to increase, its physical structure must constantly expand to meet the vast needs thrust upon it.

The development of rail communication has been recently illustrated (1927) in the Centenary of the Baltimore and Ohio railroad at Halethorpe, Md. The "Pageant of the Iron Horse," showing engines and cars of all types, was a dramatization of railroad progress. Pupils of Baltimore and Washington were excused from school for the day, to study at first hand the history of a utility which has so largely contributed to the expansion and consolidation of this nation.

The Golden Spike Ceremony at Promontory, Utah, May 10, 1869.

CHAPTER V

OUR RAILROADS OF TODAY

THE standard steam railroads of the United States, excluding those of Canada and of Mexico, with which they are closely correlated and which have more than 60,000 route-miles of line, today comprise more than 250,000 route-miles. By route-miles one means the miles of first or main-line track. To this great total may be added 37,000 miles of additional main line trackage, second or third or fourth parallel pairs of rails, and 114,000 miles of yard tracks and sidings of every sort. The grand total comes to an astounding figure, 400,000 miles. This is enough to lap sixteen times around the world at the equator.

Like the great and shadowy web of a giant spider, this railroad system covers North America. In all the United States and in Canada there is not a town, or a city of more than 3,000 population which is not served directly by it. More than this, most of these communities are reached by not one, but by two or more lines, many times by more, in competition for their traffic.

In no other nation, is the railroad so intimately entwined with social and commercial life and progress as it is here in the United States. No American city today would dare to try to exist without it. There is no doubt whatsoever as to its standing as a utility.   It is the super-utility.   It is the utility of utilities, and this, too, in the day of the glorification of the motor vehicle.   For, despite the very general use of the automobile in this country today, when there is a car for every four or five of us, and when with but little crowding the nation's entire population could at one time embark in its motor vehicles and go sailing gaily off in them, our railroads last year carried a billion passengers.

These folk rode in a variety of fashions, on fast trains and on slow.   Some went short distances and some went a very long way.   Some of them traveled on slow local trains in the sparsely settled sections of the land, while others rode upon what are said to be among the fastest trains in all creation, such as those between New York and Chicago, or between Philadelphia and Atlantic City.

Several hundred millions of travelers were the daily suburban passengers in and out of the larger cities—in ordinary parlance, the commuters.   Here, again, the railroad, is in a very large sense, a city utility, and here again it performs a large service.   If it takes 30,000 people into a city terminal in the morning and takes the same 30,000 out to their homes again in the evening, by so doing, in the three hundred working days of the year, it has added some eighteen millions to that grand total of a billion passengers a year.   It has indeed performed a very great service to the city, not only by relieving its housing facilities, but by getting its citizens to live out in the healthy open country of sunshine and fresh air.

The freight service of the American railroad lines may seem less picturesque than passenger service, but it is no less important. In some ways freight service is more important. In a recent typical year the railroads had 68,172 locomotives upon their lines and 56,842 passenger cars, in addition to about 8,800 Pullmans, but to carry the vast and unending burden of freight, it required not less than 2,352,508 cars. Two and one-third millions of cars may not seem so much at first thought, but when one comes to realize that these cars coupled end to end as a single train would extend on a vast curve all the way through Africa and Asia, across the Behring Straits, and then down North America, Central America and South America—from the Cape of Good Hope to within 1,200 miles of Cape Horn—one begins to gain some rough idea of the immensity of such a fleet.

These cars work. Upon the railroad, idleness is a sin. In a single twelve months, enough freight is offered our rail carriers to make a hundred parallel rows of loaded cars, all the way from New York to San Francisco, 3,200 miles. Of these, fifty of the parallel rows would be laden with coal and other mine products; twenty with the output of the factories of this broad land; another nineteen with the products of agriculture, including forestry. Another figure may be of interest. In an average year, the American railroad now transports the equivalent of one ton of freight 4,300 miles for every man, woman and child in all the land.

The investment in our railroads alone, represents property which it would take the entire population of the United States over a year to produce, if they worked upon nothing else whatever. To replace all the utilities covered by this book would probably take the equivalent of at least five years' labor by the entire population of the country. Inasmuch as the country could not possibly run without food, coal, transportation and other services, only a fraction of its population could ever be devoted to the replacement of these utilities. Even if a quarter of the population, which would be a high proportion, could work on nothing else, it would take twenty years.

Our American railroad system, coming close to the one-hundredth year of its life, is indeed no small business. More than twelve million people, directly or indirectly, derive their living from it. From twenty to twenty-six billion dollars already have been invested in it, and more is being invested all the time.

THE ORGANIZATION OF A RAILROAD

Some 2,000 separate corporations form the railroad system of America, although ninety-five per cent of the traffic, both passenger and freight, is hauled upon the 100 roads which report a gross business of a million dollars or upwards each year. A million dollars a year is no great sum for a railroad. Several of our lines receive gross revenues of a million dollars a day or more.

The owners of these corporations are the stockholders, each of whom owns one or more of its various types of shares and so is entitled to vote at its annual meetings in proportion to his stockholdings. These stockholders elect directors who form themselves into a board and in turn elect a chairman, a president and several vice-presidents.

In the United States the president of a railroad is the chief authority over the road. If his rule is not supreme, it is nearly so. He gives his entire time to a

TRANSPORTATION OF COAL ON THE BUFFALO, ROCHESTER, AND PITTSBURGH RAILROAD.

complicated business for which he has trained himself by long years of experience and endeavor.

As a rule, his vice-presidents are assigned to the different chief functions of the railroad that he heads. Thus, a vice-president is detailed to operation, which, though in a large sense might be thought to mean every feature of the actual operation of a railroad, is, on most of our lines in this country, limited to control of the actual movement of the trains. On a large road the addition to and upkeep of equipment alone may easily call for a vice-president; the maintenance of the track and bridges and buildings, for another one. The traffic department of the railroad—its selling organization, which also maintains its rate schedules—requires, and receives, a vice-president; so does the legal end, and on larger systems, the financial and corporate business end as well. Engineering, the creation of new structures of every sort for the railroad, is in itself a large problem. For this there is still another vice-president. In recent years the growing importance of both labor and the public relations problems have caused some of the larger roads to create separate vice-presidents for these activities.

Sometimes size enters into the reckoning. A road which must, of necessity, maintain its chief headquarters five hundred or a thousand miles from a highly important city, may establish, to improve all of its relationships in that city, a resident vice-president. This is a policy which within the past few years has developed rather rapidly.

Beneath the president and his immediate family of vice-presidents there are, on any sizable road, many other officers, filling posts of authority and responsibility. For instance, in the operating end alone, there is a great human structure gradually developed through years of experience and trial.   The chief unit of this operating structure is the division superintendent. He is, if you please, a prince who rules over a real principality. His division may consist of from a hundred to five hundred miles of main line trackage, depending very largely upon the congestion of the territory and the volume of the traffic. He has headquarters at some point, central and convenient to his division, and to help him in the many, many details of his work, he probably will have one or more assistants.

A group of superintendents, men who are apt to be at all times in most intimate touch with all the phases of the working of the line, report to a general superintendent.   In turn, a group of general superintendents report to a general manager.   On even a reasonably good-sized road there may be but one general manager and he may also bear the title of vice-president.   On the larger roads, however, there are certain to be two or three or even more general managers, all of whom report to the vice-president in charge of operation, at the general headquarters.

The same form of organization is followed, to a greater or a lesser degree, in the other departments of the railroad.   Its traffic, its engineering, its maintenance and its motive power departments follow rather closely the division units of the system.

In the details of administering authority, there is divergence. For instance, the division engineer on some roads reports directly to the superior officers of his own department.   He may have offices in the same building with the superintendent of his division; yet the

Ore Yards and Docks, Pennsylvania Railroad, Ashtabula, Ohio.

relationship between these two men is purely a friendly one. Officially they have no connection, save from the fact that they both are working for the same railroad. They co-operate in many, many ways, but to give *official* instructions to the division engineer, the division superintendent must communicate through the higher officers of his department, who confer with the higher officers of the engineering department, who, in turn, may issue the instructions to the division engineer.

This is called the departmental system of railroad organization and it works with surprisingly little delay or obstruction, particularly when one considers the many steps that must be taken in it.

The other system, the divisional one, raises the division superintendent to a post of really high authority and gives him immediate supervision over the officers of the other departments who are in his immediate neighborhood and territory. While much quicker and more direct in its workings, it has disadvantages, and so it is that some of the largest of the railroads of the United States refuse to accept it, and cling tenaciously to the departmental system.

THE OPERATION OF THE RAILROAD

With this general structure of the organization of a large steam railroad clearly in mind, let us proceed to the actual operation of trains upon the line.

Trains divide themselves, quite obviously, into freight and passenger trains, although there are cases on branch lines of slight traffic, where both freight and passenger will be consolidated into a single train, rather adequately described as *mixed*. In both the freight and the passenger services of the railroad there are also many classes of trains. In the first of these may be placed the fast or preference or merchandise freights, which make a speed quite as swift as many of the passenger trains, the special trains devoted entirely to the hauling of such perishable or extra-valuable commodities as fruit or meats or raw silk or even bullion, and then the slow-moving ones for the haulage of coal, of lumber, grain or other bulky materials for which speed is not the greatest object.

Passenger trains divide themselves into express and local trains—the first, moving at high speed and omitting most of the smaller stops, *en route*, and the second, sacrificing speed in order to take care of the travelers into and out of the smaller stations. There are two or more classes of express trains, ranging from those almost local in their spirit of accommodation to the smaller intervening stops to non-stop *de luxe* trains of swiftest speed, composed entirely of parlor, sleeping, dining, club and observation cars and for which an extra fare is often charged.

Commodities, aside from the personal baggage of the passengers, frequently move on passenger trains; in fact they are carried on almost all of them except the fastest *de luxe* expresses. On many passenger or semi-passenger trains are transported the sizable tonnage of the mails—letters, newspapers, magazine and parcel post packages, all under the direct control of the United States government—and the packages of the privately owned and operated express companies. By an odd tradition, the collection and distribution of milk and cream, in these days a large factor in the railroad business, have always been assigned to the passenger service. This is chiefly because milk cars have

The Twentieth Century Limited of the New York Central Railroad.

generally been attached to certain classes of passenger trains.

The operation of all these trains, both freight and passenger, is in accordance with a master timetable, made and maintained in each division headquarters but subject, of course, to a general and detailed supervision from general headquarters. It is a somewhat complicated chart, accurately ruled and measured in its two dimensions, the one way for every mile of the division, and the other for each hour (and minute) of the twenty-four. The course of a train therefore may be indicated by striking a line diagonally down across the face of this chart. From the intersections of the time lines and the distance lines may be picked out the arriving and leaving times of each train at each station, or in case there is to be no stop, the passing time.

These lines are first platted in colored strings, so as to admit of easy readjustment, and the men who do the platting come to be very swift and very expert in it. It is a form of mathematics, with much charm.

The timetable which is given you at the nearest railroad station probably shows only a small number of the trains that are indicated upon the complicated master timetable at headquarters. Freight trains, except those named as *mixed*, are never shown save on the so-called working timetables which are printed and issued only to the employees of the division, and even on these there are many freight trains that are never shown. Freight traffic fluctuates greatly, not merely from season to season, but even from day to day.

Therefore the bulk of it is carried upon *extras*, the possibility of whose existence is indicated on the master time card, but which may or may not be put into operation on any given day. If it is decided that any one of these *extras* should be ordered into service on any given day, a crew and a locomotive are ordered out for it, and its movement over the road is announced by telephone or telegraphic advice to all concerned. Frequently, not always, the extra is designated simply by the number of the locomotive.

Extra passenger trains are operated in much the same way, their movement or operation being left to the judgment of the chief train dispatcher, whose instructions are followed out through the train dispatcher who in turn issues orders from time to time as the train moves over the division, as he has full charge of all train movements in his district.   The train dispatcher would, if possible, run an extra as a section of a regular train in order to facilitate its movement against other extra trains, as the movement of extra trains over single track lines, without delay, is usually a difficult task and requires very close, constant supervision.

THE MOVEMENT OF A TRAIN

While the superintendent has general supervision, still the movement of any one train is under the immediate control of the dispatcher who issues orders by phone or telegraph (signing each with the initials of his superintendent) for its movement and who keeps in close touch with it on its way over the road.   The trainmaster sees to it that the engineer and fireman, as well as the other members of the crew, have reported for duty well in advance of the starting hour from the terminal.

The engine part of the crew sign for the locomotive at the round-house or other designated point, first

making a superficial inspection to make sure that it is
in good working condition.   When they are done with it
at the far end of the run, there will be other formalities
of *"signing off"* before it is turned over to the round-
house crew there.   There is system always in the
operation of a modern railroad.   Similar *signings* are
in order by the conductor of the train, not merely at
terminals, but at important intermediate points.   There
is no guesswork anywhere.

The conductor of the train is not only like unto the
captain of a ship, but to the purser as well.   He is responsible for carrying out train orders; he is required
to report any unnecessary delay; he is responsible for
the discipline of the train crew and the comfort of the
passengers; and finally he collects tickets or railroad
fares.   In this last work, on some roads, he is assisted
or relieved by special auditors.

On freight trains, instead of tickets, the conductor
has *waybills*.   In truth, a waybill is a sort of ticket for
freight shipment.   One copy of it travels with that
shipment, duplicate copies being held by the shipper
and by the forwarding office.

So it is that the little red caboose at the rear end of
the freight train is not only a resting place for the
conductor and his train crew but also a small traveling
office.   At his desk, the freight conductor sorts and
resorts his waybills, makes up his record of the train
and its contents—first, by the numbers and the initials
of the roads owning the cars, and second, by their
contents, as indicated by his waybills.   If he leaves a
car, he leaves its waybill; if he receives a car en route,
he demands its waybill.   If there is no waybill, he
probably will refuse to take the car.   His rights and his

obligations, he understands definitely. It all is as precise as the laws of the Medes and Persians.

Across the broad face of America, thousands and tens of thousands of these trains are making their way each day of the year, each hour of the twenty-four. The railroad knows no sleeping hours. The bulk of the traffic comes in the day or at night, depending on conditions, location and seasons. Effort is made to handle local freight by daylight. Day and night the traffic still rumbles forward. It is unending. It is flowing all the while, like the great unquenchable tide of commerce that it really is.

At night, the greater part of the six thousand sleeping cars, most of them owned and operated by the Pullman Company, go into active service. Each accommodates comfortably from twenty to thirty-two people. If all of them were filled, they would house more than 175,000 human beings nightly. On an extremely modest average of half-filled, they would still be carrying more than 80,000 folk, who sleep and, it is to be hoped, sleep soundly as they travel. It is the biggest hotel system, by far, in all the world.

THE MODERN CITY—AND THE RAILROAD

Without the railroad, the modern American city would be, as has already been said, virtually helpless. It is true that the railroad is dependent upon the city for its traffic, for the freight and the passengers that come and go upon its trains. Yet but few railroads are dependent upon any one city, no matter how rich or how valuable its traffic. But there is not a city that is not dependent upon the railroad— if not upon any one road or system, then upon them all, as a common system. The interrelationship between a railroad and the communities that it serves is close, and growing closer all the while—a healthy state of affairs, which is being shown more and more by a real desire for co-operation between the parties to this partnership. One of the most recent efforts of this sort has been the creation by the railroads of the United States of regional shippers' boards, to act as conference boards between the roads and their patrons in little matters of disagreement connected with service and car supply that may arise in the course of a year. Most of the matters are now settled, instantly and amicably, without reference to court or regulatory commission of any sort whatsoever. This is real progress.

The threshold of the railroad in the American city is its chief passenger terminal. There it is that it puts its best foot forward. The upkeep and the appearance of its passenger station is apt to be an index to the upkeep and the morale of the railroad that owns and operates it. There it is that the great volume of individual patrons come to do business with it, to buy tickets, perhaps, or perhaps merely to make enquiries of its agents behind the ticket windows or the information booths. These men are a railroad's first contacts with many of its patrons. Therefore it endeavors to pick only men of great courtesy, understanding and experience for these positions.

Sometimes a group of roads will combine in the use of a single station, for their own convenience as well as for that of their patrons. This then becomes known as a *Union Station*. But whether this is done or not, there is almost always apt to be a distinct effort in the passenger terminal, architectural and otherwise, to please the traveler, outgoing or incoming. For his convenience many facilities are added to the station: news-stands, restaurants and lunch-counters, rest rooms, toilets, public and private, check-rooms, information-booths, and sometimes barber-shops, private baths and drug-stores. A railroad station in a sizable city is a fairly complete organism. It generally represents a considerable expenditure of money, particularly if there has been an effort to make it an elaborate structure architecturally.

Stations like the Grand Central Terminal and the Pennsylvania in New York, South Station, Boston, the Union Station, Washington, the Union Station, Chicago, and the Union Station, Kansas City, are not only huge in extent—each representing the expenditure of many millions of dollars—but most of them are distinct monuments in the cities which they adorn.

Their vast public rooms are as handsome as the great halls of any palace in Europe; the baths of the old Roman emperors did not exceed in size or in beauty the great main hall of the Pennsylvania Station in New York, which is modelled after one of them. In the main concourse of the new Grand Central in that same city, the New York City Hall, belfry and all, could be placed without touching walls or ceiling at any point. In the similar section of the Washington station, twenty-five thousand beings could be marshalled at one time under the one roof which stands unsupported by pillar or post of any sort.

To the railroader the most impressive thing about any of our large passenger stations here in America, is not their architectural magnificence, but the intricate technique of their operation. To bring a thousand trains in and out of one of these stations in eighteen

Train Control Board and Operator, Grand Central Terminal, New York.

hours or thereabouts is no child's play. The passenger who boards one of these trains merely finds it quietly awaiting him in the trainshed. At the gateway to that shed a man has examined his ticket, to make sure before it is too late that he is boarding the right train. That, and the start of the train, are all that concern him. In the big and well-arranged baggage room, he has *checked* his trunks and received a small cardboard receipt for them which he knows will bring forth his property, promptly and easily at the city of his destination.

The train that awaits him will stand upon but one of six or eight, or ten or twelve, or even twenty or thirty similar parallel tracks within the trainsheds of the station. To connect all of these with the main line, tracks leading out from the station need, perforce, a network of switches. Formerly these all were handled by strong-armed men, a great task and a fairly unsystematic one, growing much worse under adverse conditions of weather. Today one or two men, in a cabin or *tower* at the entrance to the trainshed, by means of an intricate mechanism, not entirely unlike an old-fashioned square piano, by a turn of the wrist, throw switches as far as 100 or 150 feet away.

Because of other devices in this mechanism which is known as an interlocking, it is impossible for the men in the signal tower to throw, inadvertently, switches that will let two trains into the same track. They are able to move automatically the signal lights—red for danger, yellow for caution, and green for safety—that show the engineers and members of the train crews just how they may proceed. The creation of such a device was a vastly greater undertaking than the fashioning of any station in the world.

If the passenger station is the showy hand of the railroad in the city, the freight terminal may be considered as its practical one. It has its own fingers and thumbs, sometimes five, sometimes less, sometimes more, depending upon the size of and the physical conditions in the particular city which it is serving. In the case of freight there is less apt to be a common use of terminals. The union station idea has never been used extensively for it. For one thing, freight is inert. Passengers load and unload themselves, move themselves from train to train. The less they are incommoded in so doing, the better they will like the railroad. For the greater part they elect for themselves the railroads on which they travel.

But freight must always be moved. It has nothing to say about which way or how. To move it there must be installed huge *cranes* and other mechanical apparatus, both in the freight-houses where most of the package freight is handled in and out and stored momentarily while waybills are being prepared or the coming of the consignee awaited, as well as out on the tracks where the very heaviest freight is handled directly between the car and the motor truck for city "pick-up" or delivery.

In addition to these freight houses and delivery or receiving tracks, which may also have an interlocking switch and signal system, although the time factor is never so great as with the passenger trains, many important factories and industrial concerns have sidetracks of their own leading right to the doors of their shipping rooms from which they despatch or at which they receive most, if not all, of their railroad freight. Small locomotives, known as *switch engines*, distribute

The Lehigh Valley Freight Transfer Station, at Manchester, New York.

the freight cars to these sidings on the morning of each business day and collect them again at nightfall.

It becomes apparent now that all of these fingers, the great fingers of the railroad itself as well as the many little ones of the industrial sidings, must somewhere have a common meeting place. This generally is on the edge of the city, and it is known as a *yard*. Here the cars from all the freight houses in the town, and from all the industrial sidings, are gathered each evening and shuffled or distributed into separate trains, for various important outside points. More cars come in from branch lines of the railroad, starting at other cities or from other railroads, which connect with it there.

When there are enough cars to make a train, the dispatcher is notified and, as we have seen, a locomotive and crew and caboose are summoned and the train is started over the road. During the night and in the early morning, other through-freight trains will be arriving, and sometime about dawn, the sorting process of the preceding evening will be repeated, only in the reverse order.

For smaller shipments, the sort that the railroaders call *less-than-carload*, the sorting process, morning and night, is conducted in a huge building in the yard, technically known as the *transfer-house*. It has long platforms, sheltered against inclement weather and at these are placed strings of box cars.

In the evening, box cars are switched into the transfer-house from the freight stations and the industrial sidings downtown. These are known as the *trap* or *ferry* cars. Quickly they are unloaded and under the lights of the transfer-house their contents are sorted, very much as letters or packages are sorted in any post office. Certain box cars are assigned to certain outside cities; for instance, Boston, Philadelphia, Syracuse, Buffalo, Toledo, etc., etc. Any freight destined for these cities goes into the box cars standing under the printed names which show their destination. When a car is filled, it is taken out and sent through the sorting process in the main yard, while another takes its place at the berth in the transfer-house. It all sounds complicated, but really it is not. Experience and practice make the workings of the system comparatively easy. The greatest problem that comes in its administration is in constantly enlarging it to keep pace with the restless growth of most of our American cities.

Still other facilities a railroad must provide for a large city, or even for a moderately large one. It must have at some fairly accessible point, generally in connection with each of its larger yards, *roundhouses*, for storing its locomotives, as well as storage tracks for extra cars.

In connection with the roundhouse, there are sure to be shop facilities of some sort for at least minor repairs upon the locomotives, with other facilities in the yard outside for car work, both repairs and painting. If the city be a fairly sizable railroad center, it is apt to have very considerable shops, for both the heavy repairs and rebuilding of cars and engines. Once a year each locomotive upon the road should spend about a month in a bigger shop, or so-called *back-shop*, for a very complete overhauling. To do much less than this is to fail to operate the road properly.

JERSEY CITY PIER OF THE ERIE RAILROAD.

When one comes to consider all of these facilities and others, such as coal tipples, refrigerating and icing plants and the like, he need not be astonished that, even in a reasonably small sized city, the value of a single railroad terminal may easily run all the way from a million to several million dollars. There are probably few factories in the community that can compare with it in property investment. It employs many men within the city, aside from the members of its train crews who go in and out all the time. From a hundred to several thousand men would be the payroll of an average American railroad in an average American city of, say, a quarter of a million population. The money paid to such a force within a twelve-month, comes to a pretty penny. It filters everywhere through the community—to shopkeepers, to doctors and other professional men, to churches, to amusements, to taxes. Few businesses there are within the community that do not feel the benefit of it.

Partnership between the railroad and the city is no idle phrase. It is one of the great economic factors in the development of the American community. The railroad takes from the community dollars for freight tolls and for passenger tickets, but in return it pays taxes, mayhap furnishes architectural adornment to the city, probably provides an extensive employment and steady payroll and certainly gives the peace and ease and facility of free communication with the outer world. This last alone is worth all that it may possibly cost.

CHAPTER VI

THE COMING OF THE TROLLEY CAR

THOSE Americans who were fortunate enough to attend the great Berlin Exposition of 1879 saw, among the many curious new scientific and mechanical marvels that were presented there, a most unusual sort of railroad train. This, a miniature affair, consisted of a locomotive which hauled three small cars, each capable of seating just six portly Germans. It was the engine, however, that was the most unusual feature of this little train. Such a locomotive no one had ever before seen. It had no smoke-stack, no boiler, no cylinders —none of the familiar mechanisms of the steam locomotive. For, after all, this was *not* a steam locomotive. It was an electric one. The folk who were fortunate enough to go to the great Berlin Fair that year were gazing upon the first practical electric railway to be set up and operated anywhere in the world.

In the black metal box of the locomotive was a motor which gained its power from a third rail placed beside the two of the track itself. From this, the electric engine drew enough current to enable it to haul from eighteen to twenty persons, at a rate of about eight miles an hour. It was a very great novelty. Nearly everyone who went to the Berlin Fair of 1879, rode upon this train.

The idea of a *light railway*, as our British cousins like to call it, as distinguished from the so-called *standard steam railroad*, to be used primarily in the city transit, was not, in itself, new.   As far back as 1831 there was a street railway in the Bowery, and in its continuation, Fourth Avenue, in the city of New York, although this particular line had been built primarily as the southern-most section of the New York & Harlem Railroad, a steam line.   But the citizens of the New York of that early day complained most bitterly about the steam locomotive, with all its dirt and noise, in the nice streets of their brisk town, and so the New York & Harlem trains were hauled by horses, car by car, out to the city line, where they were coupled together, with an engine at their head.   On the other hand, those early New Yorkers had to admit that there was a deal of convenience about these cars in the streets.   The town was already growing to considerable length and if one did not have a carriage to command, there were only the omnibuses to serve him.   But a journey in one of these last, over the rough cobble-paved streets of that time, had nothing to commend it from the standpoint of comfort.   To ride in a bus that ran over a track of smooth iron rails was quite a different experience.

Impressed by the horse cars in the streets of New York, Philadelphia soon built for herself a similar railway, this time designed solely for local passenger use, to shorten, in effect, her rapidly growing distances. It, too, was immediately successful.   Yet, oddly enough, it was fifteen or twenty years before another of these railways was built—this time in the old city of Brooklyn.   In 1859, a line was constructed through the streets of Baltimore, for cars having flanged wheels.

After this, the street railway came into very general use in the larger cities of the United States.

It came as a result of a real necessity. The American city was bound to advance. It struggled all the while to increase the radius of its activity. Comparatively few folk owned carriages. So, until the development of the street railway, even the horse-propelled type, the average community was limited pretty strictly to an easy walking distance from a man's house to his place of business and return. Thirty minutes was a fair average for the time that a citizen would spend in such a walk, morning and evening. When the horse-car came, he had been so educated and accustomed to this thirty-minute allowance twice a day, that he was completely willing to spend it, or at least the greater part of it, in *riding* back and forth between his home and his work. The horse car could go at least twice as fast as he could walk; therefore the range of development for the American city was about doubled. This quadrupled its area. In a later day was to come the electric, or trolley, car which went twice as fast as the horse car and once again this radius was doubled. The average citizen still was willing to give one hour a day out of his valuable time to his journeys between his residence and his business. Of this, more in a moment! In a still later day, he was to have the automobile, much faster than the electric car, and still again, that radius of development was to be enlarged.

The electric car came, therefore, as the very greatest possible boon to the street railway. For long years there had been an effort to get a more efficient and less expensive motive power than horses or mules. Experiments were made in trying to adapt the steam loco-

HORSE-DRAWN STREET CAR, 1885.

motive to it, but none of these were successful.   In 1871, Andrew S. Halladie, a citizen of San Francisco, devised a form of street railway extremely well adapted to that excessively hilly city, a slotted track in the groove of which ran a continuous steel rope, or *cable*. By an ingenious device, known as a *grip*, cars were enabled to move at a uniform rate of speed, about eight miles an hour, or by dropping the cable to come to a stop.

For a time this type of railway, known as a *cable road*, enjoyed a great vogue.   Many of the larger cities of America—New York, Philadelphia, Baltimore, Washington, Chicago, St. Louis—adopted it.   But it proved to be vastly more expensive than the horse-car line, not alone for its installation, but for its operation, and so in the smaller cities of the land, it made little or no headway.   These sought anew for an answer to their problem.   They did not find it until there came the era of the electric railway.

It is believed that the very first suggestion for one of these in the United States came from a blacksmith up in the hills of Vermont, one Thomas Davenport, who developed into quite an inventor and electrician.   As far back as 1834, Davenport built and exhibited, at Springfield, and at Boston, Massachusetts, in a small railroad train, a toy motor, which operated from electric current derived from batteries.   In 1838, Robert Davidson, a Scotchman from Aberdeen, began the construction of a miniature electric locomotive equipped with a motor, which traveled at the rate of four miles an hour.

Nine years later, Professor Moses G. Farmer, an electrician in the employ of the United States government, actually built an electric car (at Dover, New Hampshire) which carried two passengers. Professor Page, of the Smithsonian Institution, at Washington, followed with something that approached vaguely the electric motor of today, set with batteries within a car. In 1851, on the track of the Baltimore & Ohio Railroad, between Washington and a suburban village, Bladensburg, Maryland, one hundred of these batteries and a Page motor, drove a crudely constructed electric car for a short time at the amazing speed of nineteen miles an hour. But within a very little while the batteries were completely destroyed.

These and other early attempts were, however, hardly to be reckoned as more than mere experiments of the most transitory sort. The little Siemens road on the ground of the Berlin Exposition, was the first to carry passengers, day in and day out for long months without showing more than ordinary wear and tear upon the equipment. Therefore it deserves to be known as the world's first electric railway.

In a similar way, the first successful electric train in the United States, even though much more crude than its German prototype, was the small engine and car for some months successfully operated by Thomas A. Edison, on the grounds of his home at Menlo Park, New Jersey. This was in the summer of 1880. It was not until five years after that an electric train was put in steady and continuous operation in this country on Hampden Road in the suburbs of Baltimore. This consisted of an old-fashioned "bob tailed" horse car, which was hauled by a small motor-engine, mounted upon a four-wheeled truck, not much larger than a gasoline-propelled railroad hand-car of today. This

EDISON'S FIRST EXPERIMENTAL ELECTRIC TRAIN, MENLO PARK, NEW JERSEY

curious contrivance took its power from an overhead copper wire suspended over the center of the track, by means of a broom-stick-like metal arm, with a grooved wheel to fit the wire. Soon they were calling this broom-stick a *trolley* and a little later the car it propelled —they soon got rid of a separate vehicle for the hauling —became known all the way across the land, as the *trolley car.*

As the trolley car, it came to conquer. Other cities, Cleveland among them, experimented with the trolley car. Almost within a decade it had succeeded in completely displacing the horse car in the streets of American cities.

The first city in the United States to have an almost complete equipment of these new trolley cars was Richmond, Virginia, which began the operation of them during the winter of 1887–8. They had a hard time of it. The capital city of Virginia is built upon rugged hills and to climb some of these was about all the little cars could do. There were many days that winter when the citizens of Richmond wished they had their horse cars back again. These were the times when there was snow and hail and ice and the tracks grew fearfully slippery and difficult. Eventually the trolley car triumphed. They kept building it stronger and better and it was not many months before Richmond would not have returned to the horse railways at any price.

Other American cities followed in quick succession. A very early installation was in Rochester, New York, where a suburban railway to Charlotte, upon Lake Ontario, nine miles distant, was equipped with the "broomstick trolley." This was in 1889.

The suburban possibilities alone of the new form of

railroad traction were almost unlimited. In common practice, the horse railroad had been limited in length to from eight to ten miles. Few persons cared to ride further than that in a horse car. Apparently there was no end to the distance one could ride comfortably in an electric one, especially as the electric cars all the while grew longer, heavier, swifter, better equipped. It was not long after their very general adoption across the land, before two four-wheeled trucks were being used instead of one, as in the case of horse cars. With two trucks a still longer, heavier, better type of car was easily possible.

With this type of car and the proper highspeed motors, electric cars were being sent greater and greater distances from the hearts of the cities. No longer were they limited to the radial area of existing horse car lines. Twenty miles, then thirty, then forty, became as nothing. After this the new form of railway began to connect cities and towns and small communities quite remote from one another.

This last type of electric railway soon began to be known as the *interurban*. For the most part it followed the right-of-way of established highroads, both state and county, although there was to come a day when some of the more pretentious of these were to have, at least in the country districts, their own private rights-of-way, just like the steam railroads. These were to put down double tracks of heavy steel, laid in solid rock ballast, to build elaborate terminals and intermediate stations and some of them were to embark quite heavily in the business of carrying express and freight traffic, as well as passengers. In a few exceptional instances, these roads were to build and

Early Type of Electric Trolley Cars Used in Rochester, N. Y.

operate parlor cars and dining cars and even sleeping cars, for their longer runs.

For the interurban in America developed quickly. By the beginning of the present century, one could ride upon trolley tracks, without a break, all the way from Little Falls, New York, in the valley of the Mohawk, to Chicago, more than eight hundred miles distant. A group of members of the Utica, New York, Chamber of Commerce once journeyed in their own chartered trolley car from their home city to Chicago and St. Louis. For a time long-distance trolley parties became quite a rage. Some folk began to say that the electric inter-urban railway would completely replace the steam rail-road, especially for local passenger service.

Of course no such thing came to pass. In some instances, certain of the steam railroads adopted the use of electric traction, not merely upon branch lines or for local passenger service, but, in a few cases, for the heavy traffic of main lines. Such early instances were the New York, New Haven & Hartford Railroad, from New York to New Haven, seventy-three miles, and the Chicago, Milwaukee & St. Paul Railway, which has more than 440 miles of line over the Rocky and the Cascade Mountains already electrified and upon these sections run the heaviest electric locomotives in the world. In the terminal services of the railroads in some of our largest metropolitan cities, electric traction has proved itself a great boon. Electric installations have gone into service in New York and in Philadelphia and a very large one has just been completed for the new Illinois Central Railroad suburban system in the city of Chicago.

Perhaps the most striking instance of the great

economic value of such electric installation is to be
found in the Grand Central Terminal in the city of
New York, where the New York Central Railroad, its
owner, by the substitution of electricity for steam as a
motive power in that terminal district, was not only
able, in a limited area, to make the Grand Central
a "double-decked" station, instead of a single-level one,
like most of the great passenger stations in the world,
but to bring back into active use as building sites many
city blocks in the very heart of one of the world's largest
communities.   This last was done by placing the entire
terminal service of tracks and switches under the level
of the street, a thing that would hardly have been
possible had the steam locomotive been retained in that
station.   After this the space formerly occupied by the
railroad yards was available for building purposes.

Electric traction has also been found of large
advantage in the operation of railroads through certain
long tunnels, not only here in the United States but in
Europe.

Suffice it to say that the electric railroad did not
supplant the standard steam railroad in a single one of
its activities.   Rather has it supplemented its larger
and its older brother.   It has reached into remote places
where the steam road could not and would not go.   It
sells its transportation at retail, rather than wholesale,
in small lots instead of big; sells shorter rides and more
of them.

Of this, too, more at another time!   It is enough
here and now to say that the electric railway in the
United States in its era of development, the thing with
which this chapter is particularly concerned, did at least
two very important things: it not only greatly increased

the radius of cities, by adding vastly to their habitable areas and so also increased their comfort of living and their efficiency, but well before the coming of the automobile, it brought the countryside into closer touch with both town and city, to the mutual advantage both of the farmer and of the city man. The motor-car in turn has supplemented and extended this interchange. But the automobile has its own distinct limitations. It operates best on improved roads and in pleasant seasons of the year. The interurban trolley car makes no distinction between the seasons. Through the hardest days of winter, in zero weather, sleet and snow, as well as in the most delightful days of the summer or the autumn, it provides a dependable service, not only passenger, but mail, express and small freight, into every part of the rural districts into which it reaches.

It is right here in America that the trolley has become a most efficient servant of the nation, and long since has earned its definite place in our national scheme of transport.

CHAPTER VII

THE STREET RAILWAY OF TODAY

EARLY in the morning the city is awake. Even before the coming of the dawn, lights are flashing in the windows of the houses of its workers. People are astir. The silence of the night is ended. The last of the night workers, the men who get out the morning newspapers and those who stand the night shifts in many of its industries, go sleepily to their homes and to their day-time rest. So, pass, on their way to another session of their endeavors, the earliest of the day workers.

Throughout the night the street railway has kept awake,—that is, if it is a street railway situated in any considerable city,—even though, like a dog, sleeping with but one eye open, it has fitfully kept its vigil. When the last of its real traffic on the preceding evening— folk returning home from the theaters and other places of entertainment—ceased, along about midnight, it began withdrawing its cars for the night. It sent most of them, but not all, to the barns. A few, at half-hourly, or even hourly intervals, were run up and down at least the principal streets. These are known as *owl cars*. Their operation is a profitless business to the street railway company. But they fill a real need for the night workers. So the street railway company,

being first of all a public servant, runs them throughout
the night at a considerable loss.   It is part of the price
it pays for the privilege of occupying the city streets.

Dawn comes, and the few lonely owl cars are aug-
mented by many others.   The great *barns* in which the
trolley cars are housed—the old phraseology of the
horse railway persists in remaining—begin emptying
them out.   Soon the rails of all the city lines are alive
with cars.   By seven o'clock in the morning, the service
is up to its *peak*.   It so continues, for nearly two hours.
After this there is a lessening of traffic and also a decrease in service but in no way proportionate to the
decrease in traffic—until about four or five o'clock
in the afternoon, when the evening peak, or rush hour
crowd, begins.   Like the morning peak, it also lasts
approximately two hours.

These peak loads twice a day are the bane of the
street railway manager's existence.   Without them,
his problem would be vastly simplified.   If, from dawn
to dark, or even later, traffic flowed as evenly as a
stream, he could easily arrange his timetables and the
working hours of his crews and also gain a maximum use
of his car equipment.

But the American city is not organized in this way.
It does by far the greater part of its work in the day-
time, and in its downtown or industrial sections.
Fortunately for the street railway manager, there still
is a slight divergence in the hours when people in
different callings begin and end their work.   For
instance, factory workers generally form the first part
of the morning peak load, and ofttimes the last part of
the evening one, although, in recent years, there has
been a steadily increasing tendency in all of our cities

to rearrange and shorten the hours of workers, both in factories and in stores. This further complicates the peak load problem of the street railway service.

Nevertheless, the factory workers are still the first to ride the cars in numbers. Upon their heels, come the clerks in the stores, then stenographers in offices, finally business heads and professional men, lawyers and the like. With these last, ride the teachers and the students in the schools and other institutions of learning. The expert street railway operator comes quickly to define these strata and to plan his service minutely to fit in accordance with them. So it comes to pass that a section of a city which is populated chiefly by factory workers receives its peak load service, in the form of extra car runs, much earlier than those parts of the town where live, chiefly, office workers and professional folk. Although this has been worked out with great care, it is subject to a more or less constant change all the while. The American city refuses to remain stationary, and so do its various public utilities. None of this is a matter of guesswork.

The street railway, like its big brother of the steam cars, runs on timetables. In an earlier chapter, we have seen the complicated master timetable of a division of a steam railroad. There is but one of these, however. While the average city railroad will have not less than three or four timetables, which for convenience, may be designated by letters. These provide for increasing volumes of service, against different conditions of traffic. For instance, schedule A may be designed for an ordinary business day in fall, winter or spring; B, for somewhat differing conditions of summer, when folk are apt to go to work a little

The "Submarine" Type Street Car, Late Model.

earlier in the morning and quit considerably earlier in the afternoon so as to get a little rest or play toward the close of the long days of the year. *C* may represent a Sabbath or an important holiday, when traffic conditions are entirely different from those prevailing on business days. It may be the timetable for a winter Sunday, with an entirely different one kept in readiness for a Sabbath in summer, when there is apt to be heavy travel to nearby beaches or other resorts.

The system has to be made even more flexible than this. When the general manager of a street railway awakes very early some Sunday morning,—perhaps it is in summer, when he is prepared to haul great throngs of folk out into the country,—and sees that the clouds are rolling up in the heavens and that an all-day rain is an extremely likely thing, he is apt to telephone his chief despatcher from his bedside and order into service for the day, schedule *C*, or whatever it is that represents the minimum service for the system. By good judgment, sometimes by being just a good guesser, he can, in this way, often in a single day, save several thousand dollars in the operation of the property.

On the other hand, it does come to pass sometimes that a rainy morning is succeeded by a very beautiful day. Let those clouds all go scurrying off by noon and brilliant sunshine follow and there will be plenty of riding on the street cars. This means that the general manager must change his plans, and his schedules, quickly.

To be provided for the unexpected is a part of his work always. Many unusual events he will be warned of in advance—the summertime visit of the big circus to town, great football matches or baseball games, perhaps the erection of an evangelist's tabernacle on one of the side streets, the annual county fair or local exposition.   All of these are apt to produce much business in the way of riding on the cars, but it is the absolutely unexpected for which he must be prepared, always. A great disaster may have come to pass in some one section of the city; in the course of an hour or even a half hour, there is a vast, an unusual demand upon the street railway system which must be prepared to meet the situation.   The real test of its completeness lies in its ability to respond to emergencies of every sort.

THE ENERGY WHICH DRIVES THE STREET RAILWAY

So much then for the externals of the operation of the city railroad!   With its appearance there is hardly a school-boy, in any sizable city in North America, who is not perfectly familiar.

It is with the internal operations of the street railway that we are now concerned.   We have seen its general operating methods, its flexibility, its readiness to meet all the tremendous demands, usual and unusual, that are made upon it.

How does it proceed to meet those demands?   What force does it summon to its assistance?   What is the great driving energy behind the street railway in the United States?   In a word it may be said that it is— *electricity.*

In the preceding chapter, we have seen men turning from the many and the very patent limitations of the horse-car to some other practicable form of motive power to meet the demands made by the constant growth of the American city.   We have seen them out in San Francisco accepting the ingenious device of the

Modern Interurban Trolley Car. Rochester, Lockport, and Buffalo Railroad Company.

cable railroad which quickly spread all the way acros
the United States, only to be rejected finally because
of the excessive cost of its installation and maintenance.
Other forms of locomotion for street cars—steam locomotives, cleverly camouflaged so as not to scare horses,
gas engines, even cars propelled by compressed air—
have all been tried, but finally rejected.

Then we saw the broomstick trolley, the electrically
driven car, come.

It was not rejected. Starting with the first crude
experiments, some of which were all but complete
failures, it went through one stage of development
after another. It became longer, heavier, stronger,
all the while more comfortable for passengers. It took
its place beside the steam train, the gas burner, the
electric light, the telephone and the telegraph as one of
the great, dependable servants of America. Electricity
has brought about this change.

Today electricity is the supreme and unquestioned
motive power of the street railways of this country.
In a central power station, it is generated. Power, obtained from the burning of coal and the production of
steam or, far more economically, from some dependable
water power, is used to turn, at swift speed, the great
dynamos, or generators, as they are now very generally
known. For railroad service, special types of these generators, furnishing the kind of current most needed, are
provided, although generally speaking, the same electric
current that lights your house or heats your flatiron
is available for that street car down at the corner.

When we come to study the origin of the electric light
we shall see how, at the very outset, its progress was
considerably impeded by the practical inability to send

the current much more than a mile from the generating station.   This was a very severe limitation—so much so that for some time it seemed as if the field of electric lighting was to be a comparatively small one.

This was because the earliest commercial installations of electric lighting systems used, almost invariably, what is known as the *direct current*.   Direct current travels at high amperage and low voltage.   To understand it best, in a non-technical way, one thinks of a slow-moving stream, sluggish but rather wide and powerful.   To conduct this electric stream in any quantity, would mean large wires of copper.   Copper is an expensive metal and so even to attempt to bring direct current over it any considerable distance, would mean an expense so very great as to be practically prohibitive.

But, as we shall see later, while the first direct current stations were being installed downtown in the city of New York, in 1882, two men overseas, Messrs. Gaulard and Gibbs, were doing some rather marvelous things with *alternating current.*

The existence of such a current long had been known to electrical experimenters.   Still being fairly non-technical, it may be said that this alternating current, as its name indicates, pulses backwards and forwards, from negative to positive and positive to negative, with very great frequency—several thousand pulses to the minute.   It is much easier and cheaper to generate high voltage alternating current than high voltage direct current. Also the transmission losses are lessened as the voltage is increased.   Consequently high voltage alternating current is used for transmission, and both alternating and direct current of low voltage are used in the actual application of the power because they are less dangerous to handle. In non-technical language, high voltage alternating current may be compared with a swiftly running stream, not wide, but gaining energy from the velocity with which it propels itself. It is nervous, quick, alert; and not being wide, it requires less copper wire for its transmission.

For the immediate use of a street railway motor, many men still prefer the direct current. Yet these admit that for the transmission from some fairly distant central generating station, there is nothing that can compare in efficiency and in cheapness with the alternating current. For years past, there has been almost endless discussion and battle between the proponents of the rival systems, but the foregoing may be set down as a fair statement of the practical compromise that has gradually been reached between them. While highly efficient alternating current motors have been manufactured, taking the so-called AC current directly from the distribution system (trolley wire or third rail) and using it to turn the car axles, these have never been used very largely in street railway work. The chief argument against these AC motors is the danger of carrying a very high voltage current in trolley wires suspended directly over the middle of a city thoroughfare. Such a current is extremely deadly. Wires that carry it must be more than ordinarily protected against human contact or even against coming into contact with other wires of any sort whatsoever.

The practical compromise, here in America, is of alternating current generated at the central power station and carried, in well protected wires or conduits, to one or more distributing stations within comparatively easy reach of the point where it is to be used, where, by use of the ingenious electrical devices known as *transformers* and *rotary converters* it is quickly changed from AC current of high voltage to DC current of low. This last is generally fixed, all the way from 400 to 600 volts. The first runs to almost incredible heights.

The transformer changes the very high tension alternating current to low tension alternating current, say 300 volts. The converter then takes the low tension alternating current and turns it into the direct current, running all the way, as has just been said, from 400 to 600 volts, although 550 volts have now become a standard generally accepted here in the United States.

For a long time 2000 volts was fixed as the highest practicable maximum for alternating current; then the figure was raised to 5,000 volts. At that, experienced electricians said it must remain. When the New York, New Haven & Hartford Railroad made its installation in its suburban zone just outside of the city of New York, and fixed the voltage of its system at 11,000, men shook their heads in perturbation. They were sure that there would be loss of life every day along the lines of the New Haven. In this they were mistaken.

From 11,000 volts to 22,000 was a step; then, before one really knew it, they were carrying electrical energy cross-country on the high transmission lines, lifted far above human contact by great steel towers, at 110,000 volts. Yet, even this was not all. Today the transmission of alternating current at 220,000 volts is commercially practicable. Today no wise electrical engineer assumes to say just where the maximum voltage of a current really is.

The transforming station is a simple, silent sort of place. The transformers look like huge tanks, while the rotary converter looks much like a generator. Sometimes both are much smaller. Both are even made portable, to fit within a railroad car. In this way, they may be hauled from point to point to meet emergency needs. A sudden demand for more cars, caused, let us say, by a summer day's rush to some popular bathing beach, means of necessity a vastly increased demand for power. The ordinary provisions for supplying it quickly become exhausted. The direct current, at a considerable distance from the nearest transforming station, becomes weak, fitful and utterly inefficient. Then it is that the wise general manager of the street railway puts one of his portable transforming stations to work, right close to the spot where the increased energy is needed. In fact if he is really wise, he does not wait for this emergency to come to pass. His portable station is on hand before it arises.

All of this has been, for the past thirty-five years or thereabouts, a matter of steady progress. In a similar way, the motors under the car have been in constant development for a similar period of years. The fact that an electric motor delivers power through a circular shaft in steady revolution, made its application to traction at first seem to be a comparatively simple thing. Wheel axles, the obvious driving power, also revolve. The steam engine, or the gasoline internal combustion engine, produces power through a rotating shaft driven by a system of pistons and rods and eccentrics, but then it is not always practical to make that first shaft the axle of a pair of driving wheels. So there must be for the street car some intermediate transmission. In the case of the ordinary steam locomotive, power is transmitted by means of slide rods and connecting rods to the spokes of the driving wheels and in the case of the automobile by means of an even more intricate system of clutch and flexible shafting and transmission gearing.

To make the axle of a pair of driving wheels of an electric car or locomotive the shaft of a motor has always been the dream of the electrical engineer. It has been done, but in the case of the street car, at least, never very satisfactorily. The shaft of a motor revolves normally at a far greater speed than would be practicable for the axle of a pair of driving wheels resting directly upon the track. To make a slow moving motor, means the creation automatically of a very large *field* for that motor. It is very, very difficult to design such a field and still have it clear the pavement of the street. Therefore it early became necessary to build a motor which, in order to keep within reasonable bounds of size, would communicate its power to the driving wheel axles by means of gears.

At first there were two sets of these gears, and so the motor, itself, became known as a double-reduction. It was far from a satisfactory construction. So much gearing not only called for much lubrication, but it ground out a vast deal of noise. In the course of a few years, a highly efficient motor was created with a single set of single reduction gears all neatly encased against wet and dirt. This is the motor in general use everywhere in street railway service today.

This is neither the time nor the place to go into the intricate details of the mechanical construction of the modern street car. It is enough to say that it has now become a highly refined and a fairly complicated piece of mechanism, requiring no little amount of upkeep.

Control apparatus is a problem in itself. In recent years the air brake has become a recognized feature of the equipment of the street car, just as standard for it as for the cars of the steam railroads.

A modern street car, of the roomy, comfortable two-truck type in use almost everywhere in the United States today, will cost all the way from $15,000 to $25,000. In recent years, in order to meet the growing wage problem of the street railway, "one-man cars," so called, have been introduced on many of the city railway systems of the land, particularly on their less important streets, or in places where traffic is comparatively light. These cars, in which the motorman, aided by ingenious mechanical devices, also acts as conductor, cut the labor cost nearly in half. With this saving accomplished, the manager of the street railway is enabled to increase his service, the number of cars in operation on any given line at any given time, and so also increase his opportunities for attracting traffic.

The really efficient street railway official must be something far more than an operating man, or a mechanical and an electrical engineer. He must be a salesman. In his plant, he manufactures a distinct product for sale, and that product is the transportation of human beings from one point to another within a city. He must be some other things as well—an expert on franchises and franchise-rights, on pavements and road materials, on corporation law and organization. He must know something of finance, and of the automotive industry in all its phases. His is a many-sided job.

THE CORRELATION OF THE MOTOR VEHICLE

The modern street railway executive today thinks in somewhat wider terms than those of tracks upon which run electric cars or omnibuses with flanged wheels, to keep them in place upon the rails. The recent rapid progress in the development of the motor-bus, driven by an internal combustion engine using gasoline for fuel, has given him much food for thought. The bus has appeared as a real competitor and, in some places, as a very dangerous one. The privately owned and operated automobile has, in many, many cases, taken much traffic from the street railways. There is a flexibility and an independence in its use that has made a great appeal to the citizen who could afford to own and operate his own car, even though, as we shall see in a moment, the ownership and operation of many of these individual cars in a single large city brings a vast complication of parking and other forms of congestion in the city streets.

The development of the privately owned and operated motor car into the so-called *jitney* of a few years ago, was quite a natural one. It, too, made a serious competitive problem for the street railway.

The jitney in practice, however, was foredoomed. Being in general practice an ordinary automobile, battered and usually second-hand, it formed no genuine solution to the transport problem of our cities, and its passing after a time came as an entirely logical result.

But the jitney idea had much to commend it. One presently saw the inefficient antiquated family

Modern Electric Trolley Cars, Rochester, New York, 1927.

automobile being supplanted by a genuine type of
omnibus, even though ofttimes crudely constructed,
with probably a home-made, carpenter-built body,
hard seats and small windows, fitted upon the chassis
of an ordinary motor truck.

Yet, even in this crude form, the motor vehicle
became again a serious competitor of the city railway.
Its flexibility, the fact that it could be on this street or
on that as temporary traffic conditions or exigencies
might warrant, the further fact that it could come to
the curb of the sidewalk in order to pick up its passengers, instead of forcing them to stand in the middle of the
street, all were large points in its favor. From crude
beginnings gradually there was evolved a very handsome and comfortable vehicle, in heating, lighting and
seating, closely approximating the modern trolley car.
Following foreign practice, it became popular to add an
upper deck upon the roof of the body, thus not only increasing its seating capacity, but also affording a very
attractive point of vantage for its passengers. Such a
bus early became an important factor in helping to
solve the problem of city transport.

Yet the street railway had its rights. Years before it
had anticipated the future of the community. Men
had expended their money in placing an elaborate track
structure through city streets in hope of receiving an
income adequate for fair returns upon their investment.
When the transformation from the horse railway to the
electric one had become both hygienic and economic,
vast new sums of capital were expended in many
instances amounting to two or three times the original
investment.

In both city ordinances and in legislative acts, these

rights are firmly recognized. More than this, a definite
policy is now being worked out in almost every American city which provides that the motor omnibus, a
recognized and highly practicable vehicle for mass
transportation in a city street, as well as on a country
highway, shall be used, not in competition, but in
correlation with the long established street railway
system. Translated into plain English, this means
that, with certain exceptions, the motor bus shall not be
used in the same streets parallel to the street cars.
For other city streets or avenues, without street car
tracks, particularly those of extra width, the motor
bus is peculiarly fitted.

In most of these cases, it can be correlated with
existing trolley car services; occasionally and under
certain conditions, it can be used to supplant the trolley
car, either completely or partially. In one important
Connecticut city, it has already been found to be good
business to tear up entirely a trolley line running
through an unusually narrow street through a populous
residential district; in another the street car tracks are
only used during the rush hours, morning and evening.
At all other times an attractive and thoroughly adequate service is rendered by motor buses. The climate
of the New England community does not lend itself at
certain seasons of the year to the operation of the
standard forms of double-decker buses, and the "single-
deckers" do not compare in seating capacity with the
long double-trucked trolley cars; so in the peak loads,
morning and night, recourse is had to the earlier form
of street transport.

Another correlation of the motor bus with the trolley
car, used in Rochester, New York, and some other

typical American cities, is a solution of the problem
of extending existing trolley lines into the outer, suburban country immediately surrounding the older
portions of the community. The cost of the installation of a motor bus service is a comparatively in-
expensive matter, particularly so when it is compared
with the building of even the simplest sort of single
tracked trolley road.

Because of this, it also is good business to let a motor
bus do the pioneering ahead of the trolley car. With it,
a simple sort of beginning transport service can be
established from the outer terminal of a trolley line
as far into the surrounding country as circumstances
may seem to justify. The response to such beginning
service is apt to be the same always, new homes going
up, by tens, by dozens, or perhaps even by the hundreds.
Following such suburban developments comes the need
for community conveniences, retail shops, churches, and
schools. Business begets business. Let this continue
for but a very few years and there will be need of a
trolley line. No bus service has yet been devised that
can quite equal the efficiency of the trolley car in the
handling of *mass transportation.*

This is the phrase to which your city transit expert
constantly reverts. In reality, it is not nearly as
portentous as it first sounds. To understand the full
meaning of it, go into the most crowded street of any
American city during the height of the evening rush
hours, when hundreds and hundreds and hundreds of
workers, of every sort and condition, are struggling to
find their way home, not merely in the street cars and
the motor buses, but in their own automobiles. Real
congestion ensues quickly and were it not for the facility

and the experience of the police, traffic presently would cease completely—would congest itself to the point of absolute immobility.

Here is a man riding home alone in his limousine. It is a large car, with a long wheelbase. Its owner, by his own efforts, has earned the right to ride home in the comfort it offers. That right, no one may fairly deny. Yet the fact remains that this large, individual motor car, carrying one single passenger home, occupies nearly as much room in the city street as a small trolley car, seating thirty-eight or forty people (although it is apt in practice to be carrying considerably more than this number) or a double-decker motor omnibus which seats from fifty-one to sixty passengers. Obviously it is better for the community to have that valuable footage in the crowded street at the rush hour occupied by the vehicle that represents mass transportation.

Still, as we have just said, the man who rides individually, or with one or two, or three or four other persons, in his own motor, has his rights, and these are unassailable. What is the answer? How, then, can the needs of the individual and of the community be met?

In the large cities it is in the creation of rapid transit lines off the surfaces of the main thoroughfares. More generally these take the form of railroads, either elevated on continuous bridge structures through the congested portions of the city, or else depressed in open cuts or tunnels beneath its surface levels. To avoid injuring property, these rapid transit lines are generally carried through the streets either over or under them. Obviously the underground method—subways—is the best. The *elevated* is apt to be noisy as well as unsightly.

Interurban Busses, a New Factor in Transportation.

But its cost of construction is very much less than that of subway construction.

So it is that in such metropolitan cities as New York,—including the former city of Brooklyn which is now a borough of greater New York,—Boston, Philadelphia and Chicago, one finds a tangle of both elevated and subway lines, just as one finds them across the Atlantic, in London, in Liverpool, in Paris, in Berlin, in Vienna and in Madrid.   Here in America, two smaller cities, Rochester, New York, and Cincinnati, Ohio, anticipating the future, have adopted the subway idea.   In each of these communities, ingenious use has been made of abandoned canals.   The advantageous right-of-way through the center of the cities that these old-time water-ways occupied has been transformed with a minimum of effort into a double-decked highway, a rapid transit railway underneath and a finely paved wide street upon the upper surface.

In railways of this type there comes, when the necessity arises, the finest opportunity of all for the handling of mass transportation,—that is, transportation of huge dimensions.   In subways the single electric car quickly may become an entire train, all the way from two up to ten cars and capable of carrying from 500 to 800 passengers, the greater part of them seated.   This is the real city transport of the future.   It becomes quickly and logically the chief means of transporting people to their work and back again each business day, as well as of transporting them to and from places of amusement, churches, office and social calls, etc.

To this, in turn, are correlated both the street railway upon the surface of the various streets, almost always the best form of mass transportation for short distances within the town, because of the convenience of access and facility for making frequent stops, and the motor omnibuses which have, as we now have seen, both advantages and disadvantages in comparison with the trolley.

An ingenious form of motor bus which is a sort of combination with the trolley car, has recently been devised and is in use in a number of American cities. It is known colloquially as the *"trackless trolley."* It runs without tracks, on rubber-tired wheels on well paved streets, but it has electric motors of the street-car type and for these it takes the current by trolley from overhead wires. This form of car or bus is far more economical to run than the gasoline motor bus, particularly in those cities which by reason of their proximity to water power are fortunate enough to have cheap electric current, while the simplicity of the construction of the line itself renders it far cheaper to install than any sort of trolley line with tracks, and disposes of any objection that may be made to the laying of railroad tracks in a city street.

The city railway has ceased to be a simple mechanism. It has developed into a vast and many-sided machine, yet one whose purpose is solely the carrying of people through the streets of communities. To this it bends its energies, night and day, ceaselessly; it struggles eternally to better itself, by the addition of each new device or idea that the restless brain of man may develop. It is never stilled. In itself it is never immobile; it is energy, nothing less. As a servant, it is tireless—the city railway.

A Trackless Trolley.

CHAPTER VIII

THE DEVELOPMENT OF CITY LIGHTING—
ARTIFICIAL GAS

THE beginning of the lighting of city streets goes well back into the past ages, where it was introduced primarily as a protection against crime and criminals. In London, more than five centuries ago (1416) the Lord Mayor, Sir Henry Barton, ordered "lanthorns" and lights to be hung out of the houses on winter evenings between All-Hallows and Candlemas. "Although this practice was continued for three hundred years," says Henry Norman, "it was not strictly observed." One old cry of the watchman who reminded the people of their lantern obligation at dusk was:

Lanthorn, and a whole light!
Hang out your light! Hear!

And a hundred and fifty years later the watchmen were calling:

A light here, maids, hang out your light,
And see your horns be clear and bright,
That so your candle may shine,
Continuing from six to nine;
That honest men that walk along
May see to pass safe without wrong.

In Paris there were attempts at street lighting as early as 1524, although it was not until 1558 that a systematized method of hanging the lanterns on the outside of the houses—based on that of London—was put into effect. Two centuries later, pitch or resin bowls were substituted for the candle lights in the streets. In certain instances, they were suspended over the middle of the thoroughfare. These lighting bowls continued in service until the introduction of gas in the French capital (1820).

In Paris as well as in London, *flambeaux* came at a later day, and the link boy, with his blazing torch to escort late farers home, became a regular and not always agreeable feature of the taverns of the town.

Gradually, fixed lanterns were applied to the fronts and corners of the old houses of the larger towns both in Europe and in the New York of colonial days. However, there was no really systematic form of street lighting in the chief city of the Americas until 1762. Prior to that time, wise citizens venturing forth after dark, carried with their stout sticks, their trusty lanterns, even though a temporary ordinance passed in the latter part of the seventeenth century required the occupants of every tenth house to hang out a lantern on a pole.

It was not until 1762 that New York purchased its first oil lamps for the streets, as well as the stout wooden posts upon which they were to be affixed. The system must have been successful, for eight years later, one finds a contract being awarded by the city fathers to one J. Stoutenburg for supplying oil and lighting the city lamps for a twelvemonth, for $750. In 1774 the city employed sixteen official lamplighters. This system of street lighting remained substantially unchanged until 1823, when the city made its first contract with the New York Gas Company.

This New York method of street lighting was followed, with some variations, in other early Colonial cities of America—Boston, Salem, Providence, Philadelphia, Wilmington, Annapolis, Frederick, Richmond, Charleston and Savannah. It was crude, but simple, and for its day, fairly effective. Any system of street lighting was vastly to be preferred to unlighted thoroughfares which, after dark, were sometimes wont to become the theaters of brawls and street fights, occasionally of a very serious nature.

THE DISCOVERY OF ARTIFICIAL GAS

One John Baptist van Helmont, of Brussels, is accredited with being the first man to make much study of a little-understood vapor, occasionally found in swamps and other dank places, which, upon being struck with flint-fire, had been known to blaze brightly for a time. Van Helmont was an important chemist of the seventeenth century. He had studied and practiced medicine and later he turned to research work in chemistry. He tinkered for a while with alchemy but finally devoted his time and his excellent laboratory at Velvorde to a study of what he was pleased to call "a wild spirit." This was not an entirely original name. The Germans had called this little-understood thing of the woods a spirit—*geist*—and that is the origin of the word "gas" by which it is known throughout the English-speaking world today.

But the real father of artificial gas as we know it today was William Murdock, an Englishman, who worked with James Watt in the early development of the steam engine. As far back as 1792, Murdock, by distilling coal in an iron retort, had succeeded in producing a gas, which he conducted seventy feet in tin and copper tubes and this he used for lighting his house in Redruth, Cornwall. This experiment worked so well that presently Murdock was conducting gas, on a larger and more practical scale, into the engine-building works of Boulton, Watt & Company, in Soho, near Birmingham. Here again, success greeted him, as a result of which he was able to assist materially in the celebration of the Peace of Amiens,—the signing of a treaty between France, Spain, Holland and Great Britain, in April, 1802. The display of the new gas lights which was made at that time excited much interest. A contemporary account says:

The illumination of the Soho works on this occasion was one of extraordinary splendor. The whole front of that extensive range of buildings was ornamented with a great variety of devices that admirably displayed many of the varied forms of which gas light is susceptible. This luminous spectacle was as novel as it was astonishing and Birmingham poured forth in numerous population to gaze at and to admire this wonderful display of the combined efforts of science and art. . . .

Soon after this, Murdock built a gas works and with it lighted the cotton mills of Phillips & Lee, at Manchester, with some 900 burners. For this achievement he was awarded a medal by the Royal Society of London.

Murdock was regarded as a queer young man. That seemed to be the fate of any inventor of those days.

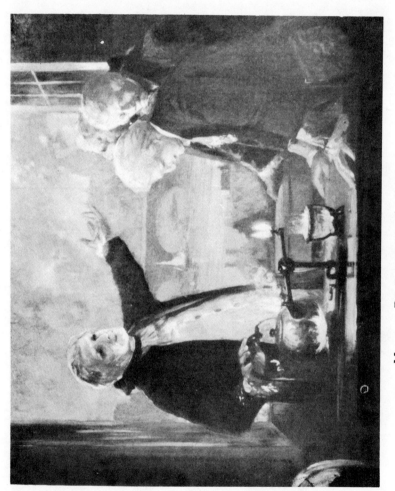

Murdoch Demonstrating His Discovery.

But it was particularly true of this one. A latter-day historian writing of him says:

He was addicted to wearing wooden hats and also made a lantern by fixing a tube in the neck of a gas-filled bladder. The sight of him, wandering about the streets at night with this strange beacon, filled the neighborhood with dismay, and some of the good people suspected him of being in league with Lucifer and consequently a person to be avoided.

Yet, despite these eccentricities, he made a serious and a very great contribution to the progress of the world, both social and economic. He followed his development of the retort for the actual manufacture of this artificial gas, as we shall see in the following chapter, with the invention of the first practical *tip* for the burning of the gas.

This, like many other inventions, came about through an accident. Murdock had desired to stop a flow of gas which was burning from an open tube. To accomplish this purpose, he picked up a thimble and clapped it over the flaming end of the tube. It so happened that this thimble had previously been pierced in a number of places and so, the gas coming through these small holes in lesser volume, was brought into contact with a greater proportion of air at the point of combustion. The result was a far better light than had before been attained, and the creation of the idea of the modern gas tip.

While Murdock was doing these highly interesting things, other men were progressing with the gas idea. In Belgium, Jean Pierre Minckelers was burning gas in his laboratory in the quiet University of Louvain, and in Paris, Philippe Lebon was lighting his house and gardens in the Rue St. Dominic with the strange new "spirit."

Frederick Albert Winsor, a German, also played a conspicuous part in the early developments. He had heard of Lebon's process, which already had been patented, and journeyed to Paris to see for himself the new illuminant. Winsor tried to buy the German rights of the Lebon process, in which wood was used as the principal material for the production of the gas, but was refused them. Lebon refused even to reveal any of the secrets of his process. Winsor then went back to Frankfort and began studies of his own in the production of artificial illuminating gas, with such success that at the very beginning of the nineteenth century, almost coincident with Murdock's display at the Birmingham celebration of the Peace of Amiens, he made a display of his own gas, also distilled from wood, before the Duke of Brunswick and his court.

The following year (1804) he went to London and in the Lyceum Theater there gave a demonstration of his illuminant. While there were many doubters in his audience, others came to have a belief that "there was something in the idea"; and in 1807 a private company, which Winsor had caused to be organized, exhibited a row of street lights along Pall Mall. Even then, scoffers were many; some of them were distinguished. Sir Walter Scott wrote laughingly: "There is a madman proposing to light London with— what do you think?—why, with smoke." Napoleon dismissed Winsor and his idea with contempt.

Winsor sought for his company the exclusive privilege of lighting by gas in all British possessions, but so sweeping a right was not granted. Parliament finally did give (1812) a charter to his London & Westminster Gas Light & Coke Company, which thus became the first gas company in all the world, and the following year celebrated its new found existence by lighting the world-famous Westminster Bridge. Says an historian of this event:

. . . the populace of London was dumbfounded by the spectacle. It was many years before the citizens of that city became accustomed to gas lighting although it was extended rapidly after the lighting of the bridge. People thought the flame came through the pipes and many objections were raised when the system was installed in the House of Commons. So little was known about gas that it was thought that the "pipes would burn the building" and they were set far away from the walls, and the members of Parliament, fearful of being burned, would not touch them with ungloved hands. Lamplighters at first refused, through fear, to light the new gas lamps, and later crowds followed them to watch their operations every evening.

GAS LIGHTING INTRODUCED INTO THE UNITED STATES

In the brisk American city of Baltimore, Rembrandt Peale, son of a distinguished American portrait painter and himself an artist of no little distinction, was conducting, in 1815 and 1816, the famous Holliday Street Theater and Museum. It is probable that Peale was a careful reader of the newspapers. If so, he must have seen in the *Baltimore American and Commercial Advertiser* for December 30, 1815, the following item:

GAS LIGHTS

We learn by the late English papers that Covent Gardens Theater and a number of the streets of London are illuminated by gas lights.   They are represented as being infinitely more brilliant, more innoxious, and vastly more economical than the common lamp light by oil.   One gas burner is equal to twenty common street lamps and the saving of expense in all cases is very considerable.   A shop may be lighted by gas for only 2d. per night, the largest room and even a whole street. proportionately cheaper.

We have been induced to notice this improvement by the curious circumstance that it was first offered by the inventor to the people of Baltimore about eight or ten years ago (1805 or 1807) but the people of Baltimore then laughed at the idea.   Now that it has been carried into effect in London no doubt our citizens will look upon it "*in another light.*"

An American inventor, it would appear, can have little credit in America until he receives the sanction of the people of London, and then he has a chance of becoming fashionable on this side of the Atlantic.

In the same newspaper appeared three days later, the following communication to the editor:

BALTIMORE, January 2, 1816.

American,

MESSRS. EDITORS:—In your paper of Saturday there was a communication relative to the warming and lighting of houses by the means of gas.

I much admire the spirit which dictated the communication; it was of the most liberal cast and had for its object the encouragement of genius and the improvement of our happy country.

But, gentlemen, these objects, important as they are, are obtained too dearly when purchased at the expense of truth. The introduction of gas for the purpose of light and heat is by no means an American invention.

In Europe it has long been known and used, particularly in France.   A French gentleman, a respectable inhabitant of this place, informed me that he saw a hotel in Rouen in Normandy, warmed and lighted in the manner alluded to more than twenty-five years ago, and that he could refer to many others who were as well acquainted with the circumstances as himself.

Be so good, gentlemen, as to make this fact known, not for the purpose of checking genius, which I admire, but to give to merit its fair and proportionate reward. In our eagerness to encourage inventions, let us not appropriate to ourselves the applause which justly belongs to the tenants of the tomb. The fact is, gentlemen, we have been much imposed upon.

(Signed) BOB SHORT.

The vigorous Mr. Bob Short is not so unintelligible as he may seem to be. The references to an American inventor of gas are unquestionably to one David Melville who, in 1806, lighted his premises at Newport, Rhode Island, by a crude form of coal-gas apparatus and seven years later set up a similar device, somewhat improved, in a cotton mill at Watertown, Massachusetts. Of the experiments in the inn at Rouen the author of this book has been unable to find a record.

It is hardly possible that the alert eyes of Mr. Rembrandt Peale could have escaped these communications in his morning paper. He must have given some serious consideration to the new illuminant which it discussed. But whether he did or no, the files of the *American* reveal, in the summer of 1816, the following notice and advertisement:

GAS LIGHTS

WITHOUT OIL, TALLOW, WICK OR SMOKE

It is not necessary to invite attention to the gas lights by which my salon of paintings is now illuminated; those

who have seen the ring beset with gems of light are sufficiently disposed to spread their reputation; the purpose of
this notice is merely to say that the Museum will be illuminated every evening until the public curiosity shall be
gratified.

REMBRANDT PEALE.

Thus it was that Baltimore, which sometimes is called
the City of First Things, became the home of the first
commercial gaslight installation in the United States.
This presently was followed by the organization of the
first commercial gas company in this country.

On the 19th of June, 1816, civic permission was given
to this concern, which was known officially as the Gas
Light Company of Baltimore, to light the streets of that
town.   Among the incorporators in addition to Peale,
was William Gwynn, then editor of the *Baltimore
Gazette*, who did not hesitate to write vigorously in his
columns in favor of the new enterprise.   It was not
until 1820, however, that it was in active force, with
its first gas works at North and Saratoga Streets, and its
first permanent installation of lights in a public building
in the old Belvedere, or "Mud," Theater close by.
The first residence to use gas for lighting in Baltimore
and in the United States was the house of Jacob J.
Cohen, in North Charles Street.   The new illuminant
came slowly.   By the end of 1820, there were only three
commercial users of gas in Baltimore city.

Yet, despite decided opposition in certain parts of
the country, the idea already had begun to spread.
It was urged, theologically, that artificial illumination
would be an attempt to interfere with the divine plan
of the world which had preordained that it should be
dark during the night time; medically, that the fumes

THE LAMP LIGHTER OF YESTERDAY.

of the gas would be very injurious, while lighted streets would induce folk to remain out of doors, thus leading to an increase of colds and similar ailments; and, morally, that the fear of darkness would disappear and drunkenness and depravity increase. The police expressed their opinion that horses would be frightened and thieves emboldened, while some sentimental folk opined that if the streets were illuminated each night, festive occasions, when it was the habit to hang out gay lanterns, would be robbed of their charm. The way of the pioneer in almost any important thing a hundred years or more ago was not exactly paved with roses.

GAS LIGHTING SPREADS ACROSS AMERICA

Yet, despite pessimism and all these kinds of conscientious objectors, the commercial use of gas in the United States made steady although very slow progress. At first used for street lighting almost exclusively, it gradually was adopted for theaters and other large public or semi-public buildings. Some of the more wealthy citizens began placing it in their homes. Early prejudice against it, vague fears of danger lurking in its use, led to the retention of candles or sperm-oil lamps for a long time for home illumination. Colonel E. L. Drake's discovery (1859) of the great petroleum fields of western Pennsylvania, which was followed by their immediate and swift development, gave great impetus to the use of oil, even though it was not until 1865 that the *kerosene lamp* was first put on the market.

The first expense of the installation of a gas-making plant prohibited its use, save in good-sized towns. The isolated rural districts obviously were excluded from adopting it. Notwithstanding these handicaps, manu-

factured gas in this country made steady progress.   In
1822 it was introduced in Boston, and as we already
have seen, it came to New York in the following year.
Philadelphia for a long time showed her traditional
conservatism in opposing it.   It did not come into use
there until 1836.   In the meantime, New Orleans,
Brooklyn, Evansville, Indiana, and even little Monroe,
Michigan, had been equipped with gas light plants.
Upon their heels came installations in Newark, New
Jersey; Charleston, South Carolina; New Haven,
Connecticut; Providence, Rhode Island; and Portland,
Maine.   In 1848, installations were made at Troy,
Syracuse, Rochester and Buffalo, New York; two years
later at Auburn, Poughkeepsie and Williamsburgh,
New York.

Chicago, although it then had a population of but
20,047 souls, had its gas works in 1850.   An account of
the occasion is given in *Kirkland's History* of that city.
It reads in part:

Among the elements essential to the health and comfort
of the inhabitants of any city are light and pure water,
the former of which has been more easily obtained than
the latter, although Lake Michigan washes the shores of
the city.

In 1849 an act was passed by the legislature authorizing
the formation of the Chicago Gas Light & Coke Company.
The work of laying mains and constructing the necessary
buildings was completed in 1850 and the city was lighted
with gas in September of that year.

This event formed an epoch in Chicago's history.   The
filling of the pipes with the lighting fluid and the bursting
forth of the brilliant flames when a match was applied,
illuminating with a new and beautiful light, stores and

streets and buildings, were watched with an intense interest and delight by an admiring crowd of citizens.

Other installations in Illinois followed rapidly, at Quincy, Rock Island, Galena, Springfield and Peoria; after which the use of artificial gas as a street illuminant in the American city increased so rapidly that it is difficult to record its exact progress. It is worthy of note, however, that it was not until the decade between 1865 and 1875 that it came into general use for house lighting. The discovery of kerosene had been a great deterrent to such use. Also there came into popular favor, almost coincident with the first development of petroleum, *natural gas*, which generally was to be found in the same fields. For two or three decades, from about 1875 to 1900 (although there is record of its having been used to light the streets of Fredonia, New York, in 1822), this lighting agent enjoyed a considerable favor. It seemed to exist in inexhaustible quantities. It was used lavishly. It was soon seen, however, that the fields were far from inexhaustible. That fact, combined with the foul odors so frequently to be found in connection with natural gas, gradually reduced it to the rank of about a fourth-rate public servant.

Gradually manufactured gas, distilled from coal, came into large and varied favor and began to have very many home uses. Robert Wilhelm von Bunsen invented in 1855 the blue gas flame burner which has been of vast use industrially and socially. By means of this ingenious contrivance it has been possible to burn gas economically, with an intensely hot but smokeless flame. In laboratory work alone, this invention has been invaluable. A number of years later there came another special lamp or burner, which became known as the Welsbach burner, from the title, von Welsbach, given in Germany to its inventor, one Carl Auer, a student at Heidelberg under von Bunsen. This came rather slowly into favor. In an inverted form it was not used until 1900, although four years earlier it was first applied successfully in street lighting.

At the great Centennial Exposition, held in Philadelphia in the summer of 1876, the gas stove was first shown. A baking powder company used it for baking bread and cake before the very eyes of delighted housewives, and so became responsible for introducing the stove itself, even though it was not until nearly a score of years thereafter that it began to come to any really popular use, both for cooking and for heating.

In the next chapter will be shown something of the vast importance that the manufacture of gas has assumed as a city utility in the United States today. Despite the all but universal use of electricity as an agent for almost every purpose, the use of gas has not merely held its own, but has increased, tremendously. It, too, has taken its place as one of the dependable and valuable servants of the American city.

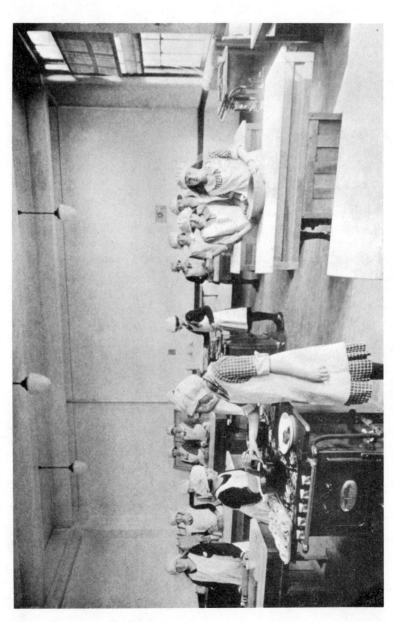

THE GAS RANGE AS USED BY DOMESTIC SCIENCE PUPILS AT JEFFERSON JUNIOR HIGH SCHOOL, ROCHESTER, N. Y.

CHAPTER IX

MANUFACTURED GAS TODAY

THE production and use of manufactured gas in the United States today is at the very highest in all its history. Its use increases steadily. Upon it, modern life remains highly dependent, not merely for light, not merely for heat, but for a wide variety of industrial purposes.

This striking increase has been due to the fact that the industrial gas engineer has accepted the challenge to enter the industrial field in competition with the exponents of other fuels and has had unbounded faith in the watchword of the industry,—"If it is done with heat, you can do it better with gas."

Of course, in the final analysis in the large majority of industries, gas is subjected to the same test as that of every other item which enters the manufacturer's costs, that of actually proving its worth on a strict and absolutely sound economic basis of dollars and cents. Electricity is not a competitor of gas in heating operations, unless other conditions in the process warrant the expenditure of the higher unit cost for fuel. Therefore, the purely economic advantages of gas to the consumer center around the fact that gas is heat in a compact form, purchased as used and delivered at the point of immediate use, absolutely free of overhead or labor charges. The advantages accruing from the use of gas as a quality product are its cleanliness and its ready adaptability to fine temperature requirements through automatic thermostatic control. Finally, under close observation, gas has demonstrated these advantages to the management of such basic industries as the manufacture of steel, non-ferrous metals, ceramics, and textiles.

The use of gas in the steel industry is as diversified as the use of steel itself.   From the pure white heat of the gas furnace which prepares the steel for the terrific impact of the forging hammer; to the soft muffled roar of the heat treating furnace, constantly holding the temperature within a narrow range for performing, perhaps, a no less delicate operation than that of heat treating and tempering an automobile or watch spring; to the vibrant chatter of the rotary carburizing furnace; to the quiet smooth-flowing operations of endless strands of wire passing through the patenter, or great blue sheets passing on to the galvanizing machines— gas will be found faithful to the task and the most dependable servant of the plant engineer.

Gas has established a similar and equally envious reputation in the non-ferrous industries, particularly in the melting of aluminum and brass, in the manufacture of battery plates, in the process of bright annealing and in the field of stereotyping, electrotyping and tin setting.

On the other hand, the gas industry has a rare treat for the æsthetic nature in the magic results produced by the heat of the gas flame in the ceramic industries. Beautiful colors in hand painted designs on china are oxidized to transparent tints and permanently fused

Modern Gas-Fired Glass Melting Furnace.

beneath the surface in special firing kilns. In this industry, gas is used in making and annealing glass of extremely high quality, from which lenses are ground, and many other grades down to the quality used in the manufacture of bottles. Large quantities of gas are used in the process of vitreous enameling in the manufacture of domestic ranges, spark plugs, hospital equipment, bath tubs and commercial vitreous lined tanks and tank cars.

The ordinary individual is familiar with the use of gas in the preparation of foodstuffs in the home, but seldom realizes how extensively it is used commercially in the same field. A few of the places in which gas has proved economically advantageous and at the same time has produced foods of a better quality, are: wholesale bakeries using large conveyor and rotary ovens; manufacturing plants for potato chips, crackers, pretzels, and prepared breakfast foods; large packing houses and markets in smoking meats; and the large candy factories. Gas is also used in roasting coffee, nuts, and spices.

One of the most significant developments in the field of domestic fuels is the trend of the public toward the use of manufactured gas for heating homes. With the exception of electricity, manufactured gas is perhaps the most expensive source of heat energy generally distributed. However, the public today is in a receptive mood for a superior heating service which will return to it dividends on its investment in comfort and convenience. Gas heating has been developed to the stage where it is entirely automatic, and safely guarded to the point where accident is practically unknown. The result is that the future will see possibly more gas used for heating homes than for any other purpose, unless it be industrial processes.

Likewise of significant importance is the development of gas refrigeration. Producing cold from heat, so to speak, as the gas fired refrigerator does, sounds rather odd at first thought. It need only be remembered that heat is energy and energy can be made to do many things. The principle of refrigeration is the compression, the cooling, and the expansion of a gas. Most of us have noticed how cold the air is as it comes from a tire valve, or a service station hose. The air has been compressed or pumped up by an electric compressor, next cooled in the tire or the tank, and then allowed to expand into the outside air which is at a low pressure.

The place where manufactured gas comes in, is in the compression part of the refrigeration cycle. Most liquids absorb gases in different amounts at different temperatures. In most of the gas fired refrigerators ammonia and water are used. When water is cold it will absorb great quantities of ammonia gas, but when heated up it expels or pushes out the gas. If we take a closed vessel with ammonia and water in it and heat it up with a gas flame we get compressed ammonia gas at the top of the vessel. If we then lead the ammonia through a pipe and allow it to be cooled and then let it expand through a valve into a medium of low pressure, we will get refrigeration in that medium. After the ammonia gas has done its work,—that is, has cooled whatever it comes into contact with in the low pressure side,—it is led back into the water and is ready to be boiled out by the gas flame again. In the gas machine the cooling is done

NEW SECTION OF THE WEST STATION GAS MANUFACTURING PLANT OF THE
ROCHESTER GAS AND ELECTRIC CORPORATION.

by city water or just air and the evaporation or low pressure side of the box is usually made of coils of pipe, which frost up and chill the air in the ice box.

There are many other uses of gas that could be enumerated in the industrial, professional and scientific fields. The printer setting type at the modern linotype knows that it is the small gas furnace within his machine that enables it so quickly to set the bars of type from which words will be printed within the hour. The manufacturer of delicate appliances of metal in his workshop, the dentist in his office, the jeweler at his bench, the scientist in his laboratory—all of these place unending and absolute dependence upon their tiny furnace wherein manufactured gas, maintained at a steady pressure, is the dependable fuel. In an industrial age the factory uses of this gas rise to a great variety and to an impressive quantity. Obviously, it must be maintained at all times at a high quality, as well as at an even pressure.

With all these things in mind, it is not so difficult to understand and to appreciate how in a certain large Eastern industrial city, typical of many, many others, where electric production for lighting and all other civic purposes, except the movement of street cars, has increased 126 per cent in the last five years, the production of manufactured gas has increased more than 158 per cent. That would seem to indicate that the older form of city illuminant was rather more than merely holding its own. As a matter of fact, an increasing amount of time and study and experiment is being placed upon it, not merely for the bettering of its quality but for the improvement of its processes of manufacture.

Of these there are three, which produce three rather distinct forms of manufactured gas: there is *coal gas*, there is *oil gas*, and there is the so-called *water gas*—this last, however, being known more technically as *carburetted blue gas*.

Coal gas and oil gas are produced by the same general processes, by the carbonizing of coal or of oil, through subjecting them to very great heat. The volatile distillate that ensues from the process is unpurified manufactured gas. Coal gas production has increased rather more than proportionately in recent years. In the United States the making of gas from oil obtains chiefly in California and other points in the Far West where petroleum fuel is appreciably cheaper than coal.

Water gas—remember always, technically, carburetted blue gas—first came into vogue about half a century ago. It is generally produced by the so-called Lowe method, which takes its name from the inventor, a famous Civil War aeronaut. Lowe, under the stress of warfare, first perfected his gas-making devices upon the actual field of battle, where he made use of them for filling his giant balloons.

In this process, steam is passed through a very hot fuel-bed of coal or coke. Under the influence of the heat in the fuel-bed, the steam interacts with the carbon of the coke. Hydrogen gas is set free from the steam, while the oxygen combines with carbon to form carbon monoxide. The mixture of hydrogen and carbon monoxide, both combustible gases, is called blue gas. It is carburetted by the addition of hot oil in heavy spray. This last portion of the process is practically duplicated in every automobile that is driven by an internal-combustion gasoline engine.

When it comes to actual commercial practice, this water gas process is done in alternate operations. Three *chambers*, *ovens*, or *furnaces* are essential to its production. In the first of these, the generator, a stout cavernous place, lined with heat-resisting fire brick, is the bed of flaming coke. For three minutes air is driven through it from below. This is the *blow* of the water gas system. You probably have seen it many times yourself, in the brilliant flare of flame against the night from some gas works in your own community. Three minutes of blow, or heating-up, are followed by three minutes of gas making.

The *run* follows the "blow." During the three minutes intervening between the flame-flares against the sky, there is no waste, either of gas or of the essential heat. The jet of air into the first generator is succeeded by one of hot, dry steam. For the next one hundred and eighty precious seconds the gas which is being prepared for commercial use passes into the second chamber or *carburetor* wherein has been built a *checkerwork* of brick. In this chamber the spray of hot oil mingles with the blue gas. Carburetion ensues. The combined gas then passes to the third chamber, the *super-heater*, also filled with a brick checkerwork, to break the flow completely and to distribute the gas throughout the entire chamber.

In the last chamber the oil vapors are finally "cracked," to use the parlance of the laboratory expert. The gas is then cooled, the small amount of tar resulting from the oil cracking is removed, the impurities are taken out and the commercial gas, now fully prepared for use, is sent into the *storage holders* on its way to the *distribution* mains and the consumer.

In recent years, however, the production of water gas has suffered something of a diminution, a little of a setback. As may be readily understood from this description of the process, it requires large quantities of oil for its production, and even though this oil be of fairly low grade, its cost mounts to a pretty penny. The tremendous increase in recent years of the gasoline motor vehicle all the way across the land has about tripled the price of oil to the manufacturer of artificial gas. He has been forced by the situation to turn his attention back to the production of coal gas, the original form of manufactured gas. In a few cases he is blending water gas and coal gas, a thing not difficult to accomplish. He can adjust the proportion between them to suit himself, for the average consumer is quite unable to recognize from the flame any variation in the blending.

Coal gas has as its great virtue today, its by-products. In fact its very salvation is due to the impressive array of these that are obtained in its manufacture. Reference already has been made to the tar recovered in the case of water gas. In the case of coal gas, the by-products are far larger, and far more important, commercially. Coke, coal-tar, ammonia, motor-fuel,— these and many others come from the coal gas process. The number of products which can be derived from these materials is almost unlimited. When it is realized that from coal tar alone, nearly ten thousand commercially valuable products are now manufactured, something can be understood of its real value. It is a tremendous base for modern drugs and medicines of a wide variety of usefulness to mankind. It also is the chief factor in the making of aniline dyes, absolutely

Sizing, Storage, and Loading Bins for Coke.   Rochester Gas and Electric Corporation.

fast colors which can be produced in every conceivable tint and shade, and in tremendous quantities. The family tree of the coal-tar by-products is a wide-spreading elm. It might almost be likened to a small forest.

The motor-fuel that comes from coal gas is of the highest grade. It not only does not carbonize within the cylinders of the motor, but it has a distinct cleansing action toward removing any carbon that may be in them. The problem at all times is for the gas works to make enough of this motor fuel to meet the insistent demands of the automotive industry.

Coke is of primary importance in house heating. It is as good as anthracite coal and cheaper.

Now why is the manufacture of these commercially important by-products valuable to the consumer? The answer is not difficult to find. It lies in the fact that the appreciable revenues that the gas company receives from them enables it to continue selling its chief product, manufactured gas, for lighting, heating or power purposes at a far lower figure than would be possible without the sale of the by-products. In recent years there has been a large increase in the cost of gas manufacture. Coal, itself the chief single expenditure in the industry, has doubled and then tripled in price. But manufactured gas has not doubled or tripled in price. The profitable sale of the by-products has kept its price to the consumer both low and stable.

Let us return to the process of the manufacture of coal gas. Even though it is somewhat complicated by the machinery necessary to remove its valuable by-products, the process itself still remains so simple that any schoolboy may readily understand it. To understand this manufacture more concretely, come with me to a highly modern coal gas plant, in the very heart of an American industrial city of more than three hundred thousand population.

The ovens of silica brick, especially made to withstand a temperature of nearly 3100 degrees Fahrenheit, are each filled with a little more than six tons of coal, and for twelve hours are subjected to great and continuous heat. In all this time there is a continuous flow of the gas off the top of the glowing coal to and through the processes of refinement. Twice a day, once each twelve hours, the ovens are empty for a few minutes, for cleaning and refilling. But there are never many out of commission in this way at the same time The cleaning and refilling is kept in rotation between them so that all the while, night and day, the gas is steadily pouring forth. The multiplication of the oven-units makes for this steady volume of production, each minute of the twenty-four hours.

This coal gas plant consumes the large quantity of 1000 tons of bituminous coal each twenty-four hours, year in and year out, and in that fullest possible working day, it sends out to the community it serves more than 11,000,000 cubic feet of gas, in addition to producing the sizable amount of by-products to which reference has already been made.

Being a modern gas works, this also is an efficient one. Within it hand labor is reduced to an absolute minimum. The 1,000 ton daily meal of this monster is fed to him continuously. Conveyor belts bring the coal from a high-set railroad siding nearby, to a storage bin. An electrically propelled lorry, or small charging car, running on rails, feeds the ovens. The situation of this particular gas plant, on the floor of a deep river

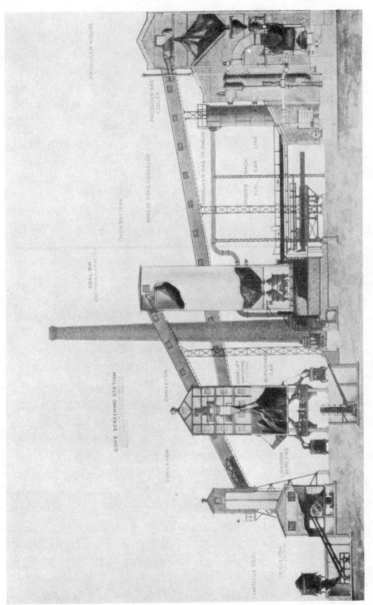

CROSS SECTION OF A PORTION OF A GAS MANUFACTURING PLANT.

gorge, makes it possible to handle the many tons of coal almost entirely by gravity and so there is a great annual saving in operating cost.

There are sixty of the ovens. Multiple equipment indeed! Each oven, it will be recalled, takes six and a half tons of coal. Sixty ovens, each consuming six and a half tons of coal each twelve hours, means 780 tons of coal each calendar day. The remaining 220 tons are used in a similar process in another plant. In turn, each ton of coal produces more than 10,000 cubic feet of gas. In the process, the coal is itself reduced to 1050 pounds of good commercial coke, today an extremely popular fuel both for domestic and industrial uses, in addition to 350 pounds of coke screenings, which the gas company can and does use for making the so-called *producer gas* which it burns to keep the ovens properly heated. For this last purpose, therefore, it is not compelled to burn good coal. Here is another of the nice economies of the process. The use of waste gases from the producers under the boilers, which generate the steam for various power uses in and about the plant, is still another fine economy. For years, practically the only waste of heat in a coal gas plant was the quenching of the white hot coke by water, after it was discharged from the ovens, which sent large clouds of steam into the air. This last item of heat like the "squeal of the pig" in the packing industry, is now saved in a process by which the heat of the hot coke is used to generate high pressure steam for power purposes.

From the ton of coal that produces the 10,000 cubic feet of manufactured gas, there also come twenty-three pounds of commercial ammonium sulphate, one and one half gallons of light oil, and twelve gallons of coal tar.

In the course of a single day's work at this typical plant, there are therefore produced 525 tons of coke, 12,000 gallons of coal tar, 23,000 pounds of ammonium sulphate and 1500 gallons of the light oils.

We have just seen the many uses of coal tar. Ammonium-sulphate, a chemical salt, is used chiefly for fertilizers furnishing nitrogen needed for plant life.

The light oils deserve a paragraph of their own. Their production was a special development of the national defense in the World War. When the country was faced with the necessity of making modern ammunition, it looked about for certain essentials for T.N.T. and other high explosives. Three of these, benzol, toluol and xylol, were particularly difficult to obtain. But, since they existed in coal gas as it came off the retorts, immediate preparations were made to collect them at the gas works of the country, including the gas plant previously mentioned. Since the war, benzol, toluol and xylol have gone out of fashion. But the light oils which contain them are now being used for the production of motor fuel, which may be used alone or mixed with gasoline, giving the excellent results which have been described.

To recover these by-products, other than the coke, and make the coal gas suitable for use by the consumer, is an extensive process. First the gas temperature must be reduced. The gas leaves the ovens at 800 degrees Fahrenheit and comes to the consumer at something like seventy degrees. In fact it enters the gas holders, the great reservoirs of the product, at that self same seventy degrees.

To bring the temperature of the gas, at a single step, from 800 degrees Fahrenheit down to seventy would be

extremely unwise.   Its heat reduction must be gradual.
Moreover, certain of its by-products will come forth
at one temperature, others at quite a different one.
Here is therefore another necessity for slowly stepping
down the temperature and for constantly watching the
process, both by testing and recording thermometers
and pyrometers.   Pressure, too, must be watched for
efficient operation.   The oven is no boiler.   Any extra-
heavy pressure upon its walls would quickly ruin the
silica blocks with which it is lined.   Therefore watch
is kept as carefully upon the pressure gauges as upon
the delicate thermometer.

Pressure controls for this process are even more
delicate than those of temperatures.   A pressure not to
exceed 13/100 inches of water equivalent to 5/1000 of a
pound per square inch must be maintained throughout
each twelve hours of the processing of the coal.

The first step for the coal gas after leaving the fiery
heat of the ovens in which it is first created, is to bring
it in contact with water.   In this process most of the
coal tar and some of the ammonia are deposited, and
the heat is brought down tremendously, from 800
degrees to about 160 degrees.

The second process is a primary "washing" of the
gas, with some more condensation of tar and ammonia
and a further reduction of the temperature, this time
down to ninety-eight degrees.   The third step is a
pumping process.   It has just been explained how the
new-born product is carried out of the ovens at a minimum pressure.   So slight is this that there is soon need
of a pump to keep it in actual motion.

Another washing process is then accomplished, like
the first, by which there is still further condensation

of tar and ammonia and a further reduction of the temperature, this time to the final seventy degrees. Then comes the final ammonia removal. Formerly this was done by passing the gas into a chamber wherein revolved great water-soaked wheels with a very large number of small holes cut into their huge paddles, seemingly a silly process, but really a most effective one.

Today these wheels no longer revolve. The gas containing the remaining ammonia is passed through a sulphuric acid bath forming ammonium sulphate and freeing the gas from this impurity. Sulphur is another impurity that, in final stages of its manufacture, must be completely removed from manufactured gas. This is brought about by a scrubbing process involving several chemicals, and in this process a precipitate of finely divided sulphur is realized that has the possibility of insecticide use.

A final process, washing, scrubs out the light oils, which as we have seen, had their first great day in the World War and which still continue to have a large commercial value. When these are all gone, the gas is as pure as any carefully manufactured product can be. It is pumped out of the gas works, carefully measured, tested, and corrected, both as to temperature and pressure, and sent off to the giant holders, awaiting its final consumption.

These holders are an essential part of gas production. It is obvious that, no matter how uniform may be the production of artificial gas, its consumption, in the very nature of things, is bound to be extremely variable. When gas was used chiefly for light in the city, the evening hours from sundown to the time when most folk went to their beds, represented the period of its

A Modern Gas Holder.

most rapid consumption. Today electricity feels most
of this particular peak-load. Yet gas is not entirely
immune from peak loads. It feels the mealtimes;
and while there is an appreciable drop in the great
gas holders both for breakfast and for luncheon, the
big pull on them comes in the hour of the preparation
of the evening meal. With this, and the definite consumption of light throughout the evening, particularly
through its earlier hours, the gas holders by ten o'clock
at night are apt to find themselves well flattened toward
the ground.

These vast holders, landmarks in almost any large
town, are quite too familiar to the average man to need
any detailed description here. Literally, they "ride the
gas." Like huge, inverted, collapsible tin drinking cups
their great weight, from the tons of steel that comprise
them, is controlled by a delicate system of guide wheels.
The slight pressure of the gas under storage within
them raises or lowers them with great facility. No
other agent moves them. As the gas comes in, at times
in far, far greater volume than it is being drawn out,
the huge rings of the sheet metal holder rise, its capacity
quickly expands, until it may be used at its fullest
capacity, rising to a height of from 150 to 225 feet
above the surface of the ground, and holding all the way
from six to fifteen million cubic feet of gas. Similarly,
when the gas is being drawn out more rapidly than it
can be produced, the holder contracts in height until
the top of the holder may come to within a very few
feet of the ground. It is tremendously elastic, and
therefore well suited to the vast variations at different
hours between gas production and consumption.

To make the gas holder air-tight and gas-tight the

gas is water-sealed everywhere.   The holder is em-
bedded in water, in a circular tank which holds water
to about thirty-five feet in depth.   The narrow circular
rings or joints between the various concentric sections
of the gas holder also contain water which prevents
leakage of gas between the sections.

Sometimes this water in the rings gives trouble,
although not often in a land of mild temperatures.
But in one subjected to really stiff winter weather, each
gas holder becomes a considerable problem in itself.   Ice
will persist in forming in the water rings, anchor ice in
the bottom of the tank itself.   Workmen, with thermometers in hand, are forever scurrying up the bleak,
cold sides of the holder to test the temperature of the
water rings, for if insufficient heat is applied to the
water, ice may form, which easily can wreak sad havoc
with the delicately adjusted great metallic reservoirs.
Hot water and steam must be brought into play to keep
the holders free from ice in any form.   It is no child's
play, any of it.

A recent innovation in this country is the dry or
waterless gas holder, a design imported from Europe.
It consists of a tank, fabricated of standard steel shapes
and plates, inside of which is a steel diaphragm.   This
diaphragm moves up and down as gas enters or leaves
the holder.   A canvas flap around the edge of the
diaphragm is pressed against the inner surface of the
tank by a series of counter-weighted "shoes."   Tar
pumped into the top of the tank runs down the inner
walls, and forms a seal in the canvas flap, which maintains a gas-tight, lubricated joint, between the shoes
and the tank.

The entire problem of distribution, of properly bring-

ing the gas from the works to the consumer, ranks in its
importance closely beside its production. In this
American industrial city of three hundred thousand
folk whose chief gas works we have just visited, there
are more than 87,000 individual consumers, so reckoned by the number of individual meters installed. To
bring the artificial gas to all these houses, stores and
factories, more than 550 miles of gas mains, enough to
stretch all the way from New York City to Erie, Pennsylvania, ranging in diameter from two inches to thirty,
are required. The task of laying, maintaining and
inspecting these, without unnecessary disturbance of the
city streets underneath which they are buried, is no
slight one.

Nor is the problem of distribution entirely a matter
of adequate mains. To keep a moderate pressure even
and dependable throughout a far-flung city and its
many suburbs, it is necessary to maintain various
pumping stations or "boosters." With this system
adopted, the gas is fed from the main holders to various
distributing centers, where there is regulation if not
actual pumping, and from which it is quickly and easily
distributed to the service mains. From these the gas
goes directly to the connection pipes to house, or store,
or factory. Great vigilance is required at the pumping
equipment and great precaution is taken by installing
automatic reserve equipment, in order to insure a continuous supply of gas. The gas man regards continuity of service as a sacred duty above all else.

No small portion of this problem of distribution is
that of upkeep. The deterioration of a vast system of
pipes and gateways buried in the damp earth is a tireless and unceasing enemy. Inspection and renewal

and repair must be equally tireless and unceasing. Reference has just been made to the winter battles against ice forming in the giant holders.   The army of men who maintain the distribution must be on constant duty during every month and week of the year. Fire, flood, a host of lesser disasters, are apt at any moment to need quick thought and instant action. The repair crews of the gas companies must be eternal in their vigilance.   Their ordinary duties, of maintenance and renewal and repair, are no sinecures. At times, in real emergencies, they may be called upon to perform services that are not less than truly heroic.

A city utility of any importance never stops.   If it is to be mended, the work must be done like an operation upon the human body, while it still functions actively. To shut off a modern city's gas supply for a single hour would be tragic, literally tragic.   Lights, unguarded, would be extinguished, automatically.   To turn on the gas again suddenly might easily mean the asphyxiation of hundreds or of thousands of human beings.   Therefore, eternal vigilance is the watchword of the many workers in this highly important city utility.   Upon their faith, upon their watchfulness await not merely the health, but the life itself of a whole city population. It is to their eternal credit that there is not yet a record of their having failed.   The gas lighting utility has stood always, like a good soldier, faithful to its task. Its long record is one not only of increasing achievement, but of absolute reliability.

We have thus seen that the process of gas manufacture produces two forms of smokeless fuel, gas and coke, each of very great economic importance to society. In the industrial world gas is proving itself superior to

State Inspector Putting His Seal of Approval on Gas Meters.

all other forms of heat energy, and hence the products of the gas works together with the products of the electric plant which is now to be described, will ultimately furnish the energy required for daily life. Through these central stations of energy will then come the smokeless city of the future, no less surely than the supply of chemicals for agricultural and industrial needs.

The gas industry is aware that its future lies in the future of the trade it serves and, therefore, it appropriates large sums of money for research in efficient heating processes. The local companies maintain a corps of trained engineers, whose duty it is to analyze the heating operations in the various industries in its territory, submit a report with recommendations and stand ready to serve their needs. Service of this nature is truly a public utility and the net results clearly indicate, to the close observer, that the trend is definitely toward manufactured gas as the ultimate fuel.

CHAPTER X

THE DEVELOPMENT OF LIGHTING—
ELECTRICITY

VISITORS to the gay Paris Exposition in the fall of 1879 noticed a new form of lamp, shown there for the first time in Europe. It was called the "electric candle" and it was the invention of a scientist named Jablochkoff. The device was regarded as a pretty toy and a most unusual one. It attracted no end of attention. Not many folk who saw it realized that they were gazing upon a device which, in a few short years, was, in a large sense, to change the face of the world; that, in particular, was to transform the streets of cities, heretofore more or less murkily lighted, by flickering gas jets, if not always into great white ways, into generally brilliant and safe thoroughfares; that was to make the advertising signboard, if not a thing of beauty at least many times a joy forever; and that was to make the illumination of buildings of every sort soft, efficient, and very beautiful, within and without.

In its first crude form, the device at Paris was hardly to be regarded as much more than a toy. Yet something more it was, distinctly; it was a symbol of a new force, awake and active in the fascinating field of invention, of a new era, fast coming to this grey, old world. Few of the folk who saw it in the French capital realized that, a few months before, a select committee of the British House of Commons had met, under orders from that august body, to look into this little known scheme of "electric lighting" and to advise, in case that wild plan ever did come to anything, just what form of franchises and protection should be put around it. The name of a young American, Thomas A. Edison, had been thrust into the conference. A scientist who was testifying, murmured something about the fact that Edison was succeeding in "subdividing the electric light," whatever that might mean. But this expert scientist apparently did not take Edison seriously, for he is recorded but a moment later, as having added:

He has never put forward any practical statement in connection with this invention that would induce any scientific man to pay much attention to it.

With this the distinguished members dropped the matter in their own minds for all time. Even as great a scientist as Tyndall, at that time, refused to take Edison seriously. This probably made very little difference to the young American inventor, a graduate railroad telegrapher, who, as early as September, 1877, was busy in his workshop at Menlo Park, New Jersey, trying to effect a commercially successful electric lamp. It will be remembered that purely experimental ones, glimmering feebly in laboratories, had been known for some years.

Edison went steadily forward. By 1879, word that something of large interest was being done in the workshop at Menlo Park began to be whispered about in scientific circles. As a matter of fact, Edison had even then devised a lamp, infinitely superior to the toy candles that were being shown at Paris, which had a commercial practicability. For a long time he had struggled with the vexatious question of a proper filament for the electric bulb. Various delicate materials, including even human hair, from China, were tried before a proper and efficient conductor finally was found.

But the lamp was only part of the problem. Electric lighting, upon any large and successful scale, meant far more than merely devising a lamp. To quote Mr. Edison's own words:

A complete system of distribution for electricity had to be evolved, and as I had to compete with the gas system, this must be commercially efficient and economical, and the network of conductors must be capable of being fed from many different points. A commercially sound network of distribution had to permit of being placed under or above ground, and must be accessible at all points and be capable of being tapped anywhere.

I had to devise a system of metering electricity in the same way gas was metered, so that I could measure the amount of electricity used by each consumer. Ways and means had also to be devised for maintaining an even voltage everywhere on the system. The lamps nearest the dynamo had to receive the same current as the lamps farthest away. The burning out or breaking of lamps must not affect those remaining in the circuit, and means had to be provided to prevent violent fluctuations of current.

Over and above all these things, many other devices had to be invented and perfected, such as devices to prevent excessive currents, proper switching gear, lamp holders, chandeliers, and all manner of details that were necessary

THOMAS EDISON AND STAFF IN HIS LABORATORY AT MENLO PARK, 1880.

to make a complete system of electric lighting that could compete successfully with the gas system. Such was the work to be done in the early part of 1878. The task was enormous but we put our shoulders to the wheel and in a year and a half we had a system of electric lighting that was a success.

Clearer exposition than this of the very beginnings of commercial lighting could hardly be made.

It was in September, 1879, the same month that Jablochkoff was showing his "electric candle" at the Paris Exposition, that Mr. Edison came out with a definite statement to the effect that he could light the entire lower portion of New York City, using no more than a 500 horse power steam engine. He proposed to establish a power house somewhere in Nassau Street. From it wires could, and would, be run as far uptown as Cooper Union, as far downtown as the Battery, and for the entire distance east and west between the East and North Rivers. He elaborated upon this plan, saying:

I propose to utilize the gas burners and chandeliers now in use. In each house I can place a small meter, whence these wires will pass through the house, tapping small metallic contrivances that may be placed over each burner. The housekeepers may turn off their gas and send their meters back to the companies from whence they came. Whenever it is desirable to light a jet it will only be necessary to touch a little spring near it. No matches are required.

This, again, was highly definite. Edison's promises had already been so followed by performance, that he now had acquired a following, not merely among ordi-

nary folk, but also among scientists and technicians.   To
such an extent was this true, that the powerful gas
companies, not merely in the United States, but on
the other side of the Atlantic, became alarmed at his
prophecies.   In London, some of the gas companies'
shares fell as much as twelve points overnight.   On the
other hand, all of this was a great stimulus and help to
him in the organization of and securing of financial
aid for his first commercial lighting company, which
began its career in the city of New York.

In the meantime, there were public demonstrations
of the new lighting system.   On December 21, 1879,
the *New York Herald* published an astonishing full-
page feature article upon Edison and his wonderful new
invention.   Similar articles appeared at about the same
time in *Harper's Weekly*, and in *Leslie's*.   The result
of all of this was an immediate public clamor to see
the new light at work.   To this, Mr. Edison yielded.
On the last night of that eventful year, 1879, more than
three thousand folk, scientists, journalists, capitalists,
prominent citizens of every sort, went out to Menlo
Park on special trains.   All were filled with curiosity
and excitement over the new device.

For a long time afterward people continued to flock
to the little New Jersey town.   Of these visitors Mr.
Edison has written, in his own carefully prepared
notebooks:

In the early days of my electric light, curiosity and
interest brought a good many people to Menlo Park to see
it.   Some of them did not come with the best of intentions.
I remember the visit of one expert, a well-known electrician,
graduate of Johns Hopkins University.   We had the lamps
exhibited in a large room and so arranged on a table as to

illustrate the regular layout of circuits for houses and streets. Sixty of the men employed in the laboratory were used as watchers, each to keep an eye on a certain section of the exhibit, and see there was no monkeying with it. This man had a length of insulated wire around his sleeve and back, so his hands would conceal the ends and no one would know he had it. His idea, of course, was to put this across the ends of the supplying circuits and short-circuit the whole thing—put it all out of business without being detected. Then he could report how easily the electric light went out and a false impression would be conveyed to the public. He did not know that we had already worked out the safety fuse and that every little group of lights was protected independently. He slyly put this jumper in contact with the wires and just four lamps went out on the section he tampered with. The watchers saw him do it, however, and got hold of him, and just led him out of the place with language that made the recording angels jump to their typewriters.

These first demonstrations were followed by the installation of a pioneer commercial plant in downtown New York. Pearl Street, rather than Nassau, was chosen for the power station, and because of the newness of the entire thing, the work, at the outset, dragged a bit. The Edison Electric Illuminating Company of New York, with an impressive list of directors, was incorporated in 1880, but it was not until two years later that its first plant began to function. The current officially was turned on, for commercial service, September 4, 1882. There were at the beginning fifty-nine customers for the company.

Of that important September evening there are many records in the New York newspapers. The *Tribune*, for instance, described the lamp as "a small blazing horseshoe that glowed within a pear-shaped globe, pendent beneath a porcelain shade." The *Herald* was a bit patronizing. It spoke of the new invention as "supplanting the dim flicker of gas" and then added that "last night it was fairly demonstrated that the Edison light had a very fair degree of success." The *Sun*, as ever, was personal and picturesque. It said very little about the remarkable invention, but commented chiefly upon the fact that Mr. Edison on the eventful night wore a square, white derby. The *Times* following its traditions, was more detailed. It explained that to get the light, all you had to do was to turn a switch. On behalf of men who worked at night in newspaper offices, it burst forth in loud praise for this new, efficient light. A little later it actually installed the strange device in its own building in Printing House Square.

From 59 customers in September, 1882, the new lighting company jumped to 203 before the end of the year, who, all told, used between them 5,228 incandescent lamps. The banking house of Drexel, Morgan & Company, and the Stock Exchange were very early patrons. This was encouraging. The fact that concerns of such magnitude and conservatism saw fit to install the new light was a large point in its favor. From the beginning of 1883 orders began to come in more rapidly than they could possibly be filled.

One great barrier and problem confronted this earliest electric lighting company, and the others that began to follow at its heels. To supply to large and congested cities direct current, the first and fundamental sort of electric current, in quantities sufficient to light any large number of lamps, there apparently must be separate power stations at intervals of approximately every two miles, for a mile seemed to be about the practicable limit for reaching out from the generating dynamos. Beyond that, the cables required for low voltage, direct current, would necessarily be so large and so heavy as to make the expense of installing them almost prohibitive. While direct current arc lamps could be used at greater distances, it seemed for a time as if the use of the incandescent lamp was to be limited to within fairly close reach of the power house, and the incandescent type already was being recognized in most instances as the more efficient and the more economical of the two lamps.

While the pioneers in the electric lighting industry struggled with this particular problem, other pioneers were developing the alternating current field. Mr. George Westinghouse, who had already acquired fame and wealth as the inventor of the air brake, as well as some other important railroad devices, gave it as his impression that a high-voltage alternating current could be introduced successfully for taking the current from the power station to the lamps over very considerable distances, perhaps quite a number of miles. He based his opinion upon the experiments of a Frenchman and an Englishman, Messrs. Gaulard and Gibbs, in Italy and in London. By high-voltage alternating current they had succeeded in successfully carrying lighting current from Rome, Italy, to Tivoli, more than twenty miles, where they transformed it back into low-voltage current for the actual lighting of incandescent lamps.

So great was Mr. Westinghouse's faith in this phase of the electric power problem, that he purchased the

American rights on the Gaulard and Gibbs' patents, and with these, together with those of the Sawyer-Man incandescent lamp, rivalling the Edison lamp in priority, and certain ones obtained by Mr. William Stanley, founded the large electrical manufacturing business that to this day bears his name.

For a long time there was much opposition to George Westinghouse and his alternating current scheme. It made little difference in an electric light whether the current was direct current or alternating current as the light is produced simply through the generation of heat, caused by the passing of current through the filament, bringing it to a point of brilliant incandescence. Electricity, however, was coming to be used for power purposes, and the direct current motor was, at that time, much more satisfactory than the alternating current motor. In fact, it was not until Nikola Tesla invented the induction motor that the alternating current could compete on even footing with the direct current for power purposes. The direct current system operates at low voltage and does not adapt itself readily to transmission of current any great distance. On the other hand, alternating current systems operate at almost any desirable voltage and are readily adaptable for transmitting current great distances.

It all sounds very easy and simple now, but for several years in the middle of the 'eighties there was a great deal of contention over the matter. Mr. Edison did not accept the alternating current plan quickly or easily. When at Auburn, New York, in 1887, a convicted murderer, who was the first to take the electric chair, was executed, and the alternating current used for the act, this was taken up as a form of popular argument against that method of transmission. Prejudice was aroused against the new form of current.

Nevertheless, Westinghouse kept faithfully to his task of introducing and of making popular the alternating current system. A crude pioneer experimental system in an abandoned factory at Great Barrington, Massachusetts, in which this method was used, was followed, a little later, by a commercial installation at Lawrenceville, a suburb of Pittsburgh, Pennsylvania. In 1886, Buffalo, New York, ate its Christmas turkey by electric light, which was furnished by alternating current.

By this time there was no longer any question in the United States as to the popularity of the electric light. The problem became one for the manufacturer to produce generators (*dynamos*), transmission systems, and lamps fast enough to meet the popular demand for them. Towns vied with one another for its installation. By the beginning of the final decade of the nineteenth century, it was a poor sort of American town that could not boast its electric lighting plant. True it was that these early power stations not infrequently broke down and sent folk scurrying back to gas, or oil lamps or even candles, and a good many communities followed the thrifty practice of extinguishing their street lights on supposedly moonlight nights. Yet they all had electric lights of one sort or another.

The culmination of this first wave of popularity of the new illuminant came also in that same decade of the 'nineties, in the blaze of glory that accompanied the World's Columbian Exposition at Chicago from May to October, 1893. The Chicago Fair, as it came quickly to be known, was made more beautiful, more dazzlingly beautiful, than anything that had ever preceded it any-where in the world. Electricity accomplished the transformation. Much time and thought had been expended upon the architecture of the great fair, both in its mass and in its detail, and the giant white build-ings, even in the blinding light of midday, were undeni-ably lovely. But when night came and deep shadows nestled down over the White City and thousands of electric lamps glowed here and there and everywhere upon the surfaces of the buildings, along the walks and paths, and canals, and lagoons, folk caught their breath and were silent for long minutes in the presence of the supremely beautiful new thing.

Eight years later, at Buffalo, New York, the Pan-American Exposition was to show great advances in the development of this exterior illumination of huge and monumental buildings by the use of myriads of small electric lamps. It, too, was very beautiful. But it was the Chicago Fair that had first awakened the eyes of America and of the whole world to the purely decorative possibilities of electric lighting. From that spectacular beginning, its progress has never been checked, until the fine illumination of the exterior of a handsome building, either by projectors hidden along its façades or by "flood lights" placed upon the roof of some nearby structure, is today well known. Perhaps the most beautiful single instance of this is the nightly illumination of the great dome of the Capitol at Washington by dozens of powerful flood lights, hidden within the shrubbery of the park which surrounds it.

Immediately following the Chicago Fair, there came another dramatic advance in electric lighting. Niagara Falls was to be put to work. In other words, the giant

ILLUMINATION OF ADMINISTRATION BUILDING, CHICAGO WORLD'S FAIR, 1893.

cataract, to which men had journeyed for two centuries, just to gaze upon its spectacular beauty, was to be harnessed to the service of mankind. After many unsuccessful attempts, a group of men finally devised a practical plan for making use of at least a sizable part of the water power going to waste there. They had to proceed with great discretion. Obviously, it would not do to ruin the appearance of one of the great natural wonders of the world, by robbing it of the unceasing flood of water which goes to make its eternal beauty. Public opinion would never have permitted such a desecration.

Under the sharp supervision of the governments of the United States and Canada, a limited diversion of the waters of the Niagara River for power purposes finally was permitted. The two countries were to share equally in the power benefits. It was planned to make the largest possible use of every cubic foot of the water that was so diverted. Yet ungainly factories were not to be permitted on the very brink of the picturesque Niagara gorge. Schemes were brought forward to transmit this power from the cataract by the use of compressed air, or even by wire or rope cableways. All of these finally were rejected, as being too clumsy or inadequate, and it was decided that the electric current, of alternating type, was the best medium for the transmission of the vast power. Experience has since shown this to have been a very wise decision.

By the summer of 1895, a power canal and tunnel and power house were finished in the city of Niagara Falls, New York, and were at once put to work. Ten powerful alternating current generators, each of 5,000 horse power capacity, formed the original dynamo plant.

From them ran the feed cables, at that time carrying current at 12,500 volts, which since has been very greatly increased, to the various transformer stations. These early generators were of the so-called umbrella type, which means that the revolving field was actually a huge metal ring, in this case 11 feet 7½ inches in its outer diameter. With this ring revolving at its normal speed of 250 revolutions a minute, the outer periphery of it actually moved at the tremendous speed of about 9,300 feet a minute, or about twice as fast as the very fastest railroad train

This plant was the pioneer large power house of the world and still stands as a monument to the vision and energy of the men who conceived and built this vast electrical industry. Since that time tremendous improvements have been made in the efficiency with which the water, diverted from the Niagara River, can be used, and the size of the individual units has been increased over twelve times. The use of these larger and more efficient units, together with an improved intake tunnel and a discharge tunnel or draft tube for handling water, results today in the generation of more than twice as much power, from approximately the same amount of water. While the American and Canadian Governments have made slight concessions to power companies from time to time, generally speaking there has been little change in the amount of water that they are allowed to divert from the Falls.

At the outset, thirty years ago, one spoke of "harnessing Niagara," an extremely popular newspaper phrase of that day, as a boon to nearby cities for their community electricity *power* requirements, chiefly lighting and street railways. It did not take long to extend the

ELECTRIC TOWER AND TEMPLE OF MUSIC, PAN-AMERICAN EXPOSITION,
BUFFALO, 1901.

power transmission lines from the Falls, to Buffalo, Rochester, and Syracuse in New York state, and to Hamilton and Toronto, in the Canadian province of Ontario. But it soon was discovered that the most efficient use of Niagara power was in certain manufacturing processes where a vast deal of energy is required, and where the processes can go forward each hour of the twenty-four. For, after all, there is no real "harnessing" of Niagara. No engineer has yet been able to come forward with a practical plan for conserving its energy in dull hours in some sort of an impound, or reservoir. It is not possible to store its power in water form before it comes tumbling down, over the mighty cataract and into the deep gorge at its foot, and neither is it possible to conserve this power after it has been converted into electric energy. Nothing comparable with the giant holders of the gas companies has yet been devised for the storage of electricity.

Storage batteries have been perfected, and are used very extensively for the purpose of protecting the large direct current systems in our larger cities from interruptions. In fact, the operation of such large direct current systems would be impracticable without the protection to the service afforded through the use of these batteries. Even in their present stage of perfection, however, the cost is so high that it is absolutely impractical to use these batteries as a means of storing up energy during dull hours and delivering it during the hours of greater power demand in order to give the generating plants a uniform load, as is done with gas.

As a rule electricity has to be used the instant it is created, which meant, therefore, at Niagara, where there was no possible chance of impounding the waters of the greatest inland lake system in the world, that continuous manufacturing processes must be sought. This presently was done and Niagara became a great center for the production of such extremely valuable modern base metals and chemicals as aluminum, carborundum, and calcium carbide as well as their various alloys and by-products. It has been said that America could never have taken her present foremost place in the production of motor cars and motor trucks if it had not been for the establishment and development of this specialized manufacturing industry at Niagara. That industry, also, was of vast help in our efforts in the World War.

Not always is water power so easily available for the generation of electrical energy, although, as will be seen in the next chapter, the potential possibilities of this sort of power in the United States still are very great. Then steam becomes the next best thing. It is, in one respect, far superior since it can be utilized to its fullest capacity in the hours when there is the heaviest demand, the greatest need, for electrical energy. Between these times, boilers can lie banked and fallow, the steam engines absolutely stilled. It is but a matter of minutes to bring the boilers to full heat, and engines once again to the fullest working capacity.

The first electric dynamos were run by almost any sort of steam engine that was available. Quite obviously a high-speed engine was always to be preferred. Edison and Westinghouse and the others of their kind spent much time in discovering just what kind of engine was best suited to the generation of electricity. Almost every conceivable form of straight line and reciprocating

INTERIOR OF THE OLD PEARL STREET STATION, EDISON ELECTRIC ILLUMINATING COMPANY.

steam engine was tried and finally rejected. Eventually the *steam turbine* was the mechanism that was found best adapted to the tremendous power now required to drive the generators.

There is nothing particularly new in the fundamental idea of the turbine. As far back as 120 B.C., Hero invented one in the ancient city of Alexandria. Through all the centuries scientists have tinkered with it, have sought, in more recent years, to make it adaptable to steam energy. Yet it came but slowly into usage. Long years went by, without much development of it. In 1835, a farmer near Syracuse, New York, was using one to operate his saw-mill. This is one of the very earliest practical steam turbines of which there is record.

Neither is there anything particularly complicated in the turbine's fundamental idea. Take an ordinary electric fan, tightly encase it in a housing and with an exhaust outlet, blow steam against the fan and you will have a steam turbine. The fan will turn and its shaft will be the shaft of your engine. Increase many times the number of blades in the fan, perfect the details of its operation, and you will have, in effect, a modern steam turbine.

It is evident that the higher the velocity with which the steam is blown against the blades of the fan or turbine the more rapidly the fan will revolve and the greater the amount of power it will generate. Hence an essential part of the turbine in addition to the large number of blades required is a means for converting the high pressure of the steam into high velocities, and this is accomplished by passing the steam through nozzles of proper shape so that the pressure energy of the steam is converted into velocity energy. This conversion is commonly called the expansion of the steam and may take place uniformly throughout the entire turbine or may be divided up into stages.

Consequently, two types of turbines have been developed. The first is known as the reaction turbine. In it the expansion of the steam is carried on gradually throughout the entire body of the turbine. This machine is made up of stationary blades set in the casing and rotating blades set in the rotor, with the steam expanding uniformly through both sets of blades. The second type is known as the impulse turbine. In this the expansion occurs in stages, the steam passing through stationary nozzles, something like the nozzle of a fire hose, in each stage and then striking the rotating blades. No expansion of the steam takes place in the rotating blades. Turbines of the first type are manufactured by the Parsons Company of England, the Westinghouse Electric and Manufacturing Company of this country and others. Turbines of the second type are manufactured by the General Electric Company under the Curtiss patents in this country and by a number of European manufacturers.

It became the practice to connect more and more directly the turbine engine to the generator. No longer was a complicated system of belting necessary. Not even gearing was required. It was found to be perfectly feasible and practical to use what becomes, in effect, the same shaft for the steam turbine and the electric generator. When this was done these two were regarded as a single unit and were given a common name—*turbo-generator*. Slowly, but surely, this combined device has driven out the former detached steam engines and electric dynamos in all modern power stations. By the combination of the two major machines great efficiencies and economies in space, in power and labor have been accomplished, and the evolution of the modern central power station has been rendered more complete.

CHAPTER XI

MODERN ELECTRIC LIGHT AND POWER

You walk into an unlighted room, touch, in accustomed fashion, a tiny switch beside the door jamb, and instantly the place is flooded with brilliant, yet soft and well diffused light. There are several bulbs in the room and in this way you can regulate the light to suit your own convenience, or your necessities. In an inverted bowl close to the ceiling, are two or three more of the incandescent bulbs. You do not see the lamps themselves, but the translucent bowl throws some of their energy against the white ceiling and so by reflection down into the room, while it also permits still more of the light to filter through its semiopaque body. This sort of fixture replaces the garish chandelier of yesteryear, in many cases a rather awkward and ungainly bit of house furnishing. There are also, perhaps, sidelights on the walls probably set in handsome sconces and softened by silken shades.

Upon the tables there may be other lamps, intended primarily for reading or for study. These are fed by long, flexible cords, attached to half-hidden sockets in the walls. If you wish, you may remove the lamp cord and replace it with one leading to an electric heater, or some highly modern form of cooking appliance, such as an electric toaster or a chafing-dish. Mother may put the cord for her sewing machine into that same socket and know that her dressmaking is not to be a matter of racking physical labor, for hours. The very current that makes the room glow with light, at the same moment performs many of the former tasks of manual labor about the house. In another room it may be freezing artificial ice, cooking the family dinner, washing, ironing, or cleaning the dishes after a meal. Today, it may also be used for operating the family radio outfit.

It is all sightly and attractive and, of course, odorless and smokeless. Those of us who have lived in no other age, cannot easily realize all of the many very real luxuries of the Electric Age. We can hardly realize the vast benefits, the real labor saving it accomplishes so quickly, so efficiently, so neatly. We do not always appreciate the resultant benefits to the human race, in bodies, eyes and labor saved. Think of Abraham Lincoln, as a boy, studying through the long winter evenings by the flickering light of the fireside or of the tallow dip, and then think of dropping easily into a comfortable chair, turning a tiny switch and having a flood of brilliant and dependable radiance descend upon your printed page. Wonder not, then, that civilization, that education, that man's intellectual attainment have ever gone hand in hand with his progress in the manufacture of artificial light.

Whence comes this energy, this unseen force, that takes that tiny glass phial held firmly in a socket at your elbow and makes it glow as brilliantly as if it really were aflame?

In the preceding chapter we have read of the birth of the electric light, of the struggles of the pioneers to make it effective, efficient and economical. We have seen Thomas A. Edison and George Westinghouse and Nikola Tesla and the rest of the early inventors creating the practical dynamo or generator, the motor, the proper sorts of lamps for varying purposes and the elaborate transmission and distributing systems that must always connect the generator with the lamp as well as the power producing device. That was the chapter of development. This one tells of the well developed thing, functioning in twelve million homes, great and small, all the way across the land; of its per capita consumption in the United States doubling each five years, for there are today comparatively few homes in this land within reach of the constantly extending electrical circuits, which are not now equipped with at least some simple form of electric light and power equipment. There is no instance known of one which, once having been so fitted, has ever reverted to any other form of illuminant.

When the electric light comes, it comes to stay. Fire risks are reduced, household cleanliness and efficiency enhanced. The installation of the lights is apt to be followed, rather quickly, by the household labor-saving devices to which reference has just been made, and which are constantly increasing in variety and in number. That the electric current is such a versatile agent, always is very much in its favor.

Electricity was first used in the production of light, and it was thought that this would be its great field of development. The epoch-making discoveries of Tesla,

Westinghouse, Steinmetz and others in the development of the alternating current systems have resulted, however, in the development of these systems for power to a point which completely dwarfs the magnitude of the use of electricity for lighting.   The vast installations of today would be commercially impossible, if this use of electricity for power had not been brought to its present stage of perfection.   This electric power covers a vast range of applications, from a tiny motor that you can easily hold in your hand, to the vast motor, developing 15,000 to 20,000 H.P., used for driving our largest battleships or rolling huge steel ingots into forms readily usable for structural steel.

Millions of homes today are using not only electric lights, but electric fans, washing machines, sewing machines, and hundreds of other useful appliances, and when electricity once makes its way into the home through the medium of these devices, its great convenience and flexibility in use make it one of the fundamental features in our modern civilization.

Obviously, the starting point of the entire system is the power station in which the electricity is generated. The electric generator may be driven either by water power or steam power.   We have seen, briefly, the first large water power station developed at Niagara Falls. This, in turn, has been followed by additional water power stations in the same location and by others located where reliable hydraulic power is available.

It must be remembered, however, that the Niagara power plants are unique among the hydraulic stations of the world.   The quantity of water in storage is so great that the small percentage allowed by the government to be diverted for power is always and continuously available at all times, on account of the tremendous storage of water in the Great Lakes.

Few localities in the world are as fortunate as Niagara in this respect, and it is only occasionally that hydraulic generating plants are so located that sufficient water is available at all times to furnish enough energy to drive the generators at full load. This is particularly true of hydraulic generating plants located upon rivers. As a consequence, the power companies find it necessary to build other power stations, equipped with steam driven electric generators, capable of producing this energy at a time when the hydraulic generating stations are suffering from lack of power due to low water. Other communities whose power demands are very great, are located in districts where no water powers are available, and consequently we have seen a tremendous development in the building of large steam generating plants, used to supply either the entire power demand of the district or to supplement the power supplied from hydraulic stations during low water periods.

If you will come with me to a great modern power station, we shall try to see for ourselves in a simple and non-technical way a typical generating plant for electric current upon a large scale. This station happens to be one where steam power is used exclusively. It is one of but two or three which are supplying the current, not only for electric light and hundreds of smaller varied industrial uses, but also for the street railways of a city which, with its closely adjacent suburbs, now claims for itself a population of a million folk. This means that it is a huge station indeed. Its rated capacity is 225,000 horse power, or about one-sixth of that which is now generated by water

MODERN HYDRAULIC POWER STATION.

in the colossal power center of Niagara, although upon occasion it has been known to exceed this output.[1]

Because this station burns more than two thousand tons of coal a day, the problem of the transport of its fuel ordinarily would be a fairly difficult one. In this instance, it is solved, most ingeniously, by placing the power station close to the entrance of a coal mine, which is owned by the same company that owns the power station and the electric lighting and the street railway utilities in the adjacent metropolitan city. A short industrial railroad, barely two miles in length, connects the mine entrance with the bunkers of the power station. Between them there is a carefully prepared yard in which there is kept stored, at all times, many thousands of tons of coal, as a reservoir or

[1] The last decade has seen a tremendous development in these large generating plants here in America. They now burn coal at the rate of thousands of tons a day, and the mechanical equipment is so designed that the coal is never touched by hand from the time it leaves the mines. Except in the case where the plant is located alongside the coal mine, this coal is usually delivered to the plant in freight cars carrying from fifty to seventy tons per car. These cars are placed in an unloading device capable of turning the car upside down, thus dumping its entire load of coal at one operation.

In the old days coal was shoveled into the furnace by hand and burned on flat grates. Today this is all done mechanically, by using either stokers which feed the coal into the furnace, or the more recently developed powdered coal equipment in which the coal is burned in a very finely pulverized condition. When using stokers, the coal is first crushed so that none of the lumps are larger than two inches. This crushed coal is then sent from an overhead bunker by gravity to the stokers which, in turn, feed the coal into the furnace where it is burned.

In burning these large amounts of coal, reliance can no longer be placed upon the natural draft produced by a chimney to supply the necessary air for combustion, but large fans are used, capable of handling thousands of cubic feet of air per minute to drive this air into the furnace. A single furnace will burn as much as fifteen to twenty tons of coal an hour.

safeguard against any emergency which might temporarily tie up production in the mine. A longer emergency or tie-up would have to be met by the purchase of coal in the open market.

The coal is burned precisely as it comes from the mine except that it is crushed to smaller size. To attempt to cull or clean it would mean a large and quite unnecessary expense. In the great heat of the furnace fires any small bits of refuse that may come through with it are quickly and easily reduced to ashes or slag.

The coal goes continuously into the furnace, night and day. As in the case of the highly modern coal gas production plant that we saw but a little time ago, it is started at the top of the huge power station building. From these *bunkers* up in the attic it descends as it is wanted, into the fire boxes of nineteen water tube boilers. Fourteen of these take the "run of mine" coal. For the other five, whose type is today largely experimental, it must be pulverized so fine that it will float easily in the air. It is claimed that in these last the time and cost of pulverizing the coal is more than compensated for by the more efficient results gained.

Under all the boilers, a fire box heat of not less than 2,400 degrees Fahrenheit is maintained when steam is being delivered at a pressure of 270 pounds to the square inch. You may gaze at the fires if you wish, through a tiny hole covered with heavy glass. As an extra protection you are urged to look at the flames only through deep blue glass, which mounted in a large board, serves as a needed protection to the eyes. The board also keeps off the excessive heat. Twenty-four hundred degrees of heat ordinarily is not easy to comprehend, but if you once look at it, in

A Steam "Stand-by" Station.

such a boiler as this, you will begin to get a faint idea of the vast and terrifying power of fire. It is almost inconceivably great.

Because the production of steam, the first essential in a power station such as this, is quite as dependent upon water as upon fire, the engineers who built these stations always looked first for an adequate water supply close at hand. The river would seem to assure it a plentiful and pure water supply, yet in this instance, at least, this is not the case. The mountain river may be a famous one, but it is a highly tempermental one as well. In a long, dry summer it sometimes shrinks to almost nothing; and at times, when its waters are raging and very high, they are also so roily as to make them absolutely unfit for boiler use. This river that flows by the power house walls, and which sometimes has been known to bring coal to it in barges, is far from dependable for steaming water. The central station reaches up into the hills by a pipe line of its own to a perfectly pure water supply.

Yet as a matter of actual fact, it makes very little use even of this pure mountain water. Being highly modern, it clings to condensation methods, which in themselves require far more water than is needed for the steam itself. In the words of a popular manual on the subject:

While large savings are sometimes possible by the erection of large electric light and power stations at the mouths of coal mines, the location of most of such mines is such that these savings are not realizable. It is not always appreciated that in the production of electrical energy from coal, huge quantities of water are necessary. Experience of

[1] N. E. L. A. Speakers *Handbook*.

even the largest electric light and power companies of the country shows that for every ton of coal burned under the boilers, from 300 to 600 tons of water must be pumped for condensing purposes. The smaller amount of water is required in winter, and the larger amount in summer in the warmer sections of the country. Unfortunately, there are few places in the country where the combination of sufficient coal and sufficient water abound. Thus the size of the station is limited, not only by the amount of coal that can be obtained, but also by the amount of water available for condensing purposes. It requires the water of a large-sized river to feed the condensing equipment of a modern steam electric station, even though in a modern steam turbine plant the water is used over and over again in making steam. So long as sufficient water is not available for condensing purposes, the vision of huge power stations at the mouths of most coal mines will remain a vision until some other method of generating electricity from coal is found.[1]

So goes water to steam, then back again, steam to water; then follows water to steam, and steam to water. It is an unending rotation. Of course, there is

---

[1] The condenser, it should be remembered, is a device for changing the steam delivered from the turbine at a very low pressure into water, and this is accomplished by passing the steam around a large number of tubes having water passing through them so that the heat in the steam is absorbed by the water in the tubes. The more recently developed and highly efficient types of such condensers require roughly from forty to sixty pounds of cold water per pound of steam to be condensed, or, differently expressed, in such a plant it is necessary to furnish from three hundred to six hundred tons of water per ton of coal burned. It is, therefore, evident why such a steam plant must be located at a point where a very large amount of water is available, and hence it is not so easy to build these large steam plants at the mine as it would seem, since the mine must also be located on a pretty good sized river or lake. A plant of 250,000 K.W. capacity will require approximately 30,000,000 gallons of water per hour, an amount larger than the consumption of most of our large cities.

more or less constant leakage. This rotation could not be repeated for a very long time without both the water and steam disappearing completely.

In most plants, this leakage is replaced by use of the best available water, sometimes treated chemically to make it better adapted for the boilers. In the very latest types of plants, however, this leakage is supplied by means of evaporators, which are simply small low pressure boilers, using high pressure steam as their source of heat rather than coal burned under the boiler and designed to evaporate the water required to make up this leakage, so that any impurities in the water do not get any further than the evaporator.

The development of these steam plants for generating electricity has been particularly rapid here in the United States since 1914 and has been brought about through the co-operation and combined efforts of the designing engineers of the manufacturers of the equipment, the engineers responsible for the design of the power plants themselves, and the engineers in charge of the operation of these large plants. The electricity which you buy today and which furnishes you light or power for the operation of anything from a sewing machine motor to a 15,000 H.P. rolling mill motor, is probably the only product for which you are paying the same price, or less, than you did in 1914, and the ability of the central station companies to market their product at pre-war prices is due solely to the vision, ingenuity and aggressiveness of the managers and engineers of this industry.

From the boilers, the steam goes to the great turbo-generators. The steam portion of the most modern turbo-generator is divided into two or three "elements," each element being, in fact, a complete turbine designed to work through a certain portion of the total steam pressure used in the entire machine. These are generally referred to as the high pressure element, receiving the steam at pressures up to 600 pounds and discharging it at pressures of approximately 20 to 40 pounds, and the low pressure elements which receive the steam discharged from the high pressure element, and, in turn, discharge their steam to the condenser. With these three elements mechanically distinct and separate, each operating its own generator, it is possible to build a machine with a capacity of 250,000 horse power combined in the three elements. In other cases only two elements are used, each of which may have its own generator, or both elements may drive the same generator. In case each element drives its own generator, the high pressure element frequently operates at 1800 revolutions per minute and the low pressure element at 1200 revolutions per minute. The low pressure element is operated at the lower speed because of the tremendous volume of low pressure steam passing through it. It is not unusual for the steam in the low pressure element to be traveling at a velocity greater than five miles a minute.

Quite recently high pressure turbines have been designed and put into operation receiving steam at a pressure of 1200 pounds per square inch, and discharging this steam at approximately 300 pounds pressure. These super-high pressure turbines may of course be operated as part of a complete unit made up of these super-high pressure elements, a normal high pressure element discharging its steam at 20 to 40 pounds pressure, and one or two low pressure elements discharging their steam to the condenser. In these "multi-element" turbo-generators, in case of difficulty with any one element, that element may be dropped out of service and the other two or three continued in operation. The only condition under which it is necessary to lose the capacity of the entire "multi-element" machine would be in case of trouble which would necessitate shutting down both of the low pressure elements.

Refer once again to the idea of an electric fan tightly encased with its blades multiplied thousands of times, and you have essentially a steam turbine. These turbines are of two types, known as the *impulse turbine* and the *reaction turbine*. In the impulse turbine steam is admitted through stationary nozzles, very carefully formed, so as to allow the steam to expand and leave the nozzle at a velocity of several miles a minute. In expanding, the steam loses pressure so that it is at a lower pressure when it comes out of the nozzle than when it went in. The steam, leaving the nozzle at this high velocity, then strikes the blades of the giant fan, causing the fan to turn the main shaft of the turbine. After passing through one row of "fan" blades, without any expansion of the steam in going through these blades, the steam again passes through another set of stationary nozzles, and is again delivered at a high speed to another set of fan blades.

In the case of the reaction turbine, the stationary nozzles used in the impulse turbine are replaced with blades similar to the fan blades except that in this case both the stationary blades and the fan blades are designed to cause the steam to expand in going through each row of blades, whether stationary or rotating.

This expansion causes the steam to travel at a high velocity, striking the blades of the fan and again causing the main shaft of the turbine to rotate.

The turbine is both one of the simplest engines in the world, and one of the most efficient. It can be built in sizes very much larger than was possible with the old reciprocating engine.

The forward and return stroke of the cylinder type of steam engine is entirely missing. In that type, the strokes had to be reduced or transformed into rotary motion; a huge fly-wheel kept that motion continuous and fairly even in speed. In the turbine there is no transformation of motion. It is all rotary and of practically unvarying power, which, with its high speed, makes it ideal for the turning of a dynamo.

The technical design of the dynamo, or generator, as it is now generally called, has no place in these pages but a brief outline of the difference between the old direct current generator as originally designed by Mr. Edison and the modern alternating current generator will be of interest.

In any generator electricity is generated in the conductors of the armature of that machine because of the fact that the conductors are mechanically rotated in a very strong magnetic field, thereby cutting "the lines of force of this magnetic field and setting up electric current in the conductor." In the direct current generator it was always the armature which carried these conductors that was rotating.

It is evident, however, that with a conductor in a strong magnetic field, you can cause the lines of force to be cut by the conductor by rotating the magnetic field just as readily as you can by rotating the conductor

INTERIOR VIEW OF A CENTRAL POWER STATION.

and for certain reasons this method is always used in the alternating current generators so that the rotating part of the alternating current generator is the field (magnetic) and not the armature. In other words, a great artificial magnet is used to set up the magnetic field and then rotated inside of a mass of coils forming the armature in which electric currents are set up by the rotating field. The currents set up in the armature coils are alternating currents, i.e., they flow first in one direction and then in the other. Generally, this complete cycle of reversal occurs sixty times per second or the current is flowing first one way and then the other at the tremendous speed of 7,200 alternations per minute. These alternations are so rapid that it is impossible to detect them by any ordinary means and consequently we have apparently a steady stream of electricity issuing from the generator.

In this particular steam-driven power house, there are two of these three-unit turbo-generators, each of a capacity of 60,000 kilowatts, or 80,000 horse power. As we have just seen, either or any part of either engine may be cut out of action when necessity or emergency so requires. In addition to these two turbo-generators, which are nearly the largest ever constructed, there are two others, which, but a few years ago, would have excited admiration because of their magnitude. These last are "single element" turbo-generators, each with a rating of 25,000 kilowatts (33,500 horse power). They are highly modern and in every way efficient engines. Only in a comparative sense, in the swift onward rush of the world today, are they small. Still, one of them alone, at times, manages very well to meet the power needs of the city, for the few "owl cars" on the street railway and the few blinking lights that never go to sleep through the dull hours from midnight to dawn. In this way it proves its own economy.

On the floor of this giant room and under it is a maze of machinery, auxiliary to these main units. There are "exciters" or small turbo-generators used to furnish the direct current required to energize the huge fields of the main turbo-generators. There are condensers, which as we have seen, take the steam exhaust from the turbines and make it into the best of boiler water once again, hot and ready for immediate use. There are pumps to force this water into the boilers, to circulate the condenser water, to gather up the seepage from the floors and cellars of the power station; also engines to raise the coal to the bunkers. The intricacy of it all nearly surpasses the imagination of the layman. Yet when an intelligent engineer explains it to you, you see readily how quickly it all falls into the general scheme of the great generating station.

One feature, and a most important one, of the generating station still remains. Obviously there must be a central directing point, a grey-mattered mind, to this Frankenstein of modern days. There is. It is called the *switchboard* and it is located aloft on one of the upper floors of the building, with a balcony which looks down into the great generator room. Through the windows of that balcony, the most responsible person on duty in the plant, the switchboard man, can keep a more or less observant eye on the workings of the generators. Yet this is not his chief duty. His great task is to keep his mind, if not his eyes, on the slate or composition bench or table that runs the long length of the switchboard room.

The switchboard itself, consists of a series of slate
or composition panels, upright, and also running the
length of the room.   Its face is covered by an intricacy
of small lamps and switches, dials and indicators.   The
entire structure is capable of being covered in a single
glance from the trained eye of the operator.   But his
direct control of all the mechanism is from the long
table right in front of him.   Upon the top of it there is
a map, in miniature, of the electrical system of the power
house.   Generators, transformers, and "busses," as
the main transmission circuits within the station are
called, are all indicated in this model.   Current at the
12,000 volts at which it is generated is shown by brass
rods; circuits carrying 66,000 volt current, the voltage to
which it is transformed for transmission into the city, by
nickel.   The difference is easily discernible.   It must be.
There must never be the slightest bit of confusion in the
mind of the switch-board man as to what is going on
before him.

Upon occasion, certain of the small indicating lamps
upon the upright board will suddenly flash.   That
means trouble.   It may mean that a thunder storm is
raging in some part of the metropolitan area and that
part of the equipment is burning out, or it may mean
trouble of almost any other sort, within the station
and without.   But it is a signal for action, instant
action, on the part of the switchboard operator.   He is
in charge, like the engineer of the locomotive, or the
captain on the bridge of a great ship.   He must think
right and act quickly.   But the service must not stop.
Again, as in the case of the gas works, tragedy might
follow a break in the service.   Suppose that in some
distant hospital a surgeon is involved in a delicate

operation, that a human life is at stake, when the light upon which he depends suddenly goes out! That is a case where seconds count; and so the coolheadedness, the experience, and the correct judgment of the switchboard operator become all-important. As a mechanical guard against even momentary breakdown of the electrical service, equipment everywhere is furnished in duplicate and in triplicate. It is but a matter of seconds, or of a fraction of a second, to *cut out* one set of apparatus and *cut in* a fresh one in its place. But in the last analysis, here, as in almost every other form of industry, the final dependence always is upon the human factor, upon the faith and the ability of man, his cool, resourceful mind and the nerve and muscle control that brings the command of that mind to the action of his fingers. This is shown in no more striking fashion than in the control of a modern electric central power station.

Underneath the switchboard control room are several floors of low ceilinged narrow halls, lined with yellow brick and brightly lighted, yet passage-ways in which the human foot rarely ever treads. In some ways, they are not unlike a stack-room in a modern library, where tens and hundreds of thousands of books, carefully classified, are kept, awaiting their readers. Back of these yellow brick walls and guarded by small doors, carefully closed and padlocked, are the vast switches by which the current is taken from this machine or that, and placed in this transformer or that; or is taken from the transformers and sent upon this transmission cable or that. In reality then, this is the switchboard. The room above is but an indication of all this. The delicate apparatus that the upper room holds is but the series of keys that control these giant switches.   To move the switches by hand, is, in most cases, quite impossible.   But an electrical device makes it easy for the operator in his high set eyrie to operate them with no more effort than he would use in striking a loud note on a piano.

Ordinarily the only persons who visit these lonely corridors are the maintenance and repair men.   They alone have the keys that unlock the prison cells of the great control switches.   These switches are, in a certain sense at least, potential murderers, and it is no wonder that they are put in cells and kept carefully locked up. Every possible safeguard is placed about them, for human life means nothing whatsoever to them.   The slightest error on the part of the repair man may bring his death so quickly that he never will have dreamed what happened to him.

Therefore the most elaborate protective devices are placed around these repair and maintenance men in their delicate and dangerous calling.   Their every movement among the switches is known to the operator overhead.   On his board and on his table are more safeguards, some of which make it physically impossible for him to throw a switch while a man is working upon it, perhaps three or four stories underneath, for the slightest error on the operator's part, and that repair man would be but an inanimate mass of human clay.

To understand the actual transmission of the current, let us pause for a moment and find a simile for it.   Take water, water running in a stream, if you will.   There are two factors by which you may measure that stream. First you measure it by its volume,—i.e., the product of its depth by its width and by its velocity; and eventually you have the engineer's way of rating a stream, so many thousand cubic feet per second. A certain portion of the creek or the river will hold, or may be made to hold, approximately so many hundred thousand gallons, as storage against the period of low water or smaller flow. Then you take depth of fall, or head or pressure into consideration, and the product of volume times pressure will equal work or horse power.

Electricity responds to the same methods of measurement. The volume of the current, the number of gallons, is measured by amperes. The force, or potential, head or pressure, is obtained in volts. The work or energy corresponding is the product of volume and pressure, or amperes times volts equals work—watts or kilowatts.

In the central power station in which we have spent this half-hour together, we have seen thousands of amperes of current, when all the machines are at work, coming at the potential of 12,000 volts to form the enormous energy of 225,000 kilowatts. In the chapter which precedes this, we saw how impracticable it was at the outset to carry large volumes of electrical current, and how George Westinghouse made his most valuable contribution to the electrical industry in the United States by introducing here the use of alternating current, which permits the carrying of the same energy by the use of much less volume of current and greatly increased pressure or potential.

To carry the 225,000 kilowatts of energy out of this very power station and to the distant city, even at the high voltage of 12,000, would mean a vast expenditure for copper transmission cable. Copper, these days, costs a pretty penny indeed. Therefore it is economical to transform it, right at the power house, to the still higher voltage of 66,000 volts alternating current. This is high, but it is by no means a record figure, 220,000 volts having been reached and higher voltages already being in contemplation.

The huge transformers by which the current is stepped up from 12,000 to 66,000 volts, stand, four in number, not far from the switchboard corridors. They are barrel-like affairs, more than a dozen feet in diameter and about twenty-five feet in height. In them there is no mechanical motion, either seen or unseen. Their work is a silent as well as a motionless one. It is accomplished by a technical process of induction through coils of the one voltage being placed within the coils of the other and all immersed in oil. The induction between them is absolutely unseen, unheard. Yet by it great heat is created. Therefore there must be elaborate water cooling devices for the entire mechanism. This is the only thing that even faintly resembles motion about the entire apparatus.

The transformers send their high powered current direct to the roof of the station; and from that station the elaborate system of carriers starts on its way into the town. Great care is taken to keep the different circuits from interfering with each other. There can be harmful induction, as well as beneficial.

In the city, the transforming process is reversed and the voltage stepped down radically to about 110 volts, ready for lighting or other domestic or industrial use. The transforming stations in the city are placed at frequent and convenient points. In the very best modern practice, they are made entirely automatic. Under ordinary circumstances, there is neither reason nor need for assigning an operator to them. A portion of the alternating current may also be changed into direct current through the medium of rotary converters for the use of the street cars, or an Edison D.C. system.

Central stations, where water is the chief or sole source of power, do not differ radically from the steam stations, either in design or in operating method, save that in them the electrical generators are apt to be vertical in design, rather than horizontal, as has come to be the usual steam-station practice. The main shaft of the dynamo again is connected directly to the main shaft of the water turbine; for the encased fan principle of power generation is as applicable when a jet of water is the primal source of energy as is a jet of steam. The same methods of making the first source of energy into steady and dependable electrical current, either direct or alternating, are as easily applicable with water power as with steam.

As time goes on, the proportion of water driven stations in this land, to the steam, probably will be greatly increased. We of America have just begun to realize our potential water power possibilities. It is estimated that today the electrical energy created in the United States at any given moment is equivalent roughly to 50,000,000 horse power. The United States Geological Survey, as well as other experts who have gone into the matter, feels that as much as this great figure, or perhaps more, may yet be realized from our water powers which have not yet been developed. It is even proposed, seriously, to use the tidal actions of the sea, at the northeastern corner of Maine, where the tides have extreme variation, for generating power. From 300,000 to 500,000 horse power, it is estimated,

WHERE POWER FROM NIAGARA FALLS IS RECEIVED AND TRANSFORMED
AT ROCHESTER, N. Y.

can be developed at this point alone and a responsible company is now being formed to make fullest use of this hitherto entirely undeveloped source of energy.

Similarly, the great natural flow of such rivers as the Mississippi, the Colorado, the Tennessee, the Ohio and the Susquehanna, are all in process of fuller development. For some years past, the Mississippi has created great energy at the huge dam at Keokuk, Iowa. The Tennessee is about to begin grinding out electricity at Muscle Shoals, Alabama; the Susquehanna, at a point about twenty-five miles above Havre-de-Grace, Maryland. Electrical engineers are firmly of the opinion that more power can be taken from Niagara without interfering with the beauty of that cataract. In New York State the upper waters of the Genesee are about to undergo still further water power development. But in the East, the greatest promise is held in the power possibilities of the St. Lawrence, where a power plan goes hand-in-hand with one for better navigation through enlarged canals around the swift rapids of the upper portions of the river. After Canada has received her share of the power, it is estimated that fully a million horse power will remain available for the United States.

The tremendous possibilities of long distance transmission by alternating current now make these potentialities available and practicable. In the days since the World War, it has been found possible to carry electric current, efficiently and economically, at least 250 miles. As a matter of fact, in California, where transmission lines already built reach as far as a thousand miles and over, power is being carried more than half that distance.

Yet even in this favored land of abundant water power, steam plants have been built in cities in order to protect the cities against interruption to their lighting and power systems, when the power carried by the long transmission lines from the hydraulic plants, located in the mountains, is interrupted by storms, lightning or other causes beyond man's control. Great strides have been made in recent years in the interconnection of large power systems with accompanying interchange of power between regions, separated by hundreds of miles, and as we continue to use and develop these means of power transmission we shall undoubtedly very largely eliminate many of the difficulties existing today, and then reduce the present need for standby steam plants. The time may yet come when this energy may be used and be entirely dependable under all conditions at a locality a thousand miles or more from the point of generation. Niagara power already drives a sawmill in Northern New York, three hundred miles away from the eternal roar of that great cataract. That is but a beginning. What the ending will be no man may safely say.

CHAPTER XII

THE STORY OF THE TELEGRAPH

ONE of man's first wants and necessities was that of communication, particularly communication across considerable distances. To get messages from one point to another, fairly remote, was one of his very earliest problems. The ancients solved it in a somewhat clumsy way, which at the time they probably thought most wonderful, by sending light-footed messengers at swift gait across the face of the country. When a man had accomplished a certain number of miles, he was relieved by another messenger, to whom he transferred his packet of messages or small bundles, and this transaction was repeated at various intervals throughout the journey. A thousand or more years ago, this method was used by the Chinese. It became known as "relaying," and as such, with horses substituted for men, came down to comparatively recent times.

For long centuries, this remained the favorite mode of communication. There were various ways of making use of it. For instance, it is related that Montezuma, the last Aztec king, and perhaps the very greatest ruler of that ancient people, used this method of message-bearing to fine effect. On the great roads that ran out from the city of Mexico, where stood his royal palace, post houses were established, distant about two leagues from one another.   The courier who bore his despatch, in the form of a hieroglyphical painting, ran with it at top speed to the first of these stations, where he handed it to a messenger who ran to the next post house, or relay, where the process was repeated.   So the process went forward, until the final destination of the message had been reached.   It is recorded that Montezuma was wont to receive fresh food by this method.   Fish, served on his table in Mexico City, had been caught in the waters of the Gulf but twenty-four hours before; through the day and through the night, the fleet-footed messengers had borne them up to the king's table.   Here, four hundred years ago, was a predecessor of the express service of today.

Vainly, the ancients searched through long years for some mechanical method of communication which would be swifter than the fastest running man or horse.   If only they could use sound, or light!   Sound travels through the air much more rapidly than any living thing, and light is far faster than sound.   Some day, watch a steamer far off on the water; it whistles: you see quickly the white puffs of steam that mark the whistle; but appreciable space of time passes before the sound of that whistling comes to your ears.

THE VISUAL TELEGRAPH

Light, therefore, visual signals, became the thing. For many centuries, great bonfires, signal lights, were set aflame upon lofty hilltops and, through a pre-arranged code, crude messages were sent long distances. Yet, more than a hundred and fifty years ago, the French bettered this method.   There stands today in

the city of Paris, at the beginning of the Boulevard
Raspail, a most curious monument to Claude Chappe,
whom the French acclaim as the inventor of the telegraph.   Behind the seated figure of the young inventor
rises a mast, with a strange device at its head, not
unlike the semaphore signals which we use upon our
railroads here in the United States.   The blades of this
curious thing could be set in a large variety of forms,
of crude letters, if you will, in relation to one another.
It was a sort of wigwagging.

These masts placed on prominent hilltops, in a
long row across the face of the country, within clear
sight of one another, however, and each in charge of a
competent operator, could, and did, flash messages
for many, many miles.   Today, it all seems extremely
crude.   But the fact remains that, in clear daylight, the
device worked, and worked extremely well, although
under unfavorable weather conditions, it was worth-
less.   As the Battle of Waterloo was being fought, all
London hung upon the news of its details, which were
flashed by this early telegraph across the Channel
and from Dover up into the heart of the city.   Then,
at a most crucial moment, heavy fog set in and the
telegraph ceased to function.   It was not until the
following day that London knew the result of the
battle.

When the Erie Canal was opened from Albany to
Buffalo, one hundred years ago, a crude telegraphic
device was used to send, from the one city to the other,
the news that the first boat had actually traversed the
waterway from the Hudson to the Great Lakes.
Because there were few high hills upon which to erect a
visual telegraph, even if there had been time and funds

available, sound was resorted to. Cannons were stationed each six miles for the entire distance of three hundred miles. As one was fired, the men at its neighbor to the east would catch the sound of the report and in turn fire their gun. In this way word was carried all the way from Buffalo to Albany, even though several minutes were required for the process.

To the man or woman of today, the telegraph almost invariably typifies the great electrical servant which years ago proved its worth to the world. The inherent superiority of electricity to any mechanical device is at once apparent. Except in most unusual cases, electricity, as transmitted upon a wire, is absolutely independent of outside weather conditions. Day and night, it is at the bidding of man, tireless, approximately as swift as light, and far swifter than sound.

The crude beginnings of the electric telegraph overseas somewhat antedate those in the United States. Thus it was that the discovery of Stephen Gray and Granville Wheeler, in Great Britain, that the electrical influence of a charged Leyden jar may be carried a considerable distance, by means of an insulated wire, brought forth several proposals, of which one of the earliest and most interesting was a scheme to use as many insulated conducting wires as there were letters in the alphabet. Each wire was to be used for the transmission of a single letter only, and messages were then to be sent by charging the proper wires in succession and received by observing the movements of small pieces of paper marked with the letters of the alphabet and placed under the ends of the wires. It also was suggested that bells, probably of different tones, be used. Lemond, a Frenchman, felt that he could transmit twenty-six different kinds of motion through a single wire and thus form an alphabet and a simple and practical way of sending messages. Sir Humphrey Davy, one of the most distinguished of early English scientists, also labored for a time endeavoring to perfect an electric telegraph.

S. F. B. MORSE AND HIS TELEGRAPH

But to an American, Professor Samuel F. B. Morse, is generally given credit for having invented the highly practical electric telegraph of today. Morse, who began life as a portrait painter,—and a very good one he was,—working in the old University of New York, in Washington Square, in 1832, constructed a crude working model of a recording telegraph. For this, he developed a complete alphabet, made up of a combination of dots and dashes—in the making and breaking of an electrical circuit, not difficult to form. This, as the Morse Code, has endured until today. In fact, his machine also, with the assistance of Alfred Vail of New Jersey, soon was perfected to a point where it remains today with minor changes as to its details.

In reality therefore, the telegraph as it is used today in this country is an American invention and, notwithstanding claim to the contrary, it preceded by a number of years, the first practical European telegraphs. Morse, with his machine well perfected by 1837, sought to make commercial use of it here in the United States. Being possessed of no large private means, he turned to Congress for aid. For a time that body was lukewarm to his appeals. But he was persistent and the idea gradually took root at Washington that this "painter fellow" from New York had hit upon something very real and vital. An appropriation of some $30,000 finally was voted by Congress and with it Morse started to build the first telegraph line, from Washington to Baltimore, forty miles distant. This location came as a matter of circumstances. He had found that the officers of the New Jersey Railroads were opposed to placing the pioneer telegraph along their right-of-way, because they feared that eventually it might hurt their business, by discouraging travel, and in his perplexity he turned to the men in control of the Baltimore and Ohio Railroad. They were interested; finally co-operative. So Morse and his associates stretched their first line along that railroad.

This was in 1843. The first idea was to bury the telegraph line, with its wires insulated in copper wire and encased in solid lead pipes. A ploughshare, drawn by sixteen oxen, was to go along the railroad, beside the tracks, and in a single operation cut a trench, two inches wide and twenty inches deep, into which the lead pipe was to be fitted. For a time, this scheme was carried forth. Yet not only did it prove very expensive, but it soon was found that the crude type of insulation did not work well. In the spring of the following year, when the line was pushed through to completion, the underground method was abandoned and the wire strung on short, unbarked poles along the line of the fence that marked the edge of the railroad right-of-way.

One end of it was in the Supreme Court Chambers of the Capitol at Washington, the other at the passenger station of the Baltimore and Ohio, in downtown Baltimore. On May 24, 1844, the line was formally completed and was opened to business for the first time.

PROFESSOR MORSE SENDING THE FIRST TELEGRAM, WASHINGTON, MAY 24, 1844.

Miss Anne Ellsworth, daughter of the Commissioner of
Patents, who had happened to be the one to inform
Professor Morse of the original Congressional appropriation, was given the honor of preparing the first
message.   She took a quill pen and wrote slowly the
following words:

"WHAT HATH GOD WROUGHT!"

Those four words of magnificent inspiration, Professor Morse, himself, dispatched over the telegraph.
A minute later, he sent another telegram, a message of
love from the famous Dolly Madison to her very dear
friend, Mrs. John Wethered, the wife of a Baltimore
congressman.

This was the beginning.   From it there came a rapid
growth.   Over the copper strands of the Magnetic
Telegraph Company, as Morse's pioneer organization
was known, went in rapid succession, business messages,
personal messages, news dispatches of the press.   The
Baltimore Patriot, on the day after the line was opened,
printed a telegram from the Capitol saying the House
had just decided to go into a Committee of the Whole
to discuss the Oregon situation.   This was the first
printed newspaper dispatch.   Many of them followed.
Two years later, almost to the day, the *Baltimore Sun*
printed the President's Message, transmitted in full by
means of the "magnetic telegraph," as they always
called it in those days.

In the meantime, the telegraph system was steadily
being extended.   It had long since reached Philadelphia.
The opposition of the railroad across New Jersey had
finally been overcome and in June, 1846, the thin strand
of copper wire had reached Jersey City, just across the

Hudson River from New York City, to which messages for a time were carried by messengers. It was a number of years before the difficult task of trying to place a cable on the muddy bed of that river was even attempted.

In 1847, the telegraph was in Cincinnati and so was beginning its steady progress across the North American continent which was to take nearly fifteen years to complete. In 1848 an efficient telegraph was in operation between New York and Boston.

Morse's original company began to be beset by many rivals, some operating under licenses which he had given, and others experimenting with rival devices, some of which were afterwards found to have infringed upon his valuable patents. Yet the majority of the public were still rather skeptical about the real value of this new "magnetic telegraph." They did not even begin to appreciate its commercial possibilities. They regarded it as being applicable possibly to great emergencies and occasions of exceptional character, but as having little relation to ordinary social and business affairs. A great awakening was yet to come.

Among the rival devices that were brought forward at this time, was the so-called "printing telegraph," which had been invented by Royal E. House, of Vermont. The great point in favor of this last apparatus was that the messages it received were printed on a paper tape in plain Roman letters, ready for immediate delivery to the person addressed. This developed and perfected, is the device that to this day is used in most European countries.

The Morse messages were received in the now-familiar code of dots and dashes, which of course had to be

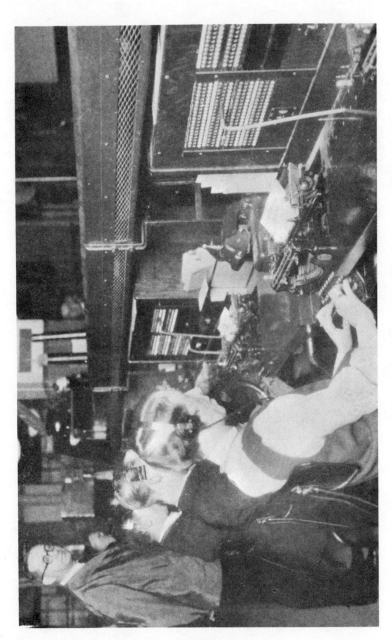

WHERE TELEGRAPHIC COMMUNICATIONS IN MORSE CODE ARE TRANSLATED.

translated and written out by the operators and so made intelligible before they could be delivered. The apparent superiority of Mr. House's telegraph won many friends for it and it was not only part of the original installation of the New York and Boston line, but of an early one between New York and Philadelphia, which was established as a competitor to the Morse company.

THE BEGINNINGS OF THE WESTERN UNION

Among the men who were promoting the House system in that very early day, was Judge Samuel L. Selden, of Rochester, New York, who secured a license for the extension of that system throughout the rest of the United States. Judge Selden at once began to plan a line from New York to Albany and Buffalo, paralleling the main lines of the New York Central and Hudson River railroads. Of all the places along the route of the new telegraph, he found his home city of Rochester the most enthusiastic over it. The result was that there he located the headquarters of his company, which eventually became the Western Union Telegraph, by far the most powerful single telegraph organization in all the world. For many years, it retained its chief headquarters in Rochester. One of Selden's staunchest supporters was Hiram Sibley, of that city, who previously had been the sheriff of Monroe County. Mr. Sibley showed great brilliancy and ability as an organizer and an executive and he it was who personally was largely responsible for the swift extension of the lines of the Western Union.

That company's original name was rather cumbersome—the New York and Mississippi Valley Printing

Telegraph Company.   It had had an ambitious scheme to build a double line (two wires) all the way from Buffalo to St. Louis; whence came its title.   At the outset it was very short of money, and finally it was obliged to shorten its main line, by bringing it into Louisville instead of St. Louis.   It barely managed to build a branch line out to Chicago.

Bad times in America began to reflect themselves upon the promoters of the telegraph.   Capital, when it came at all, came slowly to their assistance.   One by one, the early companies went into bankruptcy, even including those started by Morse himself.   Only the company in Rochester seemed to manage to keep afloat, and it, too, had vast difficulties.   But Selden and Sibley and their associates stuck to their task and eventually they were able to buy a large number of the struggling concerns and consolidate them into a single large organization; hence the name, Western Union.   By this move, they not only acquired honest rights to the valuable Morse patents and licenses, but in many cases they were able to discard the House machines which, while marvelously complete in their mechanism, were difficult and expensive to maintain and were forever breaking down.   In the long run the simple Morse apparatus proved itself more dependable, as well as more economical, in every way.

The Western Union now controlled an extensive system covering all the states north of the Ohio River, as well as parts of Iowa, Minnesota, Missouri and Kansas. In December, 1857, it paid its first dividend.   Of the six large companies that were then in existence in the United States, it was by far the largest and most prosperous.

Western Union Telegraph Office, Toledo, Ohio.

Paying dividends, it commanded credit, and with credit it prepared to push its lines farther and farther west.   Yet before California, the golden mecca of every early builder of railroad or of telegraph, could be reached, a most interesting form of early communication had been revived, successfully.   This was the Pony Express, and because it forms so interesting a chapter in the history of the commercial development of this country, it shall be given a few paragraphs, here and now.

THE PONY EXPRESS

The great gold rush to California began with the opening of the sixth decade of the last century.   Gold was discovered near Sacramento in 1848 and within a twelvemonth thereafter the news having filtered through to the East, the great hegira began.   Men found that there were two ways by which they could reach the new land of promise.   They could take a ship from New York or Boston to the Isthmus of Panama, transfer their goods across the fifty miles of mountain and morass that formed that neck of land, and then reëmbark for San Francisco; or they could risk the Indians and other hardships of overland travel and cross from the railheads by stagecoach to Sacramento. Between the two routes, there was small choice.   Both were very hard and wearisome.   The stages, for the most part operated by Wells, Fargo and Company, or by Ben Halliday, took about two months for the journey of two thousand miles from the banks of the Missouri to the California capital, Sacramento.   In national communication alone, such tedious delay was well nigh unthinkable.   In the decade of the 'fifties men racked their brains to expedite the movement of letters from the one coastal border of the United States to the other.

The Pony Express came as the result of their efforts. Long months of planning and of organization gave birth, in April, 1860, to a courier system far longer and more regular in its operation than any that the ancients had brought forth. Daily, rain or shine, a messenger left St. Joseph, Missouri, ferried across the river, and rode sixty miles toward the setting sun. In the six hours that were allotted him for this ride, he changed mounts five times. For each ten miles, a fresh pony, well-fed and rested, was furnished him. For the rider to transfer himself and his saddle-bags, containing the United States Mail, was a matter of seconds, rather than of minutes.

At the end of the sixth lap of his run, there was waiting not only a fresh pony, but a fresh rider. Yet the relay process was hardly longer. Receipts were given, the mail exchanged, the new messenger off on his way toward the west, almost before the thing could be realized.

Night and day, this process repeated itself. For, under the stars and through the storms, these young men raced their way. It was a task that called not merely for fortitude and endurance, but for quick thinking and for real ability as well. Because of the obviously limited capacity of the mail pouches in the saddle bags, letters for them could only be written on the thinnest of paper and even then carried heavy excess postage. The messengers themselves were limited in weight. Hardly more than boys in almost every instance, they automatically were out of their

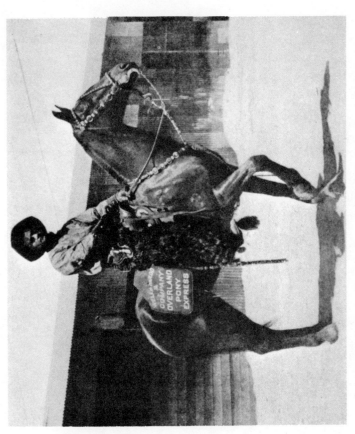

A Pony Express Rider, from a Motion Picture Adaptation.

jobs if they permitted their weight to exceed 110 pounds.

Since the two thousand miles between St. Joseph and Sacramento presented almost every possible variety of natural obstacle, the marvel of the Pony Express is not alone that it worked at all, but that the entire distance was covered regularly, week in and week out, in a steady average of twelve days. Upon occasion it was done in even less. Buchanan's final message as President was carried through from St. Joseph, the temporary western terminal of the telegraph as well as of the railroad, in nine days and twenty-three hours; the news of the election of President Lincoln in eight days; and his first inaugural message in seven days and seventeen hours. This still remains a world record.

That was about all. In October, 1861, a brief sixteen months after its inception, the Pony Express ceased to function. Telegraph lines, simultaneously built east from California and west from the Missouri, met one another at Salt Lake City, and thereafter San Francisco was in instant touch and communication with New York and the rest of the East. But the Pony Express had made an enviable record for itself. It had filled a gap with great credit and no little glory. Its story is a thrilling episode in history.

THE FIRST TRANSCONTINENTAL TELEGRAPH

The completion of the first transcontinental telegraph line came as a natural sequence of a real demand for it, even though its construction was regarded by keen men, both east and west, as well-nigh impossible. It was predicted that insuperable difficulties would have to be overcome. It was said for instance, that the

Indians would tear down the wires as fast as they were put up, and that the poles would be swept away by the irresistible movements of the immense herds of buffalo that then roamed the plains. In addition to this, more practical difficulties loomed as real menaces: not merely the construction of the line—remember that in 1860 there was no railroad west of the Missouri and therefore no adequate means of transporting the poles and wire for the telegraph—but the meagre amount of business that probably would be given to it, once it had been constructed. Congress recognized these difficulties, as well as the vast strategic necessity, military and commercial, of a line that would give almost instant communication all the way across the continent, and because of all this, it voted the enterprise an annual subsidy of $40,000 for ten years. This, however, was never considered particularly generous aid.

Nevertheless, the telegraph companies, of which the Western Union was now the dominating factor, decided to go ahead with the great national enterprise, if only a contractor could be found who was brave enough to undertake it. An advertisement for bids brought forth only one man who had the courage to say he would tackle it, and that man was Hiram Sibley, of Rochester. For the purposes of construction, the Pacific Telegraph Company was organized and Mr. Sibley given the uncoveted contract. He engaged a great number of ox-teams to transport the poles and other material; contracted with Brigham Young, of Salt Lake City, for labor and for the poles themselves; and sent his representatives all the way to California to organize the building of the line eastward. As a piece of organization, the entire thing forms one of the epics of American national progress. Sibley showed himself at once to be immensely capable; the line was connected early in 1861 and this marked the completion of a task whose importance was said to be such that it insured the holding of California within the Union at a time when she was sorely needed.

This great achievement finished, Mr. Sibley gave himself to the preparation of an even greater one. He planned to build, with the aid of a comparatively short length of cable beneath the Behring Straits, an overland telegraph from San Francisco to Moscow, Petrograd and Paris, by the way of Alaska and Siberia. The very size of the proposal, even today, when the world has grown so relatively small, staggers the imagination. Yet Hiram Sibley went to St. Petersburg, dined there with the Czar of all the Russias, and secured his imperial assent to the plan, as well as the promise of generous financial aid to it. Moreover, he actually began to build the line. Against the most terrific odds, he constructed seven hundred miles of it in British Columbia and Alaska.

That eventually it was found more practicable to rely upon the trans-oceanic cables rather than to build so many, many thousand miles of overland telegraph line is no reflection upon Mr. Sibley's judgment. For no one who knew him doubted that, once the word had been given him, he would have built the vast line, and with remarkable celerity.

The telegraph, having attained its great goal of spanning the continent, sought to extend and to better itself, in every corner of the land. It came to America in the hour when it was most vitally needed, when hundreds of thousands of the country's young men were in the field fighting for its preservation, and the hundreds of towns, big and little, all the way across the land, hungered for constant information of their loved ones. Through the four dark years of the Civil War, the telegraph ministered a vast comfort to the nation, by promptly bringing the news of the conflict to its distant corners.

Sometimes this was not easily accomplished. There is a record in the birthplace town of the Western Union, which reads after this fashion:

An anniversary of the Sunday schools of Rochester was announced for Sunday night, March 9, 1862. It was a time of deep public anxiety and alarm. The rebel ram, *Merrimac*, had appeared in Hampton Roads, and had commenced her destructive mission. She had sunk, March 8, the *Cumberland* and the *Congress*, and on Sunday, March 9, attacked the *Minnesota*. The Federal navy was in imminent danger. Just then a devastating fire occurred in Troy, which burned down the telegraph masts, which at that time bore the wires across the Hudson, and Western New York was isolated. James D. Reid was at that time superintendent of the state telegraphs. On Saturday he ordered a wire swung across the Highlands of the Hudson River above West Point to secure communication at the earliest moment and arranged to have reports sent to him at Rochester each hour of Sunday until connection was secured. At 3 P.M. word was sent him that the wire was up and at the same time a telegraphic communication reached him concerning the arrival of the *Monitor* in Hampton Roads and the particulars of her victory over the *Merrimac*. No one else in that anxious city knew of it. He was announced as one of the speakers at the anniversary in the evening. As if in expectation of some great event

the house was packed.   The national dangers could be read
on the solemn and anxious face of every citizen. . . . Passing up to the organist Mr. Reid told him to keep himself
ready for a signal from him during his address.   It was now
Mr. Reid's turn.   In vain he tried to postpone the an-
nouncement that was to make the nation laugh with joy.
Taking from his pocket the dispatch, he had scarcely
finished reading it when a small boy in the gallery shouted
in a shrill voice, "Hurrah!"   Instantly a shout of general
joy arose.   The organist, with stops all out, started the
national hymn, which was sung amid almost transporting
fervor. . . .

All the way across the face of the land, these instances
multiplied.   Weekly newspapers, assured now of
prompt dispatches, by the dozen changed into dailies.
Fighting generals used the telegraph to direct the
movements of their forces.   No longer was there any
question as to its popularity.   It became part of the
bone and fibre of the nation.

So came the telegraph to be a recognized American
institution.   It extended its lines, until today there is
hardly a town in the United States large enough to have
a name that does not also have a telegraph wire.   In
the first fifteen years of its existence, the Western
Union extended the mileage of its lines from 550 to over
75,000 miles.   Today it has 200,000 miles of line, over
which more than 150,000,000 messages are flashed
annually, and shares with its competitor, the Postal
Telegraph Company, the telegraph business of the
nation.

THE BEGINNINGS OF THE ATLANTIC CABLE

The tremendous and almost instant success of the
telegraph overland soon prompted inquiries as to why

it could not be made equally successful underseas, by
the seemingly simple device of insulating its copper
strand against the constant action of water, and then
dropping it upon the bottom of the ocean, or of lesser
bodies of water. Seemingly simple indeed! When
one contemplated the fact that, in rough figures, it is
three thousand miles across the North Atlantic and
that a cable would have to be made pliable yet strong
enough to drop to the very bottom of unknown depths
without severing itself, as well as perfectly insulated
for all those miles where it was forever hidden from
inspection or repair, the simplicity of the problem disappeared. It really was complex to the extreme.

Yet men persisted in thinking about it, and within
a decade of the day when Morse flashed the memorable
"What hath God wrought" over his first commercial
telegraph line from Washington to Baltimore, they
were organizing to place some sort of a similar line
from the United States to England. Already there
was a precedent for an under-water line of some sort.
In the fall of 1851 the cable was completed under the
English Channel and the stock exchanges of London
and of Paris were for the first time enabled to compare
prices during the business hours of the same day.

Cyrus W. Field of New York, a banker and citizen
of repute, was the driving force who was to carry
forward the first trans-Atlantic cable to a successful
culmination. Against terrific odds, he brought the
great project through. In 1856 he visited Great Britain and enlisted the aid of Sir Charles Bright, who
was at the head of the Magnetic Telegraph Company,
of that country. The two men organized the Atlantic Telegraph Company, the main portion of whose

stock was subscribed for in England. They went to work at once to manufacture their cable—this, of itself, a difficult and costly business. By June, 1857, it was finished and thirty days later the cable was stowed in the holds of two warships, the American *Niagara*, and the British *Agamemnon*, which had been especially prepared for the task in hand.

Despite elaborate precautions, the effort to lay the cable that summer failed utterly. Because of errors in paying it out, it snapped and the two warships had to return to Plymouth, England, with what remained of it. The following year, some seven hundred miles of new cable having been completed, another attempt was made. It was now decided that the two ships should meet in mid-ocean, there splice their cables and begin their journeys homeward bound. They made their splice on the 25th of June; and the following day it broke. The ends were respliced; yet after some forty miles had been laid from the *Agamemnon*, there came another break.

Again and again the cable broke that summer but patiently the men who determined to lay it retraced their steps, and, on the 5th day of August, 1858, there finally was a continuous copper wire all the way from Trinity Bay, Newfoundland, from which telegraphic communication already had been established with the principal cities of the eastern part of the United States, to Valentia, Ireland, where similar connections went through to Dublin, to London, to Paris and elsewhere in western Europe.

The stage was set for the rising of the curtain. It rose successfully. On August 15, President James Buchanan, of the United States, sent to Victoria,

Queen of Great Britain and her colonies, another historic message, much longer than that which Anne Ellsworth once had penned and S. F. B. Morse had tapped upon the telegraph wire. The first transAtlantic message read:

May the Atlantic Telegraph, under the blessing of Heaven, prove to be a bond of perpetual peace and friendship between the kindred nations, and an instrument destined by divine Providence to diffuse religion, civilization, liberty and law throughout the world.

Yet apparently good fortune was not immediately to be the full portion of the transatlantic cable; for after having been hailed with great public demonstrations of joy on both sides of the Atlantic, including a vast street parade and fireworks in New York and the burning of the cupola of the City Hall, the cable after a few weeks ceased to work. The trouble seemed to be that no one really knew the proper current for such very long-distance transmission. A high potential was tried and found ineffectual. Then weaker currents were used, with better success. But the high potential had done its work. It had ruined the insulation of the cable, which presently sputtered itself out to a weak and inglorious end.

For seven years thereafter, the entire Atlantic cable scheme was a matter of derision and scorn. But Field and his associates on both sides of the ocean never lost faith in it. Patiently they set out to secure new capital with which to lay another strand, an undertaking doubly difficult because of the utter failure of the first, and eventually they succeeded in their attempts.

It was decided that in the next effort it would be

better to have one ship rather than two to lay the line. In the seven years intervening since the earlier attempts a colossal ship had been built in England, which acquired a vast fame, although as an ocean liner it was never successful. This was the *Great Eastern* and it was many years ahead of its time. A failure as a passenger liner, it was almost ideal for cable-laying purposes because of its enormous hold capacity. It was chartered and started west from Valentia in July, 1865, to make a trip right through to Newfoundland. After all, the *Great Eastern* did not cross the Atlantic that year. Fault after fault developed in the cable as it was being payed out, and so it had to be halted and repaired. Finally, at 1200 miles it snapped and fell into the sea. Efforts to locate it were fruitless, and the *Great Eastern* returned to Europe.

But still the cable builders persisted. In the following year, 1866, they were at it again, the *Great Eastern* once more was ploughing her way across the Atlantic, this time paying out a vastly better cable from her stern. Moreover, on this second trip, she succeeded in picking up the severed section of the cable of the preceding year and making a splice with it in mid-ocean. Once again, New York could talk by telegraph with London. Thereafter there were no serious interruptions to the service.

The cables of 1865 and 1866 were not long-lived, however. By 1877, both of them had broken down and were useless. But before that day, other and parallel cables had been laid across the Atlantic until there were four others, including the direct line from Duxbury, Massachusetts, to Brest, France. The multiplication of these lines has continued from that day to this, as their extensions also have gone down under each of the world's seven seas. Almost in the snap of a finger, messages now move half way round the world. Some of the fastest service rendered over the Atlantic cables is in the cotton business, messages sent from Liverpool sometimes being delivered in the Cotton Exchange in New York within from two to three minutes.

Yet with all of this perfection, with the development of the marvelous multiplex machinery by which at least fifty separate messages can be sent simultaneously over a single strand of copper wire without interference with one another, cable construction and maintenance still remain one of the highly hazardous enterprises of the world. Despite the construction of ships of intricate design, especially built for the work, unforeseen emergencies still arise constantly.

Take as recent an instance as the break in the Bay Roberts-Penzance No. 2 cable, which occurred in 1915. A report of it to Western Union headquarters reads:

The break was about 650 miles from the Newfoundland side. It was decided to grapple first for the Bay Roberts end and then for the Penzance end. The ship chartered for the work, the *C. S. Faraday* arrived at the position of the western end of the break on September 10, but it was not until midnight of the 16th that wind and weather conditions permitted grappling. The sea rose again so quickly, however, as to make it unsafe to raise the cable. On September 26, a cyclonic storm blew the ship thirty miles to the eastward. The course was set back and on arrival at the mark buoy on the afternoon of the 27th, the weather having slightly moderated, steps were taken to pick it up. There was considerable motion of the ship and during one pitch the strain rose

The "Colonia," the Largest Ship Engaged in Cable Laying.

to over nine tons, breaking the rope and losing over 12,000 fathoms of moorings. Thereafter continuous fog prevented observations until September 30. The ship had then been on the ground twenty-five days, and had made but two dredges, one of which could not be completed, and on the other, the cable although hooked, could not be raised owing to a gale. During all the time exceptionally strong and variable currents increased the difficulties of the work. On the fifth dredge, made October 3, a short piece of cable was recovered and abandoned; on the seventh, made October 6, the cable was picked up. It was evident, however, that the break was west of the ship. This necessitated a change in the program and grappling was commenced for the Penzance or eastern end. In spite of a very strong current the Penzance end was successfully hooked on the ninth dredge, on October 8. A splice was made, thirty-six miles of cable laid and the end buoyed shortly after midnight. On October 11, weather conditions having improved slightly, the ship proceeded to pick up the two mark buoys.

Yet this could not be accomplisned; one was adrift and was found to have collapsed; there was too much wind and sea to pick up the other. If both could have been brought together, the two ends of the severed cable which they held could easily have been spliced and the whole thing then dropped into the ocean to resume its important work of international communication. But the weather increased in force and gales became hurricanes. There were two serious accidents aboard the ship, which finally on October 20, put into harbor at St. Johns, New Brunswick, to restock with food, fuel and supplies.

For ten days, she remained in port. Then she sailed and picked up the buoy which held the eastern end, with much difficulty and in the face of increasing seas. For twenty-seven days she hunted for the buoy which held the western end of the cable. When it finally was found, it was picked up with all care. The solution of the thing seemed finally at hand. Yet at the last minute as it was being drawn aboard the buoy fouled its cable and snapped it. The labor of long weeks was lost. For fourteen additional days the *Faraday* held to her task. But ultimately she was compelled to abandon it in the face of swiftly oncoming winter over the North Altantic.

The next time the telegraph boy runs up the steps of your house and hands you that white-enveloped message which has come from the other side of the Atlantic, give a bit of thought to all the human labor and patience that made it possible to send this message across the ocean in the proverbial twinkling of an eye.

No wonder it was that the world hailed with joy the coming of the wireless, and none more so than those toilers of the sea who labor so hard to keep instant wire communication between distant lands. That a man, sitting at an apparatus in Washington, could send messages of indefinite length and of great precision thousands of miles through the air without wires or visible physical connection, quickly became one of the great wonders of all creation.

The wireless, or the radio, if you please to call it such, took an instant position in the commercial life of the civilized world. Its greatest immediate value unquestionably lay in the fact that, for the first time in all history, instant communication was rendered possible with ships far at sea. Of this phase of its operation alone, a whole book of romance might easily be written.

Jack Binns, the wireless operator on the sinking *Republic*, bringing aid through the telegraph key so that not one life was lost; the *Titanic*, sending her tragic S. O. S. after her collision with the iceberg; these, and many other instances are on record where the wireless has saved hundreds of human lives. Mysterious sinkings and disappearances of ships at sea, like those of the *City of Portland* and of the *Arctic*, are practically no more. The radio patrols the lanes of the open seas, like a policeman on watch within the city streets.

Yet the physical cable, on land as well as on sea, has by no means lost its great value to the world. On the contrary, each year sees added burdens being placed upon its competent shoulders. Its strong appeal is in its dependability. Radio still is strangely subject to the whims of weather. All of these have not yet been overcome. But the telegraph, which sends its tapping message over land or under sea through a copper wire, is almost absolutely free from weather influence. The greatest danger that it faces always is with its overhead lines. Storms of sleet and ice come at times to wreck sad havoc with these, and crews of expert linemen duplicate, in no small measure, the privations and toil of those who labor on the cable ships upon the tossing sea. In recent years, however, there is a steadily increasing tendency toward placing the lines of the overland telegraph, as well as those of the long-distant telephone, in ducts or conduits connecting the more important cities of the land, and so, a return is being made to the method by which Professor Morse originally sought to build his line from Baltimore to Washington.

MODERN TELEGRAPH SERVICE

If the message the telegraph boy brings up the steps of your house is in the more familiar yellow, or blue, envelope, instead of the white, pray do not disparage it. For the sending of even the simplest telegraph message, between two nearby communities or perhaps within the confines of a single sizable town, is a fairly complicated process. To handle your telegram promptly and efficiently, no matter how short a distance it is destined to move, the telegraph company has built up a delicate, but dependable organization. Its first thought is accuracy; its next, privacy; after that speed. To ensure the first, it begins by thoroughly training its employees and then by insisting upon their using methods which make inaccuracy all but impossible. Figures, difficult and unusual names, and code and cipher combinations are spelled and repeated; if necessary, more than once, to make sure there is no mistake. The slightest error in this regard may lead to serious loss and misunderstanding. Moreover, the purely mechanical factors in the transmission of a telegram or a cablegram are constantly and minutely inspected and tested. The factor of the machine of copper and brass and steel must at all times be maintained to the full efficiency of the human one.

The necessity for privacy needs little or no explanation. The telegraph is on honor to respect the secrecy of the desires or the feelings of its patrons. It regards each message filed with it as confidential and takes every possible precaution to safeguard its contents. It not only guards its operating rooms where the wire messages are actually sent or received, but it puts each of its employees on honor to hold their secrets inviolable.

It is not enough that it is a penal offense for an employee of a telegraph or telephone company to divulge the contents of any message entrusted to him or her, but the company makes it a matter of an employee's loyalty, a matter of morale, to enforce this precept, personally, to the most minute degree.

These things then are the beginnings, the human precautions, if you please, that safeguard the message that comes to you in the little envelope, or which, perhaps in these modern days is delivered into your ears over your home telephone. The mechanical ones also are many. Some of them are sizable, others are small but still very valuable, such as, for instance, the regular half-hourly inspections made of all operating rooms to make sure that no messages have fallen to the floor and have thus been delayed in their transmission. The telegraph company is proud of its promptness in handling dispatches. That is the reason why it prints on each of them both the hour and the minute it was filed for transmission and the hour and the minute in which it came into the receiving office.

Always then, the telegraph company must be on its guard. Emergencies become almost its stock in trade. In a recent description of a highly modern telegraph system in America, the following paragraphs appear:

The normal assignment of all wires is determined by the engineers of traffic . . . and under ordinary conditions the flow of business is through the regularly designated channels. In the presence of emergencies, however, whether due to prostration of wires by flood or storm or to a sudden increase in business, an effective means of minimizing and equalizing delays is provided by a dispatching system, centering at New York and Chicago. . . . A special wire connects the two dispatching centers and special circuits radiate from each to practically all important points, thus ensuring the closest co-operation and permitting prompt rearrangement of trunk circuits in times of stress.   The dispatcher's equipment may be described as a Brobdingnagian cribbage-board, so arranged as to provide peg holes for each trunk circuit or group of circuits between any two offices in the territory covered.   Into these holes are put plugs of different colors and markings indicating the number of messages of various classes and the number of minutes' delay on the oldest of each class, so that the dispatcher is not only apprised of what traffic should be moved first, but also determines what facilities are needed to accommodate the waiting and incoming files.

Of immense help in meeting the varying requirements is a chart showing every wire in the land line service, with its number, material, gauge, the route it follows, every point where it is cut in and the cross connections between the various wires in every office.   The preparation of this chart was the work of years, but it has saved thousands of dollars' worth of wire construction. . . . It covers seventy sheets, each three feet high and five feet wide, mounted on swinging panels.   Mounted edge to edge to form one continuous map, the greatest height would be twenty-seven feet and width, sixty-five feet.

The somewhat intricate details of the machines that form the highly modern equipment of the highly modern telegraph office have no place here.   It is sufficient to say that, in addition to the key and sounder as first developed by Professor Morse, nearly a century ago, there have come in more recent years, the multiplex or automatic system of printing telegraphy,—which uses in operating a sending instrument called the perforator,—a transmitter, rotating sending and receiving distributors, with repeating relays, and a receiving instrument called a printer.

To send a telegram from a city office of the newest type to-day, the operator typewrites it on the perforator, and, as the keys of this instrument are struck by the typist, holes are punched in a moving tape. Upon it, each letter of the alphabet, as well as numerals and other characters, is represented by a combination of from one to five small circular perforations. As these are made in the narrow tape, impulses are transmitted to the line through the sending transmitter. These come to a receiving distributor and are passed thence to another distributor, or printer. As the typewheel of the receiving typewriter receives the impulses, it turns the face of the selected letter toward a message blank which is in the machine and strikes that letter. The receiving operator simply watches the message as it is being printed, after which, it is at once ready for delivery.

Through the operation of these all-but-automatic machines, eight messages, four in each direction, may be sent over the same circuit simultaneously. Each sending and receiving distributor is a disc, divided into quadrants. Each quadrant is, in turn, divided into five segments to which the five previously mentioned positions on the moving tape correspond. The impulses started by each of the four sending instruments pass to the proper quadrant and segment on the sending distributor. For the reception of these simultaneous messages this entire process is reversed. Four operators sitting at four printers at the same precise moment are receiving four entirely different dispatches. By means of an automatic control device, the sending and receiving operators can instantly communicate with each other should it become necessary during the transmission of messages.

By this method, eight messages may go forward over a single wire at the same moment, even though in opposite directions; and, as few as two, or even one, should there be a slacking in the wire demand. But the economy of the scheme in the periods of "peak load" traffic is obvious. Either a vast deal of line, which would be in use but a small part of each twenty-four hours, would have to be erected or else there would be unnecessary delays at the time of the "peak loads." The multiplex solves this problem mechanically, while the telegraph company's own selling devices are great practical aids, since they transmit at greatly reduced prices messages to be slightly deferred in transmission and sent at the company's convenience either by day or preferably by night. With these methods and many others it handles its vast and steadily growing volume of business, without permitting any stagnation or congestion in receiving or delivering the messages entrusted to it. Accuracy and privacy are indeed prime factors in the proper conduct of its business, yet speed is the foundation stone upon which it has been builded. This it never forgets. It strives ever toward the decent speed—that ensures accuracy—which it prefers to call "expedition." As an essential public utility of this country, the telegraph long since has earned its high position.

CHAPTER XIII

THE COMING OF THE TELEPHONE

WONDERFUL as it is, the field of the telegraph has, quite obviously, its definite limitations. These are the limitations that always embrace the written message of any sort. The deaf-mute always feels keenly the handicap under which he labors when he tries to carry on a conversation with one who does not understand the sign language, as talk must be reduced to a series of scribbled messages. How much freer, how far less restricted, the ordinary conversations of human beings! Questions are asked and promptly answered, all in a trice. The swiftest telegraph service requires time for the delivery of a written question and the inditing and the delivery of its answer. If there is a series of questions, each more or less dependent upon those that have gone before, the delay only becomes the greater.

Communication to no little extent is facility in speech. To be able to carry on conversation over great distances, obviously would be a tremendous extension of the usefulness of the telegraph. The wonder is that for so long a time so little serious attention was paid to it.

When it finally received the attention that was to bring about the fruition of one of the greatest of all American inventions, the telephone, the creative thought that was bestowed upon it came, not from an electrician, but from an expert in the science of acoustics—Dr. Alexander Graham Bell, a teacher in Boston University. The men who before him had tinkered with the possibility, had approached it, invariably, from the electrical side; Dr. Bell regarded the problem in large part as the creation of a mechanical organ of human speech. It carried with it, as a corollary, the making of a mechanical organ of hearing. Dr. Bell said: "If I could make a current of electricity vary in intensity, precisely as the air varies in density during the production of sound, I should be able to transmit speech telegraphically."

So definitely did this idea become fixed in his mind that some of his earliest experiments were with a human ear, cut from the head of a dead man. Gruesome as it may seem, this gave him the direct pathway of approach to the greatest single fundamental of the telephone, the delicate metal membrane which, receiving the human voice, vibrates and transmits it in electrical energy to a complement machine with another metal membrane which, in turn, converts electrical energy back into human voice. This all seems very simple now; yet, but a little more than a half century ago, here was one of the perplexing problems of science.

The telephone is now barely more than fifty years old. There is no haziness, no dispute, about the date of its coming, nor about the identity of the man whose consummate genius was to bring it into life. Dr. Alexander Graham Bell, standing in his workshop, not far from Scollay Square, Boston, invented the telephone, June 2, 1875. For months past he had tinkered with coils of wire, electric batteries, cigar boxes, tin trumpets, a vast litter of possibilities. To all this he

added his great scientific knowledge of the human voice;
for not only he, but his father and his grandfather
before him, had been recognized teachers of speech and
expression. Doctor Bell, himself, had perfected a
system of "visible speech" which he taught to deaf-
mutes. Finally he married a deaf-mute girl, the
beautiful daughter of a great Boston lawyer, Gardiner
Hubbard. With Bell, speech and its proper transmission became more than a study, more than a passion
even; to him it was life itself.

BELL INVENTS THE TELEPHONE

One can imagine the transports of joy with which he
stood on a day of the following March (1876) and wit-
nessed his first crude telephone, which for forty weeks
past had showed itself capable only of uttering unintelligible noises, talk. His assistant, Thomas A.
Watson, who had been in the basement of the Scollay
Square house, the other end of the first crude telephone line, which began its course upon the third
floor, had come running up the stairs, two steps at a
bound.

"I can hear you," he shouted breathlessly, " I can
hear the words."

Dr. Bell had just telephoned down to him, "Mr.
Watson, come here, I want you."

Down through the old house, past its closed doors,
the electrical energy had carried the voice and repeated
it to the man in the basement. Now was the telephone really born! Dr. Bell went to Washington and
there obtained his fundamental patent, in all probability, "the most valuable single patent" ever issued in
any country. For his new device, he did not, at first,

even have a name. In describing it to the officials of the Patent Office he called it "an improvement in telegraphy," although, in reality, it was nothing of the sort. The name *telephone* came at a little later time.

As such the device began to be known at the Philadelphia Centennial. It was a fortuitous circumstance indeed that brought the new invention into being just before the opening of that widely discussed international fair. Dr. Bell felt that his device should be shown there. Fortunately for him, his father-in-law, Mr. Hubbard, was one of the commissioners of the Centennial and influential with its management. The upshot of it all was that the first crude telephone finally was admitted to the show and was displayed inconspicuously upon a table in the educational exhibit. Here it was overlooked by most of the early visitors to the exposition.

Even Bell, himself, for a long time, did not see it. He had no intention of going to the Centennial. It was too expensive for him. Of modest means, the time and money he had given to the development of his invention had brought him close to poverty. He felt that he could not afford to go to Philadelphia. But when his affianced bride departed for the fair and he went to the railroad station in Boston to say "goodbye" to her, he could not resist her tearful pleadings to accompany her father and herself to the great Centennial. He threw restraint to the winds and boarded the train with them.

Again, there came a fortuitous circumstance. For on the very Sunday afternoon following his arrival, the judges were to make one of their tours of the exposition and Hubbard had exacted a promise that they

BELL'S ORIGINAL CENTENNIAL TELEPHONE RECEIVER.

would give some attention to the telephone. Herbert N. Casson, who is one of the most conscientious historians of the telephone, thus[1] describes this event, which turned out to be a most important one for Bell:

When Sunday afternoon arrived, Bell was at his little table, nervous yet confident. But hour after hour went by and the judges did not arrive. The day was intensely hot and they had many wonders to examine. There was the first electric light, and the first grain-binder and the musical telegraph of Elisha Gray, and the marvelous exhibit of the printing telegraphs shown by the Western Union Company. By the time they came to Bell's table, through a litter of school desks and blackboards, the hour was seven o'clock, and every man in the party was hot, tired and hungry. Several announced their intention of returning to their hotels. One took up a telephone receiver, looked at it blankly, and put it down again. He did not even place it to his ear. Another judge made a slighting remark, which raised a laugh at Bell's expense. Then a most marvelous thing happened, such an incident as would make a chapter in the *Arabian Nights Entertainments.*

Accompanied by his wife, the Empress Theresa, and a bevy of courtiers, the Emperor of Brazil, Dom Pedro de Alcantara, walked into the room, advanced with both hands outstretched to the bewildered Bell and exclaimed, "Professor Bell, I am delighted to see you again." The judges at once forgot the heat and the fatigue and the hunger. Who was this young inventor, with the pale complexion and the black eyes, that he should be the friend of emperors? They did not know, and for the moment even Bell himself had forgotten that Dom Pedro had once visited Bell's class of deaf-mutes at Boston University. He was especially interested in such humanitarian work, and

[1] From *The History of the Telephone,* by Herbert N. Casson. McClurg, Chicago, 1910.

had recently helped to organize the first Brazilian school for deaf-mutes at Rio de Janeiro. So, with the tall, blonde bearded Dom Pedro in the center, the assembled judges and scientists,—there were fully fifty in all,—entered with unusual zest into the proceedings of their first telephone exhibition.

A wire had been strung from one end of the room to the other, and while Bell went to the transmitter, Dom Pedro took up the receiver and placed it to his ear. It was a moment of tense expectancy. No one knew clearly what was about to happen when the Emperor, with a dramatic gesture, raised his head from the receiver and exclaimed with a look of utter amazement, "My God!—it talks!"

The die had been cast. The scientists pressed forward to see for themselves this marvelous new toy. They listened to Bell as he talked over it. Joseph Henry, of the Smithsonian Institution at Washington, a foremost scientist of that day, who had been very helpful to the young teacher of speech in solving some of the fundamental electrical problems of his invention, was the next to test the device. Following him came Sir William Thomson, afterward Lord Kelvin, the greatest electrical expert of his day. Thomson seated himself at the receiver. When he arose he expressed himself solemnly:

"It *does* speak," he said, with emphasis, "it is the most wonderful thing that I have seen in America."

After this, there was no question about the telephone. From comparative obscurity, it emerged to become the leading single feature of the great Centennial. Men crowded about one another, in their efforts to speak or to hear over the new device. It was "born in Boston, baptized in the Patent Office, and given a royal reception at the Philadelphia Centennial," says one of its historians.

PROFESSOR BELL DEMONSTRATING THE TELEPHONE AT SALEM, MASSACHU-
SETTS, 1877.

Yet it did not come quickly into power or strength or universal application. Few radical inventions ever do. The telegraph companies opposed it. It was with difficulty that Bell and Hubbard and Thomas Sanders, of Haverhill, Massachusetts, who had become their chief financial backer, leased one of their wires from New York to Boston to permit Sir William Thomson to hear conversation carried forward over a distance of 235 miles. This was the first long-distance call on record. Public opinion, always naturally conservative, did not rush to embrace the new device. It hung, hesitant, waiting to see more definitely what the telephone could do for the world.

So when, in May, 1877, a man named Emery, walked into Hubbard's office in Boston and leased two machines for use in the nearby city of Charlestown, putting down twenty dollars for the privilege, both Bell and Hubbard felt that an important corner in their progress had been turned. In their enthusiasm over this modest bit of success, they prepared an advertising circular of their telephone. In it they claimed that it was superior to the telegraph for these reasons:

(1) No skilled operator is required, but direct communication may be had by speech, without the intervention of a third person.

(2) The communication is much more rapid, the average number of words transmitted in a minute by the Morse sounder being from fifteen to twenty—by telephone from one to two hundred.

(3) No expense is required, either for its operation or repair. It needs no battery and has no complicated machinery. It is unsurpassed for economy and simplicity.

Of course, in the development of the telephone into the nation-wide instrument of swift communication that it is today, both batteries and expensive operation and repairs were, and still are, required. Bell and Hubbard prepared this circular in the earliest days of the device.   At that time, it was both an accurate and a sincere document.

FIRST COMMERCIAL USE OF THE TELEPHONE

The next step in the development of the telephone came very soon thereafter, in that same month of May, 1877, and also in the city of Boston.   A young man, E. T. Holmes, had already established a burglar alarm business, by which, upon signal from banks and other commercial houses that he had equipped with his device, he could rush special police protection to them. The telephone interested him.   He succeeded in borrowing a half dozen from Hubbard and went into six banks which were his regular customers and placed a telephone in each of them.   Five accepted the device rather good-humoredly, but the sixth ordered it removed; said it had no space for such a "play toy". The five which retained it, however, began to use it more and more all the while, and so was born the first telephone exchange in all the world, the crude mechanism in Holmes' office.

Slowly the idea began to crystallize into a rough commercial organization.   Despite the awakened and bitter opposition of the telegraph companies, chiefly the Western Union, small telephone exchanges were established in Bridgeport, in New York, in Philadelphia, and in New Haven.   Soon Hubbard was leasing

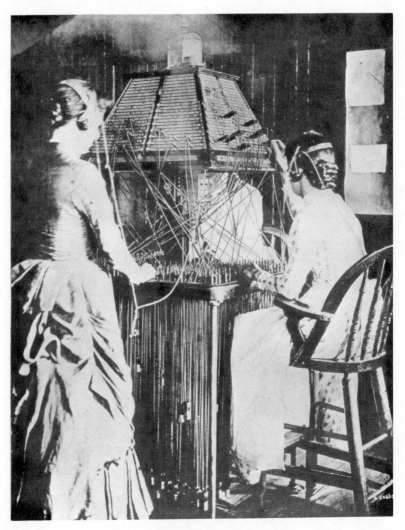

PYRAMID TYPE SWITCHBOARD, 1882.

a thousand telephones a month.   The tide had turned,
and it was in favor of Bell and Hubbard and Sanders.
They began to be a little dazed by the increasing volume of traffic that was coming their way and sought
to find a manager for their business, a sort of super-
manager, as it were, a man who had the capacity and
the talent for organizing what presently was to become
another great American industry.

Such a man was found in Washington.   He was at
the head of the railway mail service of the federal government, and was most successful at that task.   His
name was Theodore N. Vail.   He was a cousin of
Alfred Vail who, in the previous chapter we saw helping Morse develop his first telegraph.   Perhaps that
was one reason why he accepted this slender telephone
job, at a modest beginning salary of $3,600 a year.

Mr. Vail, possessed of a giant frame, a keen mind,
and an enormous capacity for work, went to his new
task with great enthusiasm.   In it, he developed great
ability as an organizer.   The national system of telephones in this country, today by far the largest and
most efficient of any in the world, is to no small extent
his monument.   Bell might have invented the telephone, Hubbard inspired him, and Sanders financed
him, but without the generalship of Theodore N. Vail,
it is very doubtful if it would have attained by this
time anything like the tremendous proportions that it
has already reached.

Yet even after Mr. Vail came to the struggling organization and the Bell Telephone Company, predecessor
of the American Telephone and Telegraph Company,
parent of all the so-called Bell companies in the United
States and Canada today, had been organized, the

progress of the telephone service was sure, rather than swift.

Take its development in the city of New York. The first paying subscriber there was J. H. Haigh, who, in 1877, had a private line stretched across the then unfinished Brooklyn Bridge from his office in John Street, Manhattan, to his steel works in South Brooklyn, five miles all told. There were only four other telephones set up in New York that year. It all was a simple beginning.

In the following year, the first New York City telephone directory was issued. It contained just 252 names and was printed on one side of a card. Most of the telephones were in business houses, although there were seventeen in New York residences, and five more in those of Brooklyn. Boys were used at the switchboards and you summoned the attention of the operator by tapping on the diaphram of your telephone with the end of a lead pencil. Seven years thereafter, the first pay station was established in New York. By that time girls had supplanted the boys at the switchboard; they were more deft and more dependable.

In another seven or eight years, the telephone service of New York City had grown to very respectable proportions, although it was nothing like the gigantic system there today. Still there were, in 1893, eight central offices, some thirty thousand miles of underground wires and about nine thousand subscribers' stations, and yet the process of expansion had hardly even begun.

OPPOSITION OF THE TELEGRAPH

As the thing had grown in New York, so had it grown

THE FIRST TELEPHONE EXCHANGE IN NEW YORK CITY.

in the other cities of America, and all the while despite the bitter and unrelenting warfare waged against it by the telegraph companies. These had become rich and strong by the time the telephone arrived and they already had entrenched themselves along the railroads, and in newspaper offices, hotels and other strategic points. The Western Union was particularly bitter. It even went so far as to engage Thomas A. Edison (who, it will be remembered, had been a railroad telegraph operator early in his career) as a consulting expert to develop the telephone for it. Mr. Edison's genius produced a transmitter of great value to the original telephone device. This valuable accessory, the Western Union used for a long time, as a club over the struggling Bell interests.

These last were indeed having a hard time of it. They were terribly hard pressed for money. Because of the extreme novelty of their idea, they were compelled to take ruinously low rates for their service. They placed a charge of twenty dollars a year for two telephones on a private line, while the rate from the private exchanges rarely exceeded three dollars a month. Moreover, there was an overplus of "deadhead" patrons, chiefly politicians and public officials. In St. Louis, one of the few cities that charged a fair price for the service, nine-tenths of the merchants refused to subscribe to it. In Boston, the first paystation ran three months before it earned as much as a dollar.

Philadelphia was a particularly hard place to inaugurate the new service. There, more strongly than anywhere else in the country, the telegraph company was entrenched with the corrupt political ring. When

Thomas E. Cornish, who had been placed in charge of the Bell telephone interests in that city, set out to locate the first wires no official would grant him a permit and his workmen were arrested when they made attempts to string them, permit or no permit. Finally Cornish was compelled to resort to strategy.

Among the men whom he had succeeded in interesting in the telephone was one of the great powers of Philadelphia, Thomas A. Scott, who, as the president of the Pennsylvania Railroad, had acquired a tremendous prestige in that city. Mr. Scott decided that he must have a telephone between his house and his office, in order that he might be in close touch at all hours with the workings of the railroad that he headed. So great was his power in Philadelphia, that a permit for the installation of his line was obtained readily, from the city officials. Under the guise of this permit, Cornish put up several lines. Before his strategy had been discovered, he had fifteen lines established and a brisk little exchange, with eight subscribers.

It is probable, however, that the Bell telephone interest might have struggled along in this way for many years without strength and without prestige, with Bell, himself bankrupt, ill and discouraged, had it not been for the invention by a young Bostonian, Francis Blake, of a transmitter that was quite as good in every way as the Edison device. This last was placed at the disposal of the Bell company. It turned the tide of favor toward it. Capital came to its aid, chiefly at first in the person of W. H. Forbes, also of Boston, a member of a very distinguished family of that city which, for more than a century past, had been engaged in the East India shipping trade, in the laying down of early railroads, and in shrewd commercial enterprises of every sort. Colonel Forbes placed his resources behind the struggling organization, reorganized it into the National Bell Telephone Company, with a capital of $850,000, and became its first president.

With financial strength at last behind them, the Bell forces were now ready to do battle with the powerful Western Union Telegraph Company. Serene in the positive belief that they had all the essential and valuable patent rights necessary to the national development of the telephone, they sought out their opponent. For a year the case lingered in the courts. Then came a day when, suddenly, both competitors went into a private conference room. When they emerged, a signed treaty of peace was in their hands. In brief, it conceded on the part of the Western Union that Bell was the original inventor of the telephone, that his patents were valid and the Western Union would retire from the telephone business into which it was preparing to enter on a large scale. For its part, the Bell Company agreed to buy the existing telephone plant of the Western Union, to pay it twenty per cent royalty on all telephone rentals, and to keep entirely out of the telegraph business.

For seventeen years, this pact, made between two of the greatest national public utilities, remained in force, and was kept by each to the letter. When it expired, there was no further need of it, for two former competitors had become firm friends. More than this they were co-operators. Each in its own field had a man-sized job.

In the telephone field, the Bell Company swept rapidly along. Its Western Union victory had added to its system, 56,000 telephones, located in fifty-five different cities of America. That was in 1880. In the following year, not less than twelve hundred additional cities and towns were marked upon its map and it began to pay dividends. By 1882 it entered upon a genuine growth from which it never has departed.

THE COMING OF "LONG DISTANCE"

Yet for a long time, the telephone's chief uses were purely local. Like the old-fashioned horse-car, it only sought to serve one city and its immediate surroundings. For long-distance messages, one still used the telegraph. This was despite the fact that the very earliest promoters of the telephone well knew that their device was quite as suitable for carrying the human voice long distances as for short. It will be recalled that, in the very beginnings of the telephone, a telegraph line was leased from Boston to New York to test its long distance powers.

Truth to tell, the problem of meeting the avalanche of demands for purely local service made it quite impossible for a long time for the telephone company to depart from that field. Moreover, the installation of long-distance lines brought complicated technical problems, of a new sort. The proper kind of cable must be used; also frequent and high-powered "relays", in order that the human voice might go in its full strength and in accurate tone for many hundreds of miles. All of these, and many others, were mechanical problems which had to be solved.

In the long run, they were solved, of course. Yet

the solution did not always come quickly.   For a long
time, the progress of "long distance" was slow indeed.
Not until 1895, did the wires from New York reach
Chicago.   The day that they thrust themselves into
Denver (in 1911) was the occasion of a sizable celebration in the Colorado capital.   Yet what was that
compared with 1915, when for the first time one could
pick up his telephone in the city of New York and
talk clearly and easily with San Francisco?   Then
again, Alexander Graham Bell talked with Thomas A.
Watson, only this time it was across a broad continent.   Beside this, all other achievements of the "long
distance" faded into the shade.   Many dinner parties
were given, on both rims of the United States, to cele-
brate this really important event.   At these affairs,
each guest was provided with an individual telephone.
He listened for himself to the swift and easy business
of making the long-distance connections all the way
across the continent, and men, sitting at dinner in New
York or Boston, almost within a stone's throw of the
Atlantic, heard in their own ears, through the magical
invention of Bell, the swish of the waves of the Pacific
against the rocks of the Cliff House, at San Francisco,
more than three thousand miles away.

TRANS-ATLANTIC TELEPHONY

Hand in hand with the development of the Trans-
Continental telephony the scientists and engineers were
engaged in perfecting the apparatus which was to make
a reality of their next goal, commercial telephone service across the Atlantic.   This too has now been accomplished.   On January 7, 1927, after an exchange of
greetings between Walter S. Gifford, President of the

American Telephone & Telegraph Company, and Sir G. Evelyn P. Murray, Secretary of the General Post Office of Great Britain, the Trans-Atlantic line was opened for public use.

The New York ceremonies in connection with the opening of the service took place in the directors' room of the American Telephone & Telegraph Company's headquarters at 195 Broadway. To the little group who had been invited to attend, Mr. Gifford briefly outlined the continuous research and experimentation that had brought to pass the realization of trans-Atlantic telephony. Then, at 8.43 A.M., with the guests listening through receivers especially installed at each chair, he lifted the receiver of an ordinary desk-set and asked for a telephone connection with Sir Evelyn Murray.

The call passed through the official board to the long lines headquarters at 24 Walker Street, and in less than a minute had been completed and the historic conversation had begun. Mutual greetings and congratulations passed between the Bell System headquarters and the British General Post Office over a circuit of wire and ether 7190 miles in length. Immediately after Sir Evelyn Murray's concluding words of acknowledgment, a long distance operator was notifying a waiting subscriber that the London circuit was ready for his call. Trans-Atlantic telephony had become a public service.

The opening ceremonies required but a few moments, but for the long distance operators assigned to the London circuit they were the beginning of a day filled with the thrill that accompanies participation in an event that was holding the world's interest. On each

side of the Atlantic were those who had "booked"
calls and were anxiously awaiting their turn to use
the new-found way of communicating their thoughts
and words across the ocean barrier. When the circuit was closed for the day, a total of thirty-one commercial calls had been handled, including messages
between banks, newspapers, business concerns, and
individuals.

TELEVISION MADE PRACTICAL FOR LONG DISTANCE
TRANSMISSION BY WIRE OR RADIO

On the afternoon of April 7, 1927, Herbert Hoover
smiled. Taken by itself, there is nothing remarkable
in that fact, yet this was an epoch-making smile, for
the Secretary of Commerce was in Washington and the
smile flashed before the eyes of an audience two hundred miles away in the Bell telephone laboratories, in
New York City.

Participating in the demonstration at Washington
and at New York were notable gatherings of leaders in
the fields of science, industry and public affairs. To
say that the guests "participated" in the program is
to describe one of the most striking features of the
event, for many persons in New York chatted infor-
mally with friends in Washington, commenting in wonder at the clearness with which the features of the latter were recreated upon the small screen into which
the observers looked as they conversed.

Not only was this application of television, for use
by individuals, most successfully demonstrated, but,
through the use of a much larger screen and a loud
speaker, the entire audience was permitted to see the
speakers at the national capital, and to "listen-in" on

the two-way conversation. Although the conversation was carried on in both directions, the visual features of the demonstration were presented only to the spectators at New York.

THE TELEPHONE IN THE WORLD WAR

One other thing needs to be told in this chapter of the development of the telephone:

As the telegraph proved itself the useful and dependable servant of man in the trying days of the Civil War, so in the equally trying ones of the World War did the telephone show itself to be man's friend. Upon its reliability, upon its absolute dependability, great generals pinned their faith, and the lives of many men rested. Men and ships and armies moved to the silently spoken orders of the telephone. It was the thin line of communication between the trench, the outpost and headquarters. Where the army moved, it also moved. The portable telephone became as much of a military adjunct as the rifle. The wiremen of the telephone corps moved with the front lines of advance. The wires they left behind them were ofttimes simply and crudely fashioned, but they met the purpose, at least until more permanent ones could be installed.

While the French, the British and other contesting armies of the earlier days of the war had very complete telephone equipments, it was left to the American Expeditionary Forces to take the Yankee telephone to France, just as they also took the American railroader and the American locomotive across the Atlantic. All of this was done with a vigor and a thoroughness which astounded our allied armies. Men, well skilled in the development of telegraphy and of telephony in this country, which long ago in the United States reached a stage many years in advance of European countries, were quickly commissioned to give our A.E.F. the finest combined system of military telegraph and telephone yet devised. This comprised the building of a trunk line for four hundred miles from St. Nazaire, the chief American port in France, up the valley of the Loire to Tours, to Dijon, to Is-sur-Tille and to Neufchateau. Auxiliary lines to this also were installed, from Bourges south to Bordeaux, and from Tours north to Paris.

At points in touch with headquarters, switchboard and branch-line installations comparable with those of good-sized towns back home, were installed, and corps of specially selected girl operators sent overseas to operate them. When President Wilson set up his own headquarters in Paris he had an American telephone from an American switchboard upon his table. So popular did these particular telephones become in the great French capital that the government of France, which controls the telephone business in that country, has been overwhelmed ever since by demands for the installation of the "*téléphone américain.*" Today in houses and places of business, not only in France, but in Great Britain, one finds an increasing proportion of our telephones. Yet, when Alexander Graham Bell went overseas in 1880 in an effort to introduce his great invention in Europe, he was rebuffed at every corner, and came home sick and thoroughly discouraged.

CHAPTER XIV

THE TELEPHONE TODAY

THAT small black instrument, looking for all the world like a sawed-off section of a rifle barrel, that proud, erect instrument, with the bright nickel trimmings, upon the desk in your office or your home, is the magic wand, the open sesame that easily can put you in immediate touch with the farthest corner of a far-flung nation. Yet nine times out of ten, ninety-nine out of a hundred, you will not be seeking that farthest corner. You will be wanting merely to tell the grocer in the next block to send around that loaf of bread, needed in a very great hurry; to remind the butcher that the chops have not yet arrived; or perhaps, to ask friend H, or cousin G, to come in to supper and partake of that bread or those chops; or in more serious emergency by far, that queer instrument will bring medicine from the corner drug-store or the family doctor, hurrying in his car. It will bring, should you be so unfortunate as to need them, the ambulance, the police, the fire department; or such simpler things as a taxi, or an express wagon. The list of its possibilities runs to great lengths. It is not merely your own personal gateway to the world, but it is your friend, your companion and your adviser.

So sweeping a category of virtues for that little black device needs some detailed explanation. How does that thing, the highly modern telephone of this highly modern day, bring the bread, or the taxi, or the fire department, or the dear friend, so quickly to you? What is the thoroughness of its function, that by day or by night its service is tireless and it is able to ferret out the answers to your demands, no matter how unreasonable they may really be?

The answer to all of this, as in so many other forms of American industrial triumph, is organization; the organization of the mechanical, the organization of the human factor; organization multiplied in all of its details to the *nth* degree; organization, perfected by study, by invention, by experience.

From that black instrument upon your desk there runs a thin strand of copper wire, which brings the outer world in direct touch with it. This wire multiplies again and again, divides, and redivides, again and again, until it has a thousand, ten thousand, one hundred thousand, a million, ten million, fifteen million terminals. Today, right here in the United States there are seventeen and a half million small black telephones, just like yours, tireless servants to you throughout the day, and the entire night as well. They start at the northeast corner of the land, Eastport, Maine, and continue to its southwest corner, San Diego, California. A man in Eastport can lift his telephone off the hook and in ten or fifteen minutes be talking to his friend in San Diego, 3600 miles away. Nay, more than this; the millions of tentacles of this highly developed national nervous system long ago leaped over the mere geographical boundaries of the country and sent themselves shooting, north into Canada, and south into Mexico.

Today, these North American highways of speech reach more than three hundred miles south of the Rio Grande, into tiny Mexican villages where the English language is hardly spoken from one year's end to the other, and north to the small lumber hamlets of northern Ontario and Quebec, where French is the reigning tongue. They touch Spanish again, as from Key West they burrow in a water-resisting cable, for ninety miles under southern seas and only emerge to come into a central station in the Cuban city of Havana. Sometimes, Chinese is the sole language spoken in the American telephone exchange. The Chinese exchanges of San Francisco long have been a tourist feature of that city.

Here, then, is the picture of our widespread telephone system, with its many highways of speech, crossing and recrossing, lacing and interlacing, and with probably at least one of them coming right into your own home or your own office, to the little black telephone upon your desk. In no other land in the world is the telephone anywhere nearly so universal in its use. Even in great and congested European cities, its adoption has not been rapid. In London, gaily uniformed "commissioners" still run errands for telephoneless folk. Paris has a clumsy and somewhat antiquated pneumatic-tube system, connected with the post office, for the expeditious sending of very small letters written upon excessively thin paper. Sometimes those letters reach their destination across the city in half a day. In ten seconds, a man in the city of New York may be in telephonic touch with any one of its almost 2,000,000 telephones; in two minutes, he may have Chicago; in ten, San Francisco; and this great facility comes just as quickly to the man in the smaller city or the village, or the remote farmhouse, as to him who has his home in the largest city on the continent.

That is all well enough, you say, but just how do I get that distant telephone by the simple process of lifting the receiver off the hook and speaking a few brief words into the transmitter?

In principle, at least, the process is not particularly difficult or complicated. We saw how, long ago, when Mr. Holmes, the burglar-alarm man of Boston, wanted to make a day use of the first early telephones that he had placed in five of the banks there as a night protection, he decided that they might use those for talking back and forth among one another, as bankers always like to talk among themselves. If there had been but two banks the problem would have been simplicity itself. A single line would have connected them. When the First National at one end wanted to talk to the Second National at the other, the First National would have lifted off the receiver at its end and rung a bell which would have attracted the attention of the people at the Second National's end of the wire. That was simplicity itself, and it was the precise way that very many of the earliest telephones were installed.

But *five* telephones meant some sort of an intercommunication between each and all of them, some central point or *switchboard* at which the five wires leading to each telephone would come together and some sort of an adjustable physical connection made between any two of them, as demand necessitated. More than this, the process of the connection must be even more than physical. The only thing that understands and reacts properly to the human voice is the human mind; when it hears, it comprehends, and then it commands. Its commands go to the muscles of the human body; these translate the commands into physical action; and so the physical action of human hands, working with the mechanical adjustments of the exchange was, and still is, the chief factor in making the physical connections at the orders of the human voice spoken into the telephone at some distant point. Keep this point, if you will, carefully in mind.

When five telephones became ten or twenty, the problem was simply the increase in the mechanical equipment of the switchboard, placing the designations that marked the ends of each telephone wire leading into or out of it in orderly and easily accessible position. But twenty telephones were not too much for the well-trained human mind of the operator to handle properly; neither, under ordinary conditions, are a hundred telephones.

HOW YOUR CALL ENTERS CENTRAL

Now see how this fascinating thing works out in actual practice. You have lifted the receiver of your telephone off the little hook on the standard on which it rests when not in use.

Instantly, on a far-off switchboard, "Central," something is happening. The call number of your telephone, let us say, is "1926." At this point it might be well to explain that your line, along with every other line in that central, is terminated on a small aperture, or hole in the switchboard, called a *jack*. Associated with this jack is a tiny electric bulb, or lamp. Since this is the point where calls originating on each line are answered, these jacks, with which the lamps are associated, are known as *answering jacks*. They are arranged in groups before each operator, varying in size depending upon the average number of calls originated by each line during the busiest hour of the day. Let us assume that this factor limits the number of answering jacks, in this switchboard we are considering, to one hundred per position. Then at the first position, line numbers and corresponding answering jacks and lamps from zero to ninety-nine appear, on the second position those from one hundred to one hundred ninety-nine, and so on; so that if a switchboard were equipped with ten thousand lines there would be one hundred operators' positions, each equipped with one hundred answering jacks and lamps. This group of one hundred answering jacks is within reach not only of the operator sitting at the particular position at which they terminate, but also of the adjacent operators on either side of that position, so that any particular originating call is liable to be answered by any one of three operators.

Thus far we have described what we might term the answering end of the line. But provision must also be made for completing calls to each line in the office. This is done by also terminating each line on jacks, other than the answering jack, and located in the so-called *multiple*. In order that every operator at the switchboard may be able to reach any line in the office, this multiple jack arrangement has been provided, above the answering jacks and lamps, consisting of the entire ten thousand lines, and this repeats itself once for every three telephone operators throughout the entire length of the switchboard. Each multiple is divided into blocks, or lamps, of one hundred jacks each, consisting of five strips of twenty jacks each. This is to facilitate the work of the operator in finding the jack of the line with which connection is desired.

At some switchboards the lamps are associated with the multiple jacks, and calls are both answered and completed direct in the multiple. As can readily be seen, however, this arrangement takes up considerable additional space and its use must therefore be restricted to the smaller central offices.

The operator's hands are kept free for swift work by placing the *receiver*, or hearing part of her apparatus, which is directly connected with the switchboard by means of a long flexible cord, in a sort of metal bonnet worn upon her head all the time she is on duty. The transmitter, or speaking part, is worn in an instrument upon her breast. In the event that a sudden rush of calls occurs at one operator's position the element of team work enters in and the operators on either side reach over with their cords and answer the calls. In case this sudden rush, variously called a traffic peak or surge, includes three or more adjacent positions, the patrolling supervisor will call off the numbers of some of the calling lines and some one of the other girls down the switchboard, not occupied at that instant in handling calls at her own position, will answer such calls in the multiple.

We are now ready to trace the course of your call following the removal of the receiver of the telephone on your line, number 1926. In front of the eyes of the girl who is seated at the position where the answering jack of your line is located, the tiny electric bulb which is the answering lamp of your line lights instantly. This operator, or one of her adjacent "team mates," pulls up one end of a long flexible cord, to which is attached a plug which just fits into the jack where she places it. She listens to your request. You want 3199, for the moment we shall assume, on the same exchange. With the plug on the other end of that flexible cord in her hand Central lets this hand trail her eye and she seeks out 99 in the thirty-one hundred block of the multiple. When she locates it, a mere matter of seconds or their fractions, she "tries" the plug in the jack opening. If 3199 is already in moment-ary use a sharp "clicking" in her receiver will indicate that fact, both to the operator and to you as she at-tempts to complete the connection and finds the line engaged, because some other operator along the switch-board has inserted a plug in one of the jacks of the desired line. Then you hang up your receiver, to try again probably in a few minutes, and the central opera-tor lets the flexible cord drop back into place. Into some of the jacks there have been inserted tiny button-headed plugs; these indicate various conditions: that the subscriber's telephone number has been changed, or discontinued, or perhaps is temporarily out of order. In cases of calls for such lines the person calling is prop-erly advised.

In most cases however the operator finds the line *free* and inserts the calling plug in the called jack in the multiple. Your line and the one you are calling are now connected by means of the flexible double-ended cord. The next thing to do is to get some one to answer the telephone on the line you called by ringing the bell at that telephone.

At this point let us consider the lamp signals by which the operator is guided in her work of answering calls and completing connections, for it is these tiny flashing lamps that keep telephone traffic moving. Just as the varicolored lamps at street corners control street traffic in busy cities so are these tiny lights in the central office the veritable traffic signals on the highways of speech. The little lamp over the answering jack of your line, which lighted when you removed your receiver, remained lighted until the answering plug was inserted in the answering jack, when it went out. These little lamp signals are now transferred to the lamps associated with the cord pair being used to complete the desired connection. They automatically indicate to the operator by their various flashings on and off, the course of the connections, such as when the ringing has started, when the called person has answered, when each of the persons talking has hung up, etc. In case you wish to regain the attention of the operator who has answered your call, either during or subsequent to the completion of your connection, a single depression of your receiver hook will start the lamp, associated with the end of the cord in your jack, flashing on and off intermittently and automatically. This automatic, intermittent flashing will continue until the operator again comes in on the connection.

The operator has connected your line with the one with which you desire connection by means of the flexible cord. By pressing a button at her position she starts the ringing of the telephone you have just called. It continues ringing automatically and intermittently until the called party removes his receiver from the hook or until you hang up your receiver. **During this**

time a distinctive "ringing sound" is being sent back
to you to indicate that the bell at the telephone you
are calling is being rung. The operator is keeping an
eye on the "traffic signals" of your connection all this
time. When, as indicated by these signals, both 1926
and 3199 have finished talking to one another and
have hung up their receivers, she pulls the flexible cord
that connected the 1926 and 3199 openings with one
another and lets it drop back into place. The call is
ended. Both telephones are now ready for other messages, either incoming or outgoing.

If the telephone business in a community could be
kept at ten thousand subscribers, about the maximum
capacity of one multiple switchboard with its largest
force of operators, the problem of the telephone manager and the telephone engineer would be simplified
immensely. But years ago the demand for telephone
service on the part of our larger cities swept past the
ten thousand maximum, a figure determined by the
outstretched length of an operator's arms. Then
it became necessary to create two or more exchanges
for a single community, and to arrange for intercon-
necting links, trunks or cables, between each of these
exchanges. It was the beginning problem of the telephone once again, with a whole exchange substituted
for a single station, the original problem magnified,
and rendered vastly more intricate.

MULTIPLE EXCHANGES

In order to illustrate it, in this larger phase, suppose now that you are living in a community large
enough to support two or more exchanges, and that the
telephone upon your desk instead of being a plain 1926

has become prefixed, after this fashion, Main 1926, and that 3199 which you are in the habit of calling has become Monroe 3199.

Now we shall repeat the process of getting the telephone call for you.

Again, you take the receiver off the hook and at the response of Central, you have asked for your number in this way, clearly and distinctly, "Monroe three-one-nine-nine, please."

At the Main exchange, with which your telephone is directly connected, the little light in front of the operator flashes on and off as before. She again makes the quick, skillful, accurate movements with the flexible cord. But the far end of it this time does not go to the number of the person who is to receive the call. It goes into an aperture which reaches over a *trunk* into the Monroe exchange.

The operator at Main, who begins this process, sits at a position in front of a long multiple board, such as we already have seen, and which in a larger system, such as this, takes the name of the *A-board*. The operator at Monroe who receives this particular call and who simply handles incoming calls off the trunks from the other exchanges, is at a *B-board*. The trunk at her end terminates on a flexible cord.

The rest of the process is simple enough. In front of the B-board operator at Monroe is a complete board for all the subscribers of that exchange up to the maximum ten thousand. She takes the incoming call from the trunk that leads back to Main and endeavors to make a direct connection with the 3199 that you desire. If it is busy, the clicking sound is heard again and she, the A-board girl at Main and you know that

the connection cannot be made at just that moment.
If 3199 is not busy the B-board girl at Monroe starts
the ringing mechanism and turns her mind to another
incoming call, from Main or some other exchange.

Of course if the call that you wanted from your Main
1926 happened to be in your own exchange, somewhere
in "Main," the transaction is immensely simpler. It
is handled from beginning to end by the A-board girl
who happens first to pick up your signal, and no "trunk-
ing" or other elaborate mechanism comes into play.
This is the reason why the modern telephone company
always prefers, when it is humanly possible, to keep
subscribers in any given territory listed in the same
exchange. It has discovered that by far the greatest
number of calls that it handles are bound for the rather
immediate neighborhood.

Sometimes the calls have complications. *Party
wires* are used where one or two or four persons are
upon the same wire and have the same number separated only by letter designations. This means the
use of a simple mechanical device by the operator which
enables her to call any one of the letters, without dis-
turbing the others. Of course, while any one of these
is in use, the wire is reported "busy" and it is physically
impossible to use the other telephones upon it at that
moment.

The telephone company also has many *pay-stations*,
in drug stores, hotels, railroad stations and other more
or less public points, and in many of these it collects
its toll in advance by means of cleverly designed automatic boxes, which receive coins of varying denominations—nickels, dimes, and quarters—and accurately
report their receipt to central. When the operator has

told the user of a coin-box pay-station the toll he or she must pay, she listens to the tiny bell-report that she gets. There is a slightly different sound for each of these three coins. When they have been received, to the correct amount, she completes the connection.

Then in many instances, there are subscribers' telephones where the service is paid for by the precise number of messages used each month. An accurate record must be made of all these, yet not by the operator. She has too many other important things to occupy her mind. When she has completed a local call from one of these telephones, known as *message-rate telephones*, and when her cord signals indicate that both parties have finished talking and have hung up their receivers a message is automatically registered on an individual adding machine, or register, for that telephone, which is located in a sealed and locked case down in the basement of the exchange. At midnight on the fifteenth of each month the readings of the individual message registers are recorded by competent employees and they are then transmitted to the accounting department of the telephone company for billing purposes.

Sometimes calls to nearby suburban points, to which toll charges apply, are handled in these "local" exchanges on a trunked basis. In such cases the operator writes a small ticket showing the calling and called numbers and the time of the conversation. These tickets are collected at convenient intervals during the day and sent to the accounting department for billing purposes.

All these things make the exchange still more intricate and complicated; and yet, when you come to see one of them for the first time, you can hardly fail to be struck by the seeming simplicity, the quiet orderliness of it all.   There is everywhere thorough organization, human organization as well as mechanical.   Intricacy has become a mere detail of operation; system almost always works for simplicity.

THE INTERIOR OF A MODERN TELEPHONE EXCHANGE

Here is a modern telephone exchange in America.   We are given an open sesame to enter it, a privilege extended to the public at large.   The telephone companies make a definite policy of welcoming interested visitors to the exchanges.   They feel that it gives the users of their service a far better idea of the many difficulties encountered in conducting it.

The heart of this very modern exchange is a long high-ceilinged room, well ventilated, well lighted at all hours and kept neat and scrupulously clean, since dust is a terrible enemy of the delicately adjusted mechanism of the telephone.   It is dominated by a single, huge, U-shaped piece of furniture, nine or ten feet in height, and which, if extended into a straight line, would reach a hundred feet or more.   It rises, like a low wall, above the heads of the row of young women who are seated before it.   It is an intricate, yet carefully and systematically planned, mass of lights, of buttons, of cams, of apertures, between some of which a network of varicolored cords connect.   The young women are constantly changing the positions of these cords, as they speak in soft, distinct tones into the mouthpieces of the telephone transmitters that, while they are on duty, they wear upon their breasts.

This is the *switchboard*, this single dominating feature of the exchange room, and these young women are, of course, the operators.   Of the functions they perform we have just read.   We know now how they are forever opening and closing the gates that lead to all the highways of speech.

For the moment we are interested in the operators themselves.   They are a fine, clean-cut looking group of girls.   They might be seniors in any smart woman's college anywhere in the land.   At the switchboard there are no old women, not even middle-aged ones. It is a job that calls for the suppleness, the deftness, the certainty of youth.   Ten years, or less, at a switchboard and one of two things almost always happens; the girl is promoted in the service or else she leaves it and gets married.

If she is promoted she becomes, in due course, a *supervisor*.   Now, six or eight or ten operators, the number depending chiefly upon the volume of business at any given time, come directly under her watchful eye.   She is there, however, more to advise and help, than to criticise.   Wearing her insignia of office in the form of the bonnet-like receiver, etc., and with her cord-plug always in her fingers, she walks up and down behind the girls under her immediate charge.   In any emergency she sticks in her plug and takes charge, generally managing to straighten out the thing very quickly.   Sometimes, too, she will temporarily "spell" the girls at their positions, even though a regular schedule of frequent relief periods applies at all times.   The telephone company believes that thus conserving to the fullest extent the comfort and the health of its workers, is not sentimental philanthropy, but the very best of

INTERIOR OF A MODERN TELEPHONE EXCHANGE.

good business. That is why it creates in each of its exchanges elaborate rest rooms and cafeteria facilities; why twice a day or oftener, there is a fifteen-minute period when the girls rise from their chairs and stand, while the windows of the room are opened and the air changed. A room which is in steady use, each minute of the hour and each hour of the twenty-four, year in and year out, needs a scientific scheme of ventilation.

There is, at the exchange, another step of definite promotion. The girl who makes a good record as supervisor may presently become the *chief operator*, which is indeed a position of responsibility and an opportunity for real service. To each exchange there are assigned to the chief operator at least six assistants, which means that in the eight-hour shift which is generally used, there are always two chief operators, one in actual charge and the other ready to serve as an instant relief to her.

Here, then, is the ideal of the telephone: continuous service, and instant. This means that there never at any time must be any more risk of breakdown in the human factor than in the mechanical.

This last is taken care of by the *wire chief* and his assistants, who are also on continuous periods of duty, in their own office, generally on a lower floor of the exchange, where they are surrounded by an amazing intricacy of wires and minute mechanism. Technically this is the *terminal room*. Into it come the *cables* from the *conduits* or the poles out in the street. Each of these cables holds hundreds of pairs of telephone wires, closely wrapped together and separated from their fellows by the insulation of paper ribbons twisted

about each separate copper wire.   A two-and-one-half
inch cable may hold over 2,000 wires.   The entire group
is protected from the action of the weather by a stout
sheathing of lead.

In the terminal room, this mass of wires is, in orderly
fashion, "fanned out" from the cables and led in a
long framework out under the switchboard, which is
located on the floor directly overhead.   The connections are so arranged that the expert wireman has
little difficulty in getting to any of them, for change,
for repair, and for emergency.   In all modern exchanges, there is left ample room for the extension of
the switchboard and its wire facilities underneath to
the maximum capacity of ten thousand lines.   Such a
huge board rarely ever is installed in its entirety at
the outset.   One-fourth that capacity may be a good
beginning.   But both the board and all its appurte-
nances are so designed that, when the traffic demands,
it may be increased easily to half-size, to three-quarters,
or to its fullest capacity.   The telephone business
demands vision at every turn.

There are also, within this terminal room, certain
special features of mechanism.   Since even the simplest telephone requires a certain amount of electricity
for its operation, a large group of them is bound to
require a very considerable amount of current.   In
ordinary practice here the telephone company generally
finds it is easier to purchase the current from the local
lighting companies.   For this purpose it has an elaborate switchboard and transformers.

Yet even the most dependable of lighting companies
may, some day, somewhere, fail to deliver the required
current in the needed steadiness and volume.   The

THE CABLE RUNS OF A MODERN TELEPHONE EXCHANGE.

telephone company cannot risk a breakdown in its continuous and instant service because of this. So each exchange must have reserve equipment for a power emergency in the form of an electric generator and a gas engine with which to drive it, as well as complete storage battery cells, a veritable reservoir of reserve electrical energy.

In the terminal room are also the pay-station and meter-station recording equipment, to which reference already has been made, and the ingenious machine which automatically rings the bells on the subscribers' telephones by the single pressure of the ringing buttons by the operator, as previously explained.

In certain very large exchanges there are special features of the service, which are reflected in special features of the equipment. For instance there is *Information.*

In order to simplify its vast problem as far as possible, the telephone company makes every effort to have all the calls given it simply in the form of exchanges and numbers, nothing else. The only exceptions are those of the police department, the fire department and the telegraph companies. To accomplish this real end it goes to great expense, and two or three times a year it publishes a huge directory showing its subscribers, their addresses and their telephone exchanges and numbers. This great list is kept remarkably simple and accurate. Therefore the company insists upon its use. No longer is it possible, even in the smallest communities boasting an exchange, as it once was in the largest, to go to your telephone, take down the receiver and say "W. G. Jones' house, please." The telephone system long ago passed the limits when the girl operator at the switchboard could carry a mental directory of it in her own mind.

Yet the telephone system is a constantly changing thing. There is not a day, save possibly Sundays and holidays, when the list of subscribers to its service is not in course of revision. Names are being added; names are being dropped. Between the successive issues of the directory there are many, many changes. The people who obtain telephones between these issues are entitled to the fullest service. So, after all is said and done, there must be some sort of human service added to the telephone directory.

This, then, is *Information*. She is a woman, generally "she" is a group of women, well-versed in telephone lore and experience, who sit on duty at a desk on top of which is a flexible directory listing, which shows almost at a single glance the exchange and number of each new patron of the local service. When the subscriber that you seek is not listed in your telephone directory, you ask for Information and state his name and address, and the number will be forthcoming in an astonishingly short time. But if you are too lazy to consult your directory you probably will be referred simply, though courteously, back to it again. *Information* is far too busy to look up numbers for lazy folk.

In more recent years and in certain of our larger cities, the so-called *automatic telephone* has been introduced, in many exchanges. With it, the burden of making the correct call is upon the subscriber, rather than upon the operator. A curious looking dial is affixed to the ordinary telephone instrument. Upon it are many of the letters of the alphabet and the digit

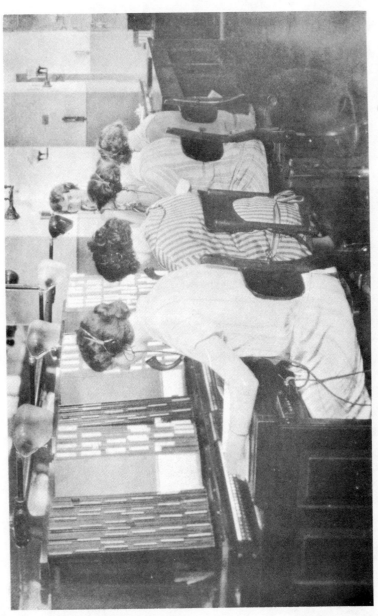

CENTRAL INFORMATION DESK, MAIN EXCHANGE, ROCHESTER TELEPHONE CORPORATION, ROCHESTER, NEW YORK

numbers. Certain combinations of three letters represent the local exchanges. With your finger you snap the dial around to these three, in their proper arrangement, and then you snap it to the exchange number desired, by use of the proper combination of the digit numbers, after which your call should be quite complete and ready for you without further effort on your part.

While this automatic system, which has been in development here in the United States for a number of years past, entails a vast increase in the central exchange equipment it compensates for this by the large savings which it makes in the human factor that it is necessary to employ there. Moreover, it does its work with a surprising degree of accuracy. Mistakes that it may make are almost always directly traceable to initial ones on the part of the subscriber.

This system is in vogue in very large cities where the labor problem for a long time past has been particularly acute; where the supply of girls who, after a thorough training that they always must undergo, are fit for competent switchboard operation, is limited; or where the facilities for getting them back and forth to the exchanges, in times of stress or great emergency, always a perplexing problem to the telephone management, are not to be depended upon at all times. In instances such as these the automatic system has proved valuable.

THE LONG DISTANCE EXCHANGE

The exchange that we have already seen might well be termed a "city thoroughfare of speech." The highways that carry human conversation afar present different and more complicated problems. Obviously the making and completing of a telephone call reaching five hundred or a thousand miles or more is a far more intricate thing than one which is handled entirely within a city and its suburban area, even in such a vast telephonic city as New York, where in certain instances purely local calls have to pass through as many as four exchange switchboards. In *Long Distance* there frequently are also many exchange switchboards to be used; also in the very nature of the service rendered there are, in many, many instances, persons to be sought out and brought to the telephone, whereupon the man originally calling is, in turn, notified and brought back to his own telephone. All of this requires time, in many cases, a great deal of time, and the resources of a huge separate organization, an organization both human and mechanical.

Suppose that this time when you lift the receiver off the telephone instrument in your home you do not ask for "Monroe 3199" or even "Main 3199," but let us say, for a purely supposititious instance, you demand Cosmopolis. Cosmopolis is about 250 miles away from your home town. It is a sizable city and there are numerous practices of telephony that will have to be complied with before your call with the man you want over there will have been completed.

When you wish to talk to Cosmopolis you do not tell that to the first operator who answers your call, you merely lift the receiver off the hook and say, "Long Distance." The operator at the A-board of your home exchange connects you with one of the trunks that leads from her position to the Long Distance switchboard and from that point on the task of completing your call becomes the business of the Long Distance operator to whom you pass your call.

Long Distance has its entirely separate board, in any good-sized city usually an entirely separate exchange. As far as possible it is kept as an entity. Long Distance also has its outgoing or A-board. When your call comes into it over the trunk from your own exchange the Long Distance operator carefully records on a small white ticket the details pertaining to the conversation in which you wish to engage. Mr. Blank, of Cosmopolis! Very well! What is Mr. Blank's telephone number? This may seem to you an unnecessary question, but it is most important, if you wish to have your call completed quickly, to furnish the called telephone number when you place or "file" your call, even if you have to go to some trouble to obtain that number beforehand. Let us assume that in this instance you do know Mr. Blank's telephone number and pass it to the Long Distance operator.

All these details she is writing upon her small white ticket as you give them to her, and then she places the exact time of your call on the ticket, exact to the tenth of a minute. A marvelously accurate clock, operated by the Western Union Telegraph Company, is on the switchboard in front of her and for her it records time, changing itself every six seconds. The advantage in figuring in tenths of a minute is that it indicates for this operator, or for any other operator who may have a part in handling your call later on in case it is delayed in completion, which of these calls that are entering themselves for Cosmopolis is entitled to precedence. In times when there is a heavy rush upon the facilities of Long Distance this becomes an important factor.

The Long Distance operator now asks you to "hold the line, please." She has in front of her a multiple of all the trunks to distant points going out of her office. Placing the other end of the flexible cord, with which she has answered your call, in one of the trunks to Cosmopolis she rings the Cosmopolis operator, asks her to ring the telephone, the number of which you have given her, and gets Mr. Blank to that telephone for you—all this while you have been "holding the line" and listening to the course of your call and all within less time than it takes to tell it. If there are no direct trunks to Cosmopolis from your city you hear your Long Distance operator requesting some intermediate office for connection with Cosmopolis before she is able to pass the called number.

If you have been unable to furnish the called telephone number, the Long Distance operator tells you she will call you and you hang up your receiver. She then places the small white ticket that becomes the record of the transaction in a compartment marked "Directory" of a steadily moving multiple belt conveyor, which all the time passes in front of her and which when it comes to a specified point on its travels, drops the ticket on a desk where sit young women with telephone directories of most of the important cities in the United States. Skilled in their use they make small work of finding Mr. Blank's telephone number and entering it upon the ticket, after which that ticket is sent on its way to another part of the switchboard to the girl who handles so-called "delayed" calls to Cosmopolis. If the directory operator is unable to find the precise number the ticket goes anyway and then the Cosmopolis office locates the correct number. But the originating office first exhausts every possibility of obtaining the detailed information pertaining to the call. In so doing it saves tying up the through telephone lines for any longer time than is absolutely necessary. Time is money when you come to the usage of a really long distance telephone trunk.

From the foregoing it can readily be seen how much the passing of the called telephone number, at the time the call is filed, expedites its completion.

When no trunks to Cosmopolis are immediately available at the time you file your call, or when the Long Distance operator who first received it runs into some other delay, such as a "busy" or "don't answer" line at Cosmopolis, or finds that Mr. Blank is not immediately available, she also informs you that she will call you and you hang up the receiver. The ticket is then sent to the Cosmopolis "delayed call" operator by means of this same conveyor belt, and thereafter it is her responsibility to complete the call.

When the Cosmopolis operator reaches Mr. Blank, whether immediately or after a delay, and you start conversation she records the precise time again in seconds on the white ticket. She does not trust this time even to her accurate eyes, but inserts the ticket in the calculagraph, the time clock operated by the telegraph company, which prints on it the hour, minute and tenth of a minute. When your call is finished the ticket again is stamped in the calculagraph and its precise length, once again, in the fraction of a minute, is stamped upon it. Periodically the tickets are collected and sent to the auditing department for figuring out the cost of each individual call from the tariff books and then making the proper charges to the accounts of the subscribers. In cases, generally those of public pay-stations, where the charge must be given at once it is calculated right within the precincts of the switchboard room.

In cases where Mr. Blank is not readily located, unless the calling subscriber gives instructions to the contrary, the Long Distance operator in your town to whom the ticket has been passed and who is thereafter charged with the responsibility for completing it, keeps at the call all the day long, yes, and far into the night and sometimes for successive days, keeping you informed at intervals of the progress of your call, until Mr. Blank is finally located for you or you definitely cancel the call. If his line has been reported "busy" she keeps trying it at automatic ten-minute intervals until she is able to get it; if "don't answer" is the report the repeated attempts are made at forty minute intervals, etc., definite intervals for re-trial being prescribed for each condition encountered. But Central persists until she gets some sort of a definite and satisfactory answer.

For she is more than an operator, this Long Distance Central; she is a saleswoman for her company, and almost always a very good one. If she cannot complete your call, the telephone company gains little or no revenue from the transaction. Therefore, she tries to complete it, and in the shortest possible time, so that the company may gain not only the revenue but your good-will and continued patronage.

For all of these reasons she must be not only courteous and interested, but expert, in making the calls.

Sometimes they are complicated and she will need every ounce of her good sense and initiative. To understand this better take some fairly concrete instances. This time we shall talk of real cities.

Here is a Long Distance A-board operator at Rochester, New York. From one of the local exchanges she receives a request to bring to the telephone a man at Columbia, Missouri. The order for the call comes through the formula that we have just seen. The operator who actually is to make the call knows that to get Columbia she first will have to get Chicago, then in turn, St. Louis, which will give the nearby small city of Columbia. If there is difficulty in getting Columbia through St. Louis, she may try Kansas City, still using Chicago as her first junction point.

There is a single high-grade direct trunk between Rochester and Chicago. If it continues to be occupied for some length of time, she may, in her resourcefulness, attempt to "build up" an entrance into Chicago, trying a direct wire either to Buffalo or to Cleveland and asking Long Distance in one or the other of those two cities to give her Chicago.

Always there is abundant opportunity for initiative, and for resourcefulness. Perhaps the call is going from Rochester eastbound. There are a dozen trunks that run direct and without interruption to Syracuse, the next large city to the east. On the switchboard some trunks bear strange symbols; at the aperture where the plug is inserted there is a tiny "o" which to the operator indicates that that particular trunk wire is connected with a relay or repeater, to strengthen the call at the other end. Some of them are marked in green and some in red; the green are the more modern and superior circuits. Obviously the superior circuits and those equipped with the mechanical repeaters should be used in preference upon "built-up" calls of which the Rochester-Syracuse trunk is but the beginning link. For calls which terminate in the two cities, the inferior circuits will serve quite as well. Central is supposed to know these things, she does know them, and the facility and the rapidity of the service she renders, and so the degree of salesmanship for her company that she shows, is largely dependent upon that knowledge.

Also, there is a B-board at Long Distance. At times thirty per cent of the operators in the room will be employed in handling incoming calls to your town, though these are never as great in number as are the outgoing calls. The number of operators fluctuates, as do the totals of the calls, for telephone traffic is a tremendously seasonal thing, always. In a single day of twenty-four hours it has many and varied peak loads, some of them expected and always anticipated, but others coming when least they might ordinarily be looked for.

TRANSATLANTIC TELEPHONY

Calls originating in this country are handled over the regular telephone circuits to the long distance office of the American Telephone and Telegraph Company in Walker Street, New York. At this point equipment is provided to separate the transmission toward London from that received from London. Eastbound transmission is carried by telephone lines to the radio transmitting station at Rocky Point, Long Island; thence by radio to the receiving station at Wroughton,

President W. S. Gifford Opens the New York-London Telephone Line

January 7, 1927.

England. From Wroughton the transmission passes by wire telephony to the long distance office of the General Post Office. At this point is located segregating apparatus similar to that in the Walker Street building. From the General Post Office long distance building the calls are handled over the ordinary telephone plant to the person called.

West-bound, the transmission from the calling person, which reaches the London long distance over the regular wire plant and is there segregated from the east-bound transmission, is carried over ordinary telephone lines to the transmitting station at Rugby, from which it proceeds by radio to the receiving station at Houlton, Maine. From Houlton to New York, as from Wroughton to London, the received transmission is handled over telephone lines and at the New York long distance office it passes through the combining apparatus and is delivered to the person called over his regular telephone circuit.

The radio transmissions both east and west-bound are on the same wave length, of approximately 5000 meters, or 60 kilocycles. This is the wave length which long experience through many years of experimentation has indicated as being the most satisfactory and reliable which the present state of the radio art makes available for this transmission. The choice of this wave length was agreed to by the engineers of the American Company and the British Post Office as being the one most suitable in the initial trans-oceanic telephone channel.

As is well known, radio transmission of every kind and on every wave length is subject to erratic disturbances and interruptions which render it materially less reliable than telephone or telegraph transmission over wires. Experience shows, however, that widely different wave lengths are not always affected to the same degree at the same time. Both very long and very short wave transmission between two points may be equally subjected to disturbances and interruption over a period of hours, days or months. It is found, however, that the periods of maximum disturbance do not always coincide. It follows that while a wave length of approximately 5000 meters is the best which present knowledge can assign for reliability on a single frequency, commercial transmission can, at times, be maintained more readily on a very short wave length.

Experiments conducted with long and short waves have indicated further that, because of the five hour difference in time which results in the afternoon of the business day in London overlapping the morning in New York, more difficult receiving conditions are generally encountered at the eastern terminus. In a word, telephoning between this country and England is more likely to be unsatisfactory because of radio conditions at the European end than at the American end.

Because of the two facts, first, of more severe natural conditions in England and, second, of non-coincidence of disturbances on long and very short waves, it seemed desirable in initiating commercial trans-Atlantic telephony, until more experience was had, to provide an alternate short wave channel for transmission from New York to London.

To accomplish this the outgoing east-bound transmission from Walker Street is carried by regular telephone lines both to the long wave transmitting station

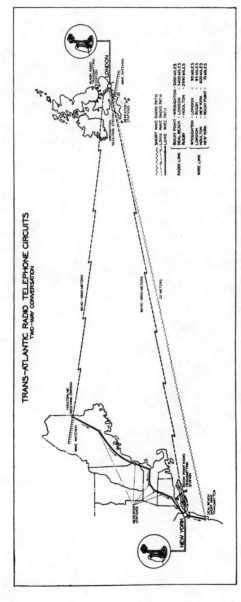

TRANSATLANTIC RADIO TELEPHONE CIRCUITS.

at Rocky Point and to the short wave transmitter at Deal Beach, N. J. The transmitter at Deal Beach operates on approximately 22 meters and the antenna is arranged to radiate in a concentrated or beam manner along the direction of the great circle to London. In England the short waves are received at New Southgate, on the outskirts of London, and carried by ordinary telephone wires to the combining apparatus in the London long distance office. With the same transmission east-bound on both the long and short waves the London operator can select at will the transmission channel which affords the best service. The short wave transmitter is thus far purely of an experimental character and further experience may indicate either that the provision of an alternate short wave channel east-bound is unnecessary or that at times of the year a corresponding alternate short wave channel may be required west-bound to insure maximum reliability of transmission.

It is, of course, well recognized that radio transmission is not, in itself, secret. The frequencies used in the transatlantic telephone circuit (5000 meters and 22 meters) are far removed, however, from the frequency range used in broadcasting and will not be heard in radio broadcast receiving sets. A further difference from broadcasting resides in the fact that the long wave trans-Atlantic transmission is of a special character, employing a single sideband and having the carrier suppressed, and cannot be received by means of the broadcasting type of receiving set. Thus, while the present trans-Atlantic circuit is not secret, no ordinary receiving set will pick it up intelligibly. Methods are now under development for increasing the degree of privacy which the circuit will provide, and these will be added as they become available.

THE TELEPHONE NEEDS OF TOMORROW

Here still is the picture of our American highways of speech, handling the constant and steadily increasing traffic that is placed upon them. The telephone service by its own excellence engenders increasing use of itself; after all, it is its own best salesman. The telephone engineer thinks therefore not at all in terms of yesterday, very little in those of today, and almost all the while in the prospects of tomorrow and of the best way of anticipating and of meeting these last. His strongest requisite is vision. He must see in every growing town, all the way across this land, the cities of ten years, twenty years, fifty years hence. For them, today, he draws the telephone plans—central stations to be added, new trunks, new branches, new equipment of all kinds to be provided. When those cities of tomorrow arrive, and tomorrow often has an embarrassing habit of coming before we are quite ready for it, their telephonic organization, in truth their high-strung nervous organism, must be ready. There can be no scrambling about, this way or that, to find makeshifts. In the telephone business makeshifts are not allowed for they are too expensive. Telephone equipment is not only intricate and delicate, but it is very costly; therefore, it does not pay to install it only to rip it right out again.

Not only is it intricate, but in these days it is tremendously varied. By means of the long distance telephone, the radio broadcasting station, America's newest and best beloved toy of the moment, picks up its program from this corner or from that.   The President of the United States speaks into a telephone at the White House in Washington, a long distance telephone copper circuit carries it to New York, and not only does a huge assemblage at dinner there hear Mr. Coolidge speak, but the great WEAF sends it out upon the wireless, thousands and thousands of miles, so that sailors on our warships lying at anchor in South American harbors hear the precise inflection of the tones of our chief executive, while skillfully designed amplifiers carry the tones of a distant speaker so clearly to a thousand diners that seemingly he might be speaking from the next table instead of from his home, three or four thousand miles away.

To meet these dramatic, almost spectacular, demands of the moment, there must be much special telephonic equipment, of one sort or another, and more skilled workmen must be employed at the American standard of good wages.   But all this costs money, a great deal of money.   Financing is always a huge problem not only to the telephone engineer but more particularly to his chief, the president of his company.   It is the problem of the man who maintains and expands the telegraph; of those who labor with gas and electric heating and lighting and power plants to keep them abreast and ahead of the increasing demands of a steadily growing nation; of the builders and the operators of the steam railroads and of the street railways; of the directors of every form of public utility.   To this highly important and fundamental problem we shall give due consideration in the chapter entitled, "Financing and Regulating the Utilities."

TELEVISION

It is no unusual occurrence to find in a New York or Chicago paper a picture marked "received by radio." This means that the photograph has actually been sent, not as a piece of paper nor as a film, but as a variable electric current passing through the air or over land wires. It was another step in advance to demonstrate that by means of suitable apparatus the living, moving image of a person could be transmitted from one place to another. This is television.

Television and the transmission of pictures by wire or radio have many points in common. In an electro-mechanical system of picture transmission it is not possible to send the entire picture all at once. It has to be sent over the circuit, or through the ether, piece by piece. Similarly, in television, the scene at the transmitting end must be carried over the wires or by radio waves, bit by bit, and the received picture must be recreated piece by piece. In the case of television, the details transmitted must follow each other so rapidly that, to the eye and brain of the observer at the receiving apparatus, the effect will be that of seeing the scene reproduced as a whole. This effect is made possible by what is called the persistence of vision, which means that the eye and brain retain for an instant the impression of an object which has been seen, after the object itself has been withdrawn from the actual field of vision.

Broadly speaking, the apparatus for television consists, first, in an electro-optical device, substituted for the eye, which "looks at" the scene to be transmitted, in most cases the face of the person placed before the sending apparatus. Viewing a small portion of this scene at a time, it transforms the variations of light and shade which it "sees" into variations in the strength of an electrical current. The present form of the sending apparatus is shown in the two figures at the left of the diagram [opposite page 270]. The next factor is the transmitting medium, which may be either wire or radio waves. The third factor is the receiving apparatus, by means of which the variations of current may be transformed back into terms of light and shadow, and the picture thus reconstructed, piece by piece, and seen by the observer. A fourth and final factor is the apparatus used to keep the sending and receiving mechanisms in step.

THE SENDING APPARATUS

In actual operation, the problem of getting a piece-by-piece view of the object before the transmitting apparatus is met in this way: a strong light from the arcs, shown in the diagram, is directed upon the space occupied by the scene, in this case the face of the young woman standing, or of the young man sitting, before the apparatus. Between the source of light and the object or scene a disc is interposed. This disc is perforated with a number of small holes, arranged near its circumference in a single spiral. As the disc rotates, the light is let through in a series of spots traveling from left to right and (on account of the spiral arrangement of the holes) progressively downward, repeating the operation again and again. The disc rotates so rapidly that the whole object is lighted up, a little spot at a time, in a fifteenth of a second.

In the box-like arrangement before which the actor

is placed are three large photoelectric cells, probably the largest ever made. The ability of these cells to conduct electricity varies in direct proportion to the light falling upon them. As any particular part of the object is lighted by the traveling spot of light, the fluctuations of current thus produced in the photoelectric cells are transmitted by wire or radio, to the receiving apparatus.

In addition to this property it is equally important that the photoelectric cell possess another quality, one in which its action is radically different from that of the eye. It has already been pointed out that for the recreating of an image at the receiving end, it is necessary that the eye possess a certain sluggishness which we have called "persistence of vision." It is equally essential that the photoelectric cell possess no persistence of vision whatever. It must be instantaneous in its response and it must instantaneously "forget" the impression to which it was last subjected. Stating this in another way, if we could look at the illuminated object at the transmitter, as the photoelectric cell looks at it, we would not see a uniformly illuminated object at all, but merely a rapidly oscillating spot of light. As this spot of light passes back and forth over the object, it is reflected in varying degrees depending upon the character of the surface, and the extent to which it is reflected determines the current which the photoelectric cell emits.

WHERE THE SCENE IS RECREATED

As will be seen from the diagram, two forms of receiving apparatus are used as shown in the two right hand figures. When the image is received by

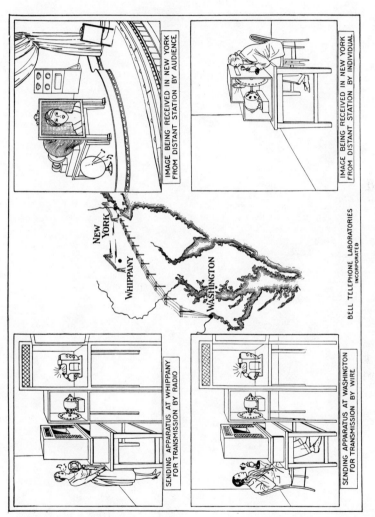

IMAGE BEING RECEIVED IN NEW YORK FROM DISTANT STATION BY AUDIENCE

IMAGE BEING RECEIVED IN NEW YORK FROM DISTANT STATION BY INDIVIDUAL

NEW YORK

WHIPPANY

WASHINGTON

BELL TELEPHONE LABORATORIES
INCORPORATED

SENDING APPARATUS AT WHIPPANY FOR TRANSMISSION BY RADIO

SENDING APPARATUS AT WASHINGTON FOR TRANSMISSION BY WIRE

TELEVISION TRANSMITTING APPARATUS.

more than one person, that shown in the upper figure is utilized.

In both forms of receiving apparatus a neon gas tube is an important element. Neon tubes, which the reader has doubtless seen used in advertising display devices, are hollow glass vessels in which the air has been replaced by neon gas at a very low pressure. Electrical discharges passing through such a tube cause it to glow, the brilliance of the light being directly proportional to the strength of the current. It will at once be appreciated that, in regard to the relation between light and electricity, the properties of a neon tube are exactly opposite to those of a photoelectric cell.

In the apparatus for use by a single individual, the entire neon tube glows according to the strength of the current being received from the transmitting station at any particular instant. The next instant the entire tube glows at a different brilliancy. Between the tube and the observer, who looks through a small aperture about two and a half inches square, there is interposed another disc exactly similar to the one at the transmitting station, rotating in step with it. The result is that the observer sees at successive instants successive portions of the field of view, each of which is illuminated by the glowing neon tube, whose brilliance fluctuates. So rapidly is the scanning of the field of vision carried out that the observer's sensation is that of seeing the scene as a whole, recreated just as it appears at the transmitting apparatus.

TELEVISION FOR LARGE GROUPS

In the apparatus for use before a large group of spectators, the neon tube is a very long, slender affair,

bent back upon itself into fifty loops forming a grid-
like square about two and a half feet on a side. Into
each loop are introduced, at regular intervals, fifty
contacts, making a total for the entire grid of 2500
contacts. These contacts are connected by wires with
a distributor which, in turn, is connected with the circuit coming from the transmitting station. The distributor revolves in step with the rotating disc at the
sending end. When a particular spot on the object
at the sending station is illuminated, its location and
light intensity are transmitted, in the form of electrical
impulses, to the receiving station, as has already been
described. In this case, however, the distributor
selects the proper connection with the neon tube and
lights a spot on the grid corresponding with the spot on
the original scene, the illumination of which set up the
impulse.

Only one spot on the grid is illuminated at a time,
but these glowing spots follow each other with such
rapidity that the audience sees the entire grid lighted
up, its degrees of illumination corresponding to those of
the original scene, thus producing a complete picture
before the eyes of the spectators. The grid may be
viewed directly or through a screen of ground glass or
other translucent material.

In keeping the mechanism of the sending and receiving apparatus in step, separate currents, or separate
waves in the case of radio transmission, are employed.
In order to insure steadiness of speed, two motors are
used at each end of the circuit. So accurately are the
sending and receiving mechanisms synchronized that
they are never out of step by more than half the width
of one of the small holes in the revolving discs, which

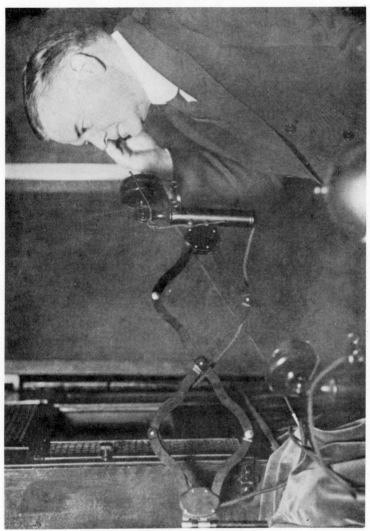

Secretary Hoover is Seen by Means of Television while Telephoning to a New York Audience.

corresponds to an interval of time of one ninety-thousandth of a second.

The electrical impulses emitted by the photoelectric cells are far too weak to carry over any considerable distance, and vacuum tube amplifiers play an important part in the operation of the television apparatus. The current sent out by radio at Whippany, for example, must be amplified 5,000 million times before it is broadcast from the antenna.

A PRODUCT OF CO-ORDINATED RESEARCH

The achievement of television in practical form, with facilities capable of transmitting over great distances, is a product of close co-operation and co-ordination of effort on the part of the members of the technical staff of the Bell Telephone Laboratories, just such team-play as has accounted for many other outstanding accomplishments in the field of telephone communication.

A series of researches and apparatus developments planned by Dr. Herbert E. Ives and carried out under his supervision by a group of his associates was necessary to bring the apparatus and technique to the point where a public demonstration seemed justified. Perhaps the most noteworthy of the contributions to the development of television, apart from those of Dr. Herbert E. Ives himself, have been made by Dr. Frank Gray and by Mr. H. M. Stoller.

Dr. Herbert E. Ives, who has many achievements in the field of research to his credit, has been connected with the Bell Telephone Laboratories since shortly after the close of the World War. Dr. Frank Gray contributed the method of scanning by a beam of light, the development of special forms of neon tubes, and the application to television of the basic principles of amplifier designs. Mr. H. M. Stoller, jointly with E. R. Morton and a group of associates, developed the method of synchronizing the sending and receiving apparatus.

What will be the economic value of television only the future can disclose. At present its status is that of an interesting experiment demonstrating the possibility of seeing across space. It may be that in time to come television will accompany telephonics in such a way that two speakers using a telephone will be able through an auxiliary apparatus each to see the other as if in actual conversation. This will tend to prevent the misunderstandings which arise when words alone convey messages without the natural interpretation given to them by facial expression. What other purposes television may be used for, it is impossible to say at present. It is an interesting invention and its development will command further attention as the years go on.

THE EXPERIMENTAL RADIO STATION OF BELL TELEPHONE LABORATORIES FROM WHICH TELEVISION BY RADIO WAS DEMONSTRATED ON APRIL 7, 1927.

CHAPTER XV

MUNICIPAL UTILITIES—STREETS AND BRIDGES

OF all the utilities of the modern city, unquestionably the most fundamentally vital to its very life and growth are the streets. Without streets it would be difficult, if not almost impossible, and most expensive, to install city railways or lighting systems, waterworks or sewage pipes, telephones or any other of our modern systems of communication. Indeed, without streets, there could hardly be a city. The one is dependent, almost absolutely, upon the other.

In the first chapters of this book we have traced the beginnings of the modern American city. We have shown how the roads or streets grow from trails, in some instances trails made by our first Americans, the Indians; how these trails gradually became more broken, more traveled, wider, more definite. Gradually, the small streams that at first interrupted their progress were overcome by *fords*, wherein horses and vehicles could cross the beds of the shallow streams with comparatively little difficulty. These fords gradually gave way to *bridges*, in early days simple affairs, usually constructed of wood, although occasionally of enduring stone.

Few of the earliest American communities had what is today known as a *city plan*. Paris, which had grown for centuries on a hit-and-miss scheme, resulting in a terrific tangle of streets and houses, under the domination of the magnificently-visioned Napoleon, was one of the first modern great cities to have a definite plan or scheme for its development, laid down in advance of its growth. The Baron Haussman worked out its details. Such broad plans were not, however, unknown among the ancients. Athens is full evidence of this.

In this country, Philadelphia probably was the first community to be laid out upon a definite city plan. The founder of Philadelphia, William Penn, in days prior to those of the great Napoleon, possessed enough foresight and vision to lay out a design of streets and open squares for the plot between the Delaware and the Schuylkill Rivers, upon which he had determined would one day rise a fine city. The exquisitely regular pattern of the streets and squares of what is now down-town Philadelphia, to this day shows the minute attention that its founder gave to the problem of the city's future development.

Savannah is another Colonial city that from the outset had a city plan, which also resulted in giving it charm and beauty and dignity as it attained its growth. Many of these qualities in that fine city today come from the broad streets and the large open parklike squares which its founders gave it nearly two centuries ago, and which have been maintained from that day to this.

Unfortunately, most of our older American cities had no such advantage of definite plan or forethought. Boston, until some eighty or ninety years ago, suffered terribly for lack of it. Her narrow, twisting streets, in some cases the gradual evolution of cowpaths, hampered both her comfort of living and her growth. The great open space of the Common, which always has been a breathing space for her, came by accident rather than by design. Yet, before it was entirely too late, she managed to develop a city plan. The result was her present-day splendid Back Bay section, with the parklike Commonwealth Avenue as its chief axis.

In a similar way, the city of New York, through nearly a century and a half of its earliest development, failed to achieve a city plan, and when it did get such a plan, along about the beginning of the last century, a very grave error, which it has never been possible to correct, was made in it. Today this century-old city plan of Manhattan is regarded as a monumental mistake. The prime need of this city for many broad avenues extending north and south, the long direction of the narrow island, was completely overlooked by its makers, with the result that the central portion of New York today possesses a superfluity of crosstown streets and a paucity of up-and-down avenues. So serious is this error that, were it not for the absolutely prohibitive cost of so doing, the city long ago would have cut additional traffic avenues north and south.

It took the courage, the brilliance and the vision of a Frenchman, Major Charles Pierre L'Enfant, schooled in the exquisite city plan of Paris, to create here in the United States, not only a well planned city, but a magnificently planned one. Our national capital, Washington, is today regarded as a world model in city planning. L'Enfant's remarkable conception of taking a rectangular block plan, such as that of Philadelphia or of Manhattan, and superimposing upon it a spiderweb design of broad, radial avenues, striking here and there and everywhere from various focal points or hubs, of which the open places holding the Capitol, the White House, and the Washington Monument, are the most conspicuous, is today regarded as a superb achievement. Even though today Washington has grown far beyond the area and the population that the far-visioned L'Enfant predicted for it, his scheme always has been closely followed in practice, as originally laid down by him for the older portions of the city, and in principle, in those portions quite outside the original mappings.

Other American cities, some of them no longer young, have followed, to a greater or lesser degree, the inspiration of the Washington plan. Among the more conspicuous examples of these may be mentioned Buffalo, Detroit and Indianapolis. Yet today there are few large cities in the United States that have not laid down a plan for their future growth. Chicago, St. Louis, Baltimore, Cleveland, Rochester, Springfield (Massachusetts), Seattle, and Hartford are but a few of the names that come to mind when one comes to enumerate those that are now making such wise provision for their future growth.

The continued expansion of our cities makes such foresight not only valuable but almost absolutely necessary. The day has passed when our communities can afford to continue to build on a hit-and-miss plan, or without any plan whatsoever. New conditions, some of them quite unforeseen, are arising continually to make demands upon our scheme of civic communication. Who, for instance, in the opening year of the present century, could have foreseen the tremendous development of the motor vehicle which has come within the last twenty-five years and which has taxed almost every American city, large or small, to find room in its streets for it? Such a single problem, in many of our communities, almost compels the entire recasting of the city plan. The civic boards which are created, not only to devise such plans but to see that town growth is made strictly in accordance with their provisions, are constantly perplexed to make provision for just this one phase of their many-sided problem.

Moreover, these boards are compelled to give much of their time and energies to a detailed supervision of the types of buildings that go up in the streets of a community that has committed itself definitely to a city plan. They must supervise and regulate, not merely the details of construction of every new or remodeled building, but the future uses for which it is designed. On certain residential streets, business may not be permitted to show its head at all, and on others, there may be only residences of a certain specified type, such as those holding but one family, or perhaps two, at the most. This is called *zoning*, and it has come to be recognized as an important and far-sighted provision of city planning. Its chief function is to preserve the fine quality of the community, seeking to separate more or less or segregate its various necessary activities, such as manufacturing, merchandising, housing and the like. Valuable, for instance, as is a gasoline filling-station, it is not often necessary that one of those highly modern minor utilities should be set down in the middle of a quiet residential street. To prevent mistakes of this sort being made, mistakes that once made cannot easily be corrected, is one of the important functions of the board or commission that supervises the practical operation of the city plan.

STREETS AND PAVEMENTS

The street, as we see it as a utility, involves in practice chiefly the matter of proper planning, not only as to location, but also as to width, gradients, curvatures and the like. Its actual construction, as well as its maintenance, usually is a comparatively simple matter. Today some form of artificial *pavement* is the demand not only for almost any form of city street, but for those streets or highways that lead off into the open country as well. For all of this the development of the motor vehicle is largely responsible.

Pavements, as such, go back many centuries. The Roman cities specialized in them. The Romans had a fine reputation as road-builders. Some of the pavements they laid in Italy twenty centuries or more ago, are still in use, stout and strong and fairly comfortable. In the Middle Ages, the art languished, and even in such great cities as London and Paris, but two hundred years ago, the street pavements were pronounced disgraceful. As a rule cobblestones were used rather generally. When they were obtainable, they were far less expensive than blocks cut from granite. But to ride over a cobblestone pavement, even in a vehicle more than ordinarily well equipped with springs, was an experience never to be sought, while the wear and tear on the wagon or carriage was a serious matter.

In this country also, cobblestones were used extensively for early city pavements. Gradually, however, the use of large *paving flags*—stones from eighteen to

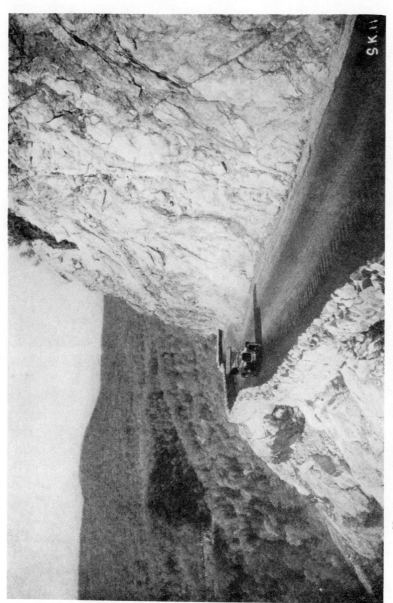

View of the Storm King Highway, along the Palisades of the Hudson River

twenty inches square, and generally set diagonally in
the street—became popular.   There was a reason for
this.   In the days when we were too wasteful of our
timber resources, many ships carried our lumber across
the oceans to lands which stood in need of wood.   These
ships, on their return trips to America, required ballast.
Paving-stones made excellent ballast.   Thousands of
tons of such stone were brought in the last century from
China to San Francisco.   In the older parts of New
Orleans, you may still see streets paved with these huge
flags.   Formerly they were common in all our seaport
cities.

Yet the flag was only relatively better than the cobblestone.   Its very size tended upon occasion to make
it slippery.   Under sleet and ice it offered extremely
hard footing for horses drawing loaded wagons.   Men
then began to cut the paving blocks into smaller units.
This made a far better pavement in every way, more
durable as well as giving better footing for horses, but
it also was vastly more expensive, both to prepare and
to put down.

Fifty years ago, brick came into use in this country
for paving.[1]   It made and still makes an excellent
pavement.   A refinement of this in Europe was the
use of wooden bricks, laid in sand and tar.[2]   In many

[1] In Tillson's *Street Pavements and Paving Material*, one finds that
brick pavements were used in Holland in the 13th century, and that
roads between The Hague and Scheveningen at a later time were paved
with the same material.   Japan is said to have had brick pavements
for more than a hundred years.   In the United States the first brick
pavements were laid in 1878, in Charleston, West Virginia.

[2] In 1839, there were 1,100 square yards of wood pavement in London, which three years later had increased to 60,000 square yards.
These earliest wood pavements consisted of hexagonal blocks of fir,
some six or eight inches across and four inches deep, laid on a founda-

ways, this last is an ideal pavement. It gives good
footing and it is almost absolutely noiseless. When
London years ago installed mile after mile of wooden
bricks within its streets, it quickly became known as
one of the quietest great cities in all the world. This,
of itself, was worth very much indeed to a huge city,
with vast street traffic at all hours.

Wood-block pavement is very expensive, however,
not only to produce, but to lay, brick by brick. It also
needs constant maintenance and repair. A real improvement came when there was discovered, chiefly in
certain portions of South America, a curious tarry sub-
stance, the result of the evaporation or oxidation of
liquid petroleum, which quickly became known as
asphalt.[1] It had many qualities that rendered it most
fit for pavement. Men began molding paving bricks
from it instead of laboriously cutting them out of wood.
Then, some years later, it was found that it was not
necessary to use the asphalt in brick form at all. Melted
in great ovens and mixed with sand or other ingredi-
ents, it could be poured out upon the street surface, to
cool, in a sheer, smooth, unbroken surface.[2] First laid in

tion of gravel. In 1872 a concrete foundation began to be used for the
blocks, which then were cut out of beech and were mineralized, by a
special process. Today the blocks, where used, are creosoted.

[1] As a matter of recorded fact, asphalt, in other forms, was used
throughout the ages. In the *Bible,* Noah was told to "pitch the Ark
with pitch." . . . While the most celebrated natural deposit of
asphalt is this South American one (on the island of Trinidad, just off
the coast of Venezuela) it is found in quantities elsewhere, notably in
our own California. The streets of European cities are paved very
largely with asphalt found in Germany, in Switzerland and upon the
island of Sicily.

[2] The modern asphalt pavement, as generally laid in this country
today, is an artificial one, containing from nine to twelve per cent of

PAVEMENT LAYING SIMPLIFIED BY USE OF MODERN EQUIPMENT.

this country at Newark, New Jersey, in 1870, this soon became the most popular form of pavement on both sides of the Atlantic. Many miles of it were laid everywhere.

More recently still another form of pavement has come into popular use, although more on highways outside of our cities than on those within them. This is concrete, long laid merely as a base or foundation for stone and brick and wood-block and asphalt surfaces. Yet the concrete, itself, makes an excellent surface for streets of every sort and of all modern pavements gives the best footing for horses. A mixture of cement and broken stone and sand, it requires no heat in its construction but is applied when freshly mixed and wet with the water used in the composition. As it "sets," it forms a sort of artificial stone, solid and unbroken, and of very great permanency. In the excavations of the early pyramids and temples of old Mexico, concrete which was applied several thousand years ago has been found, as solid and as strong as on the day it was set. Properly laid and protected against frost coming up through the ground underneath, it commends itself for strength and durability. It is for this reason, as well as for its excellent riding qualities, that more than five thousand miles of concrete roadway a year are now being laid in the United States.

BRIDGES

When the city street, or the country road, comes to a deep ravine or an open stream there is need for recourse

bitumen, the remainder being made up mostly of sand and crushed stone. It is laid upon a concrete foundation.

Sheet asphalt pavements consist generally of a wearing coat, two inches thick, composed of asphalt paving cement mixed with sand, and a "binder-course," one inch thick, of broken stone and asphalt. Again, a concrete foundation is necessary.

to some form of artificial construction to carry it over, and because it always is wise to preserve an even grade wherever it is possible, this form of construction sometimes may attain considerable length. Such construction almost always takes the form of some type of *bridge*, or *trestle* or *viaduct*.

We have seen already the early builders of our American cities using a ford where a shallow stream was to be crossed and a bridge, generally because of the expense or the difficulties in its construction, was quite out of the question. But the streams that may be crossed in this primitive fashion always are limited. A bridge is vastly more practical. In its simplest form, over a small brook, it is not difficult to construct. Upon foundations, or abutments, prepared on either bank of the stream, two or more stout timbers, or girders, are laid parallel to one another. A flooring is put down upon these, the necessary railings, to prevent people or animals stepping off accidentally, are placed, and you have the crudest form of bridge.

When the brook or small river is wider, it may become necessary to place one or more foundation *piers* midstream. Between these piers the same construction is carried forward. As the stream grows still larger, it may be found impracticable to use too many of these piers. It then is necessary to lengthen the girders—now far beyond the length of ordinary timbers—which become known as *spans*.

When single timbers became entirely too short for the fabrication of single spans, man in his ingenuity began to get the effect of a single girder by fashioning a peculiar construction of various timbers, which came to be known as a *truss*. The truss generally consists of two long girders built up of one or more *members* laid side by side, running parallel to one another and connected by upright posts and an intermediate system of latticework construction. In ordinary practice, two of these trusses were set up together and the space between them girdered and floored for the roadway of the bridge. Occasionally, three parallel trusses were used, and so a double roadway was created.

In the days of our great-grandfathers, these truss bridges were built almost entirely of wood. In order to protect them as far as possible from the snow and other deteriorating effects of the weather they usually were roofed and boarded up on their sides. They then became commonly known as *covered bridges*, and in the America of a century ago they were almost universally used. Great skill was displayed in constructing them. Sometimes they were as much as a mile long, narrow wooden tunnels, or boxes, built over a broad stream on many stout stone piers and carrying a vast traffic of men and beasts and wagons. Once in a while, as in the case of the old wooden bridge at Trenton, built by Theodore Burr, in 1804, the tracks of a railroad also were carried within the spans.

Few of these old covered bridges survive today, yet the truss type of construction that they demonstrated still is very popular with modern engineers. Fire was always a great enemy of these old structures. Moreover, the steadily increasing scarcity and cost of good lumber during the latter half of the last century, made them more and more difficult to build. In the meantime our nation was learning the wonderful possibilities of iron construction, first wrought-iron and then steel.

At the outset, iron was used only in certain places or

as certain *members*, of the truss, which continued to
be fabricated chiefly of wood. Gradually, however,
iron supplanted wood, until the truss was completely
fashioned of wrought iron. Afterwards, without essential changes in its design, it came to be built of steel.
Sometimes today the truss construction is done away
with entirely. The flexibility of steel renders it fairly
easy to make it into great girders, eighty to one hundred feet in length, or even longer, and these are sometimes placed upon the stone piers, in the simple fashion
of the very earliest bridge construction.

At other times, and particularly when the river or
gorge to be spanned is both wide and deep and so central piers are difficult or impossible, the fabricated construction of steel will take the form of a giant arch.
This form of steel bridge although very hard to put
up in the first instance, since it requires great quantities of temporary scaffolding, is not only very strong
but very beautiful. The Washington Bridge, spanning
the Harlem River, in upper New York, is a splendid
example of this form of bridge.

The arch, like the wheel, was one of the fundamental
inventions that laid the very foundations of the inven-
tive progress of all civilization. The *arched bridge of
stone* goes almost if not entirely, as far back into an-
tiquity as the simple one fashioned from a pair of logs
thrust down over a narrow brook. The stone-arch
bridges of the Romans are still to be found in Italy,
as well as in the other nations which they dominated.
Ofttimes, when the bridge attained length, multiples
of the arches were used. In fact some of the aqueducts
leading into the old city of Rome were for miles a succession of high and narrow arches, built either of stone

THE PLUSHMILL'S MEMORIAL BRIDGE NEAR PHILADELPHIA.

or of brick. Similar aqueducts are to be found on this continent, built by the Spaniards in Mexico. Once in a while the early bridges were built with tiers of multiple arches superimposed, the one upon the other. Such a construction is the Pont du Gard in the south of France, built two thousand years ago by the Romans to bring water to the nearby city of Nimes. This bridge today carries an important highway and is apparently as sound and as good as in the day when it was first completed.

In this country, stone bridges have never been quite as prevalent or as commonly used as in Europe, although there are in the United States many fine evidences of this superb and permanent form of engineering construction. One of the greatest single stone arches in the world is the Cabin John Bridge, just outside the city of Washington, built primarily to carry an aqueduct with the water supply for the capital. Stone-arch bridges, for both highways and railroads, are still being built in this country, some of them of monumental size.

Yet, in very recent years here in the United States this arched form of bridge is being constructed more and more frequently of concrete. The ease and the rapidity with which this highly permanent form of building material may be put into place counts much in favor of it. Moreover, it is easily susceptible of fine decorative treatment. Many of the fine new concrete bridges and viaducts of this country today rank among its monumental architectural structures.

The final form of bridge deserves a few paragraphs in these pages. Where a river or gorge is entirely too deep and too wide to admit of piers, and so of any ordi-

nary type of arch construction, engineers must try their
wits to find some other form of practical construction.
Sometimes, as at Niagara and Quebec, they have used
steel in a highly ingenious and delicately balanced structure, into which the simple truss frequently is combined
with that which is known as a *cantilever*, but more often
they fall back upon another early form of bridge, the
suspension-bridge.

This last type of construction goes back to the days
when primitive man wove ropes himself and suspended
them across a stream, fastening them perhaps to stout
trees near the shore.   Between them he might easily
swing the floor of a practical bridge.   As his prowess
increased, the detailed problem of this sort of bridge
also increased.   But its solution never was quite impossible.   When iron came into its own and men found
they might weave immensely strong ropes or cables
from it, by using multiples of wires, it became easily
possible to build suspension bridges of great size.

Such a bridge was the structure which Telfair built
across the Straits of Menai, in Wales, more than a
hundred years ago and which still continues to carry
the heavy traffic of an extraordinarily busy highway.
In America, John A. Roebling, of Trenton, New Jersey, seventy-five years ago became expert in this very
practical and very artistic form of bridge construction.
He had built other types first, of which one of the most
notable was the iron tubular Victoria Bridge, two miles
long and spanning the St. Lawrence River at Montreal,
since supplanted by the present modern structure.   He
also built a wonderful suspension bridge over the Ohio
at Wheeling, West Virginia, which, after having once
been blown down in a gale, was recovered, made fast,

The Old Suspension Bridge at Lewiston, Below Niagara Falls.

and restored to usefulness again. A similar bridge was placed over the same river further down, at Cincinnati, and it, too, still remains in busy service.

But Roebling's first great triumph was the famous suspension bridge over the gorge of the Niagara which he completed at the middle of the last century. Here he was confronted with a peculiar problem,—how to get the very beginnings of his bridge structure across the river from the one bank to the other. The usual method of sending a boat over with the cable was impossible in the raging torrent of the Niagara, and so Roebling flew a kite, from the United States to Canada. The kite came to the ground on the far side of the gorge. The string upon which it had been flown was used to pull heavier strings across, ropes more and more heavy, until finally an iron cable was stretched across, after which there came more and more cables. Then the weaving and rearing of the superstructure of the bridge was a comparatively easy and simple matter.

But Roebling's greatest triumph, the bridge that was to give him world-wide fame, was the so-called Brooklyn Bridge, the first to span the mighty and the busy East River which formerly separated from each other the erstwhile separate cities of New York and Brooklyn. This tremendous structure was begun a half century ago and was opened in May, 1883. During its construction, both Roebling and his son died, the task being finished by the grandson of the great engineer. For more than forty years, it has carried the greatest traffic of any bridge in all the world; and it still stands nobly to its task.

Across that same East River, in more recent years, three other great bridges, two of them suspension, the third cantilever, have come to join the parent city of New York, the borough of Manhattan, with the boroughs on the other side of the busy stream. While, in recent years these bridges have still more recently been supplemented by railroad tunnels, great credit is given to them for the upbuilding of the present great metropolitan city of New York.

The year 1927 saw the opening at Buffalo of another great bridge across the Niagara River between Canada and the United States, fittingly called the "Peace Bridge." A bridge will always stand in the estimation of mankind as a symbol of harmony and goodwill. Whether it spans a river within the confines of a nation or a river that marks an international boundary, it means that people separated by a natural barrier have overcome the difficulty, and by means of the bridge have united their commercial and their social interests. Thus bridges play their part in furthering communication and understanding among people and in establishing peace and prosperity.

BROOKLYN BRIDGE VIEWED FROM THE MANHATTAN SIDE.

CHAPTER XVI

MUNICIPAL UTILITIES—WATER, SEWERAGE AND PARKS

STREETS and, to a large extent, bridges, once built, need comparatively little maintenance. A city's *water supply* is different. Not only must there be a natural, uncontaminated, adequate and always dependable *source* of pure water, but to keep it efficient and dependable, *reservoirs* and *aqueducts* and *pipes*, *pumps* and *meters* and *filters* and much other mechanical equipment must be supplied and operated all the while. The problem, more closely than those that have just gone before, approximates that of the great privately owned and operated utilities, especially gas and electric lighting and power and heating, telephones and street railways. Because water supply is a highly specialized utility, requiring much constant service, in addition to the large original outlay for plant, American cities, although almost everywhere owning these plants, make charges for their services, quite apart from the ordinary taxes, which go to support every form of municipal endeavor.

The city, in its own enterprises, is by no means immune from the great problems of financing that continually confront the privately owned and operated utility. Its expenditures, not merely for water supply, but for its other activities, almost always very large, divide themselves into four principal groups: current expenses, debt service, utility expenses and capital outlay.

While we are upon this question of expenditure, a few brief paragraphs of explanation in regard to the financing problem of the modern American city may not come amiss. The four groups above mentioned may in turn be amplified or explained as follows:

Current expenses are those involved in the administration of general service rendered to the public, such as police and fire protection, health service, street cleaning, etc.

Debt service represents the carrying charges of interest and redemption on indebtedness incurred by the municipality.

Utility expenses are those involved in operating municipal enterprises such as water works, public markets, illuminating plants and other similar enterprises, the revenues from which usually are sufficient to pay all costs of operation.

Capital outlays are those made for projects, generally new, which result in an addition to asset or capital worth. Under this class are included such items as land, buildings, street improvements and the like.

Ordinarily, the current expense and debt service charges of a city are financed through the municipal budget, the greatest amount of revenue to finance them being obtained through direct taxation. Generally, a considerable amount of other revenue is received which is applied to the financing of these two items. These revenues tend to reduce the total amount levied in direct taxation. The latter revenues are obtained from various sources, such as state grants and state aid, departmental earnings, interest, licenses, fees, etc.

The utility expenses are financed by income received from the rates charged to the users of the particular service furnished. The rates are expected to be sufficient to pay all operating expenses, debt service, and depreciation of the utility.

Capital outlays generally are financed by bond issues. Improvements which are made by the city and which involve an assessment against the property benefited, are usually met by bonds and the receipts from collections on assessments apply toward the paying off of the indebtedness. Bonds for improvements of a general nature, charged against the city at large, are paid off from taxation and other revenue sources. The bonds may be retired by the sinking fund or serial method.

Nearly every city in America is restricted in some way in its power to tax and to borrow. Into the state constitutions, general laws, and city charters, have been written many provisions, the purpose of which is to safeguard the taxpayers against unwise and extravagant spending. The two most important limitations are the tax and debt limits. In general, tax limits have not been effective, but the debt limits have. These limitations, as a general rule, are expressed in a certain percentage of the assessed value of property. With the curtailment of public improvements during the war and the enormous demand for improvements since, municipalities have experienced considerable difficulty in meeting these demands and at the same time keeping their finances solvent.

With these things in mind, we now turn to the specific civic problem of municipal water-works.

THE BEGINNINGS OF PUBLIC WATER-WORKS

We have seen in a previous chapter how the Romans built great aqueducts, running for miles all the way across the open plain that surrounds Rome, to bring that city pure water, not only for drinking, cooking, bathing, but for the splashing fountains that for centuries have been the most cooling and refreshing delight in all the Eternal City. We have seen, too, how the Spanish conquerors, four hundred years ago, introduced the same system into the ancient city of Mexico, which they tore down and then rebuilt. Some of these aqueducts still are bringing the pure cold water of the mountains down into Mexico city.

In the United States the production of a public water supply, a definite utility, goes back nearly three hundred years, to a crude system in Boston, of which, however, few definite records are available. Two Pennsylvania communities, Schaefferstown in about 1732, and Bethlehem in 1761, were the next to show a civic attempt of this sort. It is recorded[1] that the Bethlehem works, which included the first pumps to be used in America, were begun in 1754 and finished seven years later "after severe struggles, by Hans Christopher Christiansen, a millwright and native of Denmark, the first water-supply engineer of record in America."

The older portions of the city of New York were fortunate in being built upon an island that fairly abounded in springs gushing forth the purest sort of water imaginable. These, and private wells, served it as a water supply for a hundred years. Then the growing community began to outstrip the supply.

[1] *The Manual of American Water-Works.*

In 1774 a reservoir was built between Prince and White Streets, east of Broadway. Into this, water was pumped from the wells, after which it was distributed in wooden pipes through the city. Its capacity was soon reached, however, and, but four years later, a committee of citizens recommended that the Rye Pond in Westchester be made into a reservoir, by building a dam, and that its water be brought to a city distributing reservoir through iron pipes, which would cross the Harlem River on a bridge. To this end, the Manhattan Water-Works were chartered as a private corporation, but the company got no further than to establish a bank and build a small reservoir in Chambers Street. The bank still continues, but the water-works were soon abandoned.

The beginning of the past century saw but seventeen water-works systems in the United States. It was not until 1825 that this number was doubled, while until 1850 there were still less than a hundred in the whole country. By 1875, there were but 243. The thousand mark was passed in 1885. Today it is estimated that more than ten thousand communities in the United States, and 750 in Canada, have their public water-works. The thing was a gradual development, but, once developed, grew rapidly.

Baltimore had water-works in 1804, and Philadelphia began them in 1819. In the latter city, a dam, 1248 feet in length, was placed across the Schuylkill River and pumps lifted the water from the river, fifty feet, to a reservoir in Fairmount Park, of 22,031,976 "ale gallons" capacity. These water-works were first placed in service July 1, 1822, and they speedily became one of the sights of the town.

NEW YORK'S WATER-WORKS

New York, after her first unsuccessful efforts, followed more slowly. It took several pestilences and the great and disastrous fire of 1834 to arouse her to the real necessity of water supply protection. Then she attacked the problem with all of her energy and financial resources and produced a real water-works system. She returned to the idea of going far north of Manhattan Island, and decided upon the Croton watershed, some thirty miles distant, as the proper source of her future supply of abundant and absolutely pure water. This, ninety years ago, was a tremendous undertaking, even for a city as large as the New York of that day. It involved the damming of the Croton River into a mighty artificial lake, or *reservoir*, five miles in length and the construction for miles of an artificial stone pipe or conduit or aqueduct, shaped like a horseshoe, 8½ feet in height and 7½ feet wide. To carry this great pipe on its way from Croton Lake to Central Park, across the Harlem River, involved the construction of High Bridge, which to this day remains as one of the remarkable stone-arch bridges of the continent. Twenty-five lesser streams were crossed.

At the Manhattan end of High Bridge, a lofty *high-pressure tower* was installed, while in Central Park a central distributing reservoir was built, with a secondary one in Fifth Avenue, between Fortieth and Forty-second Streets, on the present site of the New York Public Library. The total capacity of all these reservoirs was 31,000,000 gallons and it was felt that it would be at least a hundred years before their capacity would be reached.

The work of providing for and building this system

was completed in 1842. The water was turned on July 4th, amid the greatest enthusiasm of the people. In September of that year, there was a military and civic procession eight miles long, a vast amount of fire works and other forms of celebration.

Yet, within forty years the city had completely outgrown even this generous means of water supply. The original aqueduct, designed to carry some 60,000,-000 gallons of water a day, was being compelled to bring nearly 100,000,000 gallons. But even that was not nearly enough. The upper stories of the high buildings of the 'eighties, and even those of residences standing on elevated ground, could get no water at all while the limited storage capacity of the reservoirs afforded no real reserve against the possibilities of long dry spells and water famine.

So it was that in 1885 a second aqueduct was built to the city from Croton Lake,—this one with a flowing capacity of 300,000,000 gallons a day. In certain sections it is of horseshoe form, and in others it is circular, and it varies from twelve to thirteen feet in diameter. No second High Bridge was necessary to carry this aqueduct across the navigable and busy Harlem River. Engineering science, by the 'eighties, had reached the point where it was possible to burrow for the new conduit under and through the rock bed of the river, forming a U-shaped tunnel or *siphon*. To help accommodate this new water supply, a new storage reservoir was built, in the borough of the Bronx, upon the site of a former race track.

Great cities, like New York, habitually refuse to "stay put" and so it was that, at the beginning of the present century, that vast metropolitan community again was rapidly outstripping its water supply. Thousands of new hotels and apartment-houses and private dwellings were being constructed, in many cases with a bathroom to each sleeping room. No one denies that bathrooms, and the cleanly habits of daily bathing that they induce, are tremendous helps to the health of the community, but they require, in the aggregate, large additional quantities of water. In fifty years, the average daily consumption of water of the New Yorker has jumped from forty to one hundred and thirty gallons a day. This includes all the manifold uses of fresh water,—for drinking, for cooking, for cleansing, for industrial enterprise, and as the one real resource against the ever-present danger of fire.

To give the metropolitan city of New York (which has come to include the former cities of Brooklyn, Williamsburg, Jamaica, Flushing, Long Island City, Astoria and other early separate communities) adequate and generous water supply for these uses became a tremendous problem. After much thought, it was solved by going, not thirty, but one hundred miles away, into the very heart of the verdant Catskill Mountains.

At a point but a few miles back of Kingston, New York, on the west bank of the Hudson, a huge dam, a mile in length and at points more than 300 feet in height was built, a few years ago, and an artificial lake in two sections, together nearly twenty-five miles in length, was created behind this dam. Filled, this lake, now known as Ashokan Reservoir, has a capacity of 128,-000,000,000 gallons. It is fed by Esopus Creek and its many tributaries.

The aqueduct which connects the Ashokan with the

Ashokan Reservoir, Catskill Mountains. One of the Reservoirs of the Water Supply System of the City of New York.

city, almost an even hundred miles distant, is seventeen feet in height and ten feet wide. It has a flowing capacity of 500,000,000 gallons a day. In order that this may be better estimated, consider a city street of ordinary width, filled with water nearly to the height of a man's shoulder, which flows forward at about the same pace that a man ordinarily would walk.

The Ashokan Aqueduct crosses under, not merely the Harlem, but the far mightier Hudson. In each case, the huge siphon dips far below the ordinary level of the earth. For crossing the Hudson, the narrowest portion of the lower river in the Highlands just below Newburgh was chosen. In this narrow passageway, the river is extremely deep. By means of diamond drills boring far down into the rock, the precise depth of the river, until then always a matter of guesswork, finally was established and the water tunnel brought well under it, at a depth below the surface of the river of about 1,100 feet. Yet the tunnel, prior to the turning of the mountain waters through it, was so dry that a man could easily walk through it without wetting his feet.

The great capacity of the Ashokan, tremendous as it is, has not been found, of itself, sufficient to meet the steady growth of metropolitan New York. So, five or six years ago (1920), workmen began burrowing still further into the Catskills, in order that the city might always have its full-sized drink of water. This time, they went to the western slope of those mountains, the side farthest from the Hudson, took the Schoharie River, which from time immemorial has flowed north into the Mohawk, and deliberately turned its course toward the east. To do this, at the small village of Gilboa, another huge dam was erected. The reservoir that it impounded was made to pour its waters into the Esopus Creek and the Ashokan Reservoir, by means of a connecting tunnel—the Shandaken, eighteen miles in length and one of the longest bores in the world.

The problem of a proper water supply for a great and growing city is at all times a terrific one. Growth must be anticipated always; it would be absolutely fatal to permit the city to be caught with an inadequate water supply even for a month, or a week, or a day. Pestilence, or devastating fire, might come and the helpless city, without proper water protection, would go down quickly before it.

So the modern American city looks forward always to its water supply. When the water resources of the Catskills have been exhausted, or at least as much taken from them as can be spared from the needs of their local communities, New York City may find itself compelled to turn toward the more distant Adirondacks, or, what is far more likely, toward Lake Ontario, with its almost inexhaustible supply of fresh water.

The question of abundant supply is not the only one to come into consideration. There arises with it always the equally great one of purity. Drinking water, if polluted, may easily give rise to terrible epidemics of typhoid fever and other serious diseases. A small community, sometimes even a farmhouse on the bank, with its waste, may quickly pollute even a sizable river or lake. There used to be a tradition that water purified itself in the course of a few miles of transit, but this has been proved to be a tradition and but little more.

THE PURITY OF WATER SUPPLY

We have anticipated. We shall go back to the beginnings of the water-works development here in the United States. The problem of the city of New York has been, in greater or less degree, that of almost every one of the ten thousand communities in the land that have now come to find these works of the greatest necessity to their health and preservation. The larger early cities were, quite naturally, the first to avail themselves of water-works. We have seen Boston and Baltimore and Philadelphia, as well as New York, struggling with the problem. As New York went to the Croton in 1842 so Boston went, six years later, to the Cochituate. When, like the Croton, the Cochituate was exhausted, Boston went fifty miles to the west and built the great Wachusett Reservoir, back of Worcester, today the chief source of her pure water supply. In the case of Boston, closely surrounded by a group of sizable but independent municipalities, it became necessary at that time to prepare a water-works system jointly with other Massachusetts cities. Under the guidance of a state commission, this was arranged.

In the interior of the land, Rochester, New York, was one of the first cities to achieve pure water supply. From a rather tardy beginning, the city by the Genesee made rapid progress in the development of water-works that quickly became world famous because of the brilliancy of their fundamental idea. All this was more than half a century ago. For some years previous, the then small Western New York City, realizing that the Genesee, filled with silt and dirt, was not fit for drinking purposes, had been turning its attention toward certain of the so-called Finger Lakes, thirty miles to'the south. Of these, Hemlock Lake seemed to be best fitted for its use. But the building of thirty miles of conduit or aqueduct promised to be such an expensive business for a small city, that for twenty years the project was deferred. It was not until January, 1876, that the pure waters of Hemlock Lake finally were turned into the houses of Rochester, abundant reservoir facilities having been provided, both on a ridge just south of the city and on the top of a hill at Rush, almost equidistant between the city and the lake. [1]

Two things enabled Rochester to take this great step forward in American water-works progress. In the first place, she decided not to attempt to bring from Hemlock the huge quantities of water that would be

[1] The city of Rochester also acquired the right to use the waters of Canadice Lake, the neighbor of Hemlock. This lake is the same depth as Hemlock and about one-third the area. The water from these lakes is brought to the city through three conduits. (Conduit I, laid in 1873-6, consists of cast iron and wrought iron pipe; Conduit II, constructed in 1893-4, of riveted steel pipe and a six-foot masonry section extending for 12,000 feet from Hemlock Lake; and Conduit III, cast iron and steel, constructed in 1913-18.)

There are now three artificial reservoirs, one at Rush, about nine miles from the city, and two within the city limits—Highland, constructed in 1875, and Cobb's Hill Reservoir, of greater capacity, but at the same elevation, completed in 1908.

As the population of Rochester doubles about every twenty-five years, the increased use of water demands the utilization of some additional source. The present conduits are of a capacity sufficient for the yield of the watersheds now in use. Further water supply for the city can be had by pumping from Lake Ontario, or even from the Genesee River, or by gravity from other lakes or gathering grounds lying at a higher topographical elevation south of the city. In general, if not too far-distant, a gravity supply is to be preferred.

necessary for her fire protection. The waters of the Genesee were quite efficient for that purpose. So an entirely separate system of water mains, with the necessary hydrant outlets for fire hose, was provided, and great pumps set up in a pumping station, to lift the water out of the river into the mains.

With the volume of water so lessened by the provision of a separate fire-fighting supply, it was possible to bring the first aqueduct from Hemlock down to reasonably small dimensions, in fact to fabricate it out of riveted wrought-iron pipe. In that day this was much of a novelty, although such pipes had been used successfully in San Francisco some years before, and in fact a crude coated form of iron pipe had appeared at Saratoga Springs as long before as 1845. In earlier days things moved slowly. For example, it was not until 1892 that the city of Newark, New Jersey, laid the first sizable steel conduit, 42 inches in diameter, and found it entirely feasible. Steel conduit has been much used in water-works since then.

In far more recent years, the city of Los Angeles, compelled by its remarkable growth to go very far afield for pure water, has laid several hundred miles of an even larger diameter of this conduit, back into the high places of the Sierras, with their abundant supplies of magnificent water. All California cities have been to an extent handicapped by the lack of large and dependable rivers near by for their growing water demands. San Francisco, which originally found plenty in the springs and fresh water ponds of "the Peninsula" right at its back door, finally has been compelled to go away across the Bay and also to resort to the Sierras, to the isolated and beautiful Hetch-Hetchy Valley.

Purity comes ahead even of dependability;—the ability of a lake or stream or watershed to furnish abundant water even in seasons of long and continued drought. To keep a city's water supply absolutely pure at all times is the first desire of the water-works engineer. Primarily, this is accomplished by making sure that the lake, stream or watershed from which the city gets its supply is uncontaminated; that this supply is not near towns, villages or any groupings of human habitations, nor factories or other buildings that would tend in the least degree to pollute the water so that if not rendered absolutely undrinkable, still it might leave secret sources of possible disease and pestilence.

Yet in a nation which is growing as rapidly and as steadily as the United States, where already great sections of the land approximate in their congestion of towns and villages the more crowded portions of Europe, the water-works engineer cannot always find his dependable supply of such unquestioned purity. Then he must erect safeguards in another way. We live in an age of remarkable chemical development. Chemistry today is doing things for civilization that would have been deemed impossible one hundred, or even fifty, or even twenty-five years ago. It is known today that chemical process can take polluted or unclean water and make it practically as pure for human consumption as the finest stream that ever came bubbling out of a mountainside.

Even a full half century ago, they were experimenting in water purification. As far back as 1870, towns in certain parts of the United States were beginning to grow uncomfortably close together; streams which they

A Method of Aerating a City's Water Supply.

had shared in common and which they had regarded as at least reasonably pure were becoming more and more polluted.

The Hudson River, for example, in the memory of men still living, was remarkable for its annual springtime yield of shad (and the shad is a fish particularly partial to pure, clean water), but for the past thirty-five or forty years the Hudson has ceased to be the habitation of these delicious fish. Many sizable and growing towns formerly pumped their water supply from this river. Epidemics of typhoid and other serious and devastating diseases finally began to convince them, however, that the river was fast losing its purity. Then it was that we took a lesson from England and at Poughkeepsie in 1870, and five years later at Hudson, New York, there were installed slow *sand-filters*, of a type that had already been used successfully in Great Britain. But their slowness always stood against them, and so it was that, when, in the late 'eighties, rapid filters of improved mechanical construction were introduced, they came into large use. Large-sized cities, such as Philadelphia and Pittsburgh, began to make extensive use of them.

Where the mechanical filter is not enough, of itself, to secure the purity demanded by public health officers, chemical processes come into vogue. Chlorination, as the usual process is called, accomplishes wonders. A notable instance of its possibilities is in Eastern Massachusetts and Rhode Island, where sewage from the large industrial city of Worcester is turned into the Blackstone River, which is then purified by chemical process before reaching cities along the course of that stream. This point we shall consider in a little more detail when we come to the general subject of sewage disposal.

In the meantime, it may be added here that the community which has a pure water supply—pure at the source—still has a distinct advantage over the one which must always depend upon artificial purification, no matter how thorough the method. This is the thing that New York and Los Angeles and San Francisco and certain other very large cities of America have obtained by going far back into the mountains even at prodigious expense. Rochester secured it by going to Hemlock Lake and Syracuse later on when she followed the example of her sister city and reached back into Skaneateles Lake. Rochester now has from Lake Ontario an additional water supply pumped, filtered and distributed by the Rochester and Lake Ontario Water Company, a private corporation.

The handling of the water ofttimes involves large mechanical plants, although in these instances just given, the water comes chiefly, if not entirely, by gravity and so accomplishes a vast economy in its handling. We have already seen Christiansen nearly two centuries ago setting up his pumps at the small colonial city of Bethlehem, Pennsylvania. Since that day *pumping stations* have come to a high state of development indeed. Often they are worked by steam-power, not infrequently by electric, but where it is possible, water-power is used, sometimes generated by the fall of the very stream which is being used as the water source.

Because great and unending dependence must be placed upon such pumps, the equipment is always at least in duplicate. In other words, one set of the tireless pumps may break down, or be shut down for

inspection, cleansing and repair, while the other set
or sets go throbbing on their patient work for the
city's life and health and comfort. For the same reason, duplicate conduits and mains are used wherever
possible; and in the reservoirs, especially when artificial, there are generally duplicate basins, each of which
can be filled or emptied, independently of the other.
Elaborate systems of gates, in many instances mechanically or electrically operated, permit a free interchange in the use of all these systems, and in the use,
continual or seasonal, of multiple systems of filters.

One essential thing is, always and at all times, dependable continuity of water supply. To meet this
highly necessary end, the American city makes every
effort in the world, and many sacrifices too. We have
seen long since the vital necessity of the gas company's
maintaining constant pressure in its mains. The necessity is not less in the conduits of the city water-works.
An hour without adequate water supply or pressure
might be the very hour in which fire, the most devastating thing physically that we ordinarily know, might
break out and be swept by the wind into a terrible con-
flagration. The best fire department in the world
can accomplish little or nothing without abundant
water supply and pressure. Too many bitter experiences of the past go to make full proof of this statement.

SEWERAGE

When a community consists of a few scattered dwellings, the household wastes are readily disposed of either
on the ground or by lightly covering with soil. When
a water supply is introduced, together with household

plumbing, the water-carried wastes require a different treatment. Ordinarily, at first, such treatment consists either in conducting the liquid wastes into a closed vault or *cesspool*, in which the organic solids are, to some extent, liquefied while the liquid leaches away in the surrounding earth and the resultant solids are later removed and buried, or else the crude wastes are conducted by a subterranean pipe to the nearest flowing stream.

When the dwellings become more numerous and the territory is more densely occupied, these small streams are liable to create a nuisance, to avoid which they are covered or replaced by closed conduits, which not only conduct away the household wastes which enter through the branch sewers, but also carry, as in their former open conditions, rain and flood waters tributary to them.

As the American city grows, so grows the size and number of these great hidden drainage systems. Moreover, it must be remembered always that the very nature of the growing community is likely to throw increased burdens upon its sewerage. One point alone will illustrate. In the modern city the sewers must be built large enough to remove not only ordinary waste day by day, but storm waters, in the case of a sudden rain, or a torrential downpour. In older American cities, there still were left many open spaces of earth —lawns, open squares, dirt streets and the like. These, after a heavy rain, did their part in absorbing much of the precipitated moisture. Today, not only have buildings encroached more and more all the while upon open spaces of every sort, but the almost universal use of hard paving in the streets has increased the proportion

of impervious surface. So in the curbs of every paved
street there must be frequent sizable *outlets* into the
sewers underneath, with generous gutters to lead toward
all of these outlets; otherwise, a heavy storm could
easily produce conditions very similar to those of a
flood or a freshet.

No wonder then that even moderate-sized cities
today possess sewers, or giant tunnels running mile after
mile, through which a man might easily walk with
head erect without touching the top of their linings.
Years ago it was considered one of the tourist sights of
Paris to take a trip in a boat in the tremendous sewers
that run in every direction far under the streets of that
great city. American cities have not made their
sewers into sight-seeing affairs, but many of them have
these vast hidden waterways in which a boat with
passengers might ride for long distances indeed. Naturally as all of these sewers begin to converge and to
lead toward their common destination they grow to
their largest dimensions. Then it is that they begin
to be known as *trunk sewers.*

The question of that common destination is a problem in itself, an increasing one, as the land grows more
and more congested. If there is a steadily running
river of ample size near at hand, it probably will be
chosen for the sewage disposal, if possible at a point
well below the community. A large lake is ofttimes
taken. The Great Lakes have helped solve the problem for many of the cities that line their shores.

Yet there is another side to all of this, and it cannot
be ignored. The river which flows by one town and
which receives its sewage, may flow by other towns
further down its course, may even be their reliance for

drinking and other water supply. These other towns naturally do not relish the thought of drinking, even though remotely, the sewage of neighboring communities. We saw this problem lifting its head a moment ago when we were studying the purity of the water supply of the American city.[1] Even such vast inland seas as the Great Lakes are not wholly immune from the possibilities of pollution. The cities that must use their waters have the *intakes* of the waterworks as far from the shore as possible, in some cases as much as three miles out.

It is as an added precaution therefore against the further pollution of our inland streams and lakes, that our more progressive cities have sought, more and more, to destroy their sewage by mechanical or chemical processes, rather than to continue to pour it out, either into the water or upon the land. Sometimes this has been done under the initiative or order of the state health boards, which must consider the rights and needs of whole groups of communities, more or less interrelated. More often, however, it has been done because our modern American city has vast pride in its innate cleanliness and decency; this, in so many words, means that it does not feel that it has a right to pile its waste in the backyard of its neighbor. So it creates huge disposal stations into which the sewers empty and which, in their main functions, are not unlike the private cesspool or septic tank formerly operated by the individual householder, and by him generally both feared and hated.

[1] We also saw then that the city of Worcester was making provision by means of a chemical process for purifying the Blackstone River, flowing from it toward the sea.

SEWAGE DISPOSAL

Various methods in the past have been used in an attempt to clarify sewage wastes. The following outline presents the modern view of sanitary sewage disposal:

FIRST. The separation of solids and liquids.
A Removal of coarse floating and suspended matter by racks and screens.
B Removal of heavy grit by grit chambers.
C The removal of settleable solids and from forty to ninety per cent of the suspended solids by sedimentation in tanks.

The following definitions were published by the American Public Health Association in 1924:

Tank. A chamber, vat or basin through which sewage passes, or in which it is detained during its collection or treatment.

Sedimentation Tank. One in which sewage or effluent is detained long enough or in which the velocity is low enough to allow partial deposition of suspended matter but without intended anaërobic action.

Hydrolytic Tank. General term for any sedimentation tank in which, by biological processes, a portion of the suspended organic matter is liquefied and gasified.

Travis Tank. A two-storied hydrolytic tank invented by Dr. Travis, consisting of an upper sedimentation chamber with steeply sloping bottom terminating in slots through which the deposited solids pass into the lower or sludge digesting chamber. Through the latter a predetermined portion of the sewage is allowed to pass for the purpose of seeding and maintaining bacterial life in the sludge and carrying away decomposition products. This is for the purpose of inducing digestion of the sludge attended by its reduction in volume.

Imhoff Tank. A deep two-storied tank invented by Dr. Karl Imhoff, consisting of an upper or continuous sedimentation chamber and a lower or sludge digestion chamber. The floor of the upper chamber slopes steeply to trapped slots through which solids may settle into the lower chamber. The lower chamber receives no fresh sewage but is provided with gas vents and with means for drawing digested sludge from near the bottom.

SECOND. The treatment and disposal of solids.

A Screenings may be disposed of by incineration, by composting for fertilizer, or removed as garbage, in which case they may be buried, burned or reduced.

B Grit from properly constructed and operated grit chambers is usually inoffensive and may be used for filling.

C Sludge may be lagooned or dried in furrows and covered, or it may be digested in the bottom of the Imhoff tank or in separate digestion tanks, after which it may be dried on beds and used for fertilizer or for filling.

THIRD. Treatment and disposal of liquid. The liquid portion of sewage should ordinarily be oxidized to prevent nuisance due to further decomposition. This may be done by

A Dilution in lakes and streams where sufficiently isolated and sufficient water is available.

B Broad irrigation where the effluent is turned upon land growing crops.

C Filters where the effluent is passed through large areas of sand.

D Biological treatment in contact beds, on trickling filters or by the activated sludge process.

Contact Bed. An artificial bed of coarse material such as broken stone or clinkers in a water-tight basin provided with controlled inlet and outlet. It is operated in cycles of filling with sewage, standing full in contact, emptying and resting empty, in order to remove some of the suspended matter and oxidize organic matter by bio-chemical agencies.

Trickling Filter. An artificial bed of coarse material such as broken stone, clinkers, slate, slats or brush over which sewage is distributed and applied by drops, films or sprays from troughs or drippers, moving distributors or fixed nozzles and through which it trickles to the under drains giving opportunity for organic matter to be oxidized by bio-chemical agencies.

Activated Sludge Process. Sewage treatment in which sewage standing in or flowing through a tank is brought into intimate contact with air and with biologically active sludge previously produced by the same process. The effluent is subsequently clarified by sedimentation.

Sludge. Semi-liquid and largely organic sewage solids as deposited in tanks or as subsequently treated.

Effluent. Sewage, partially or completely treated, flowing out of any sewage treatment device.

An example of a large Imhoff tank installation is the Irondequoit Sewage Disposal Plant of Rochester, New York, put into operation in 1917, at which time the plant contained the largest installation of this type yet constructed. Rochester also has three other Imhoff tank plants, the Brighton Plant, put in operation March 1, 1916, where the tank is followed by a trickling filter, the Charlotte Plant put in operation in 1921 and University District plant, put in operation in 1924. The largest plant employing the activated sludge process has been constructed by the city of Milwaukee.

GARBAGE DISPOSAL

Other forms of city waste necessitate some attention at this time. They include the material which the householder formerly burned himself, although in most towns he probably would now go to jail if he attempted to do that very thing today. When American towns became big enough to begin to organize their civic enterprises at all, they began the collection of this larger waste—old paper boxes, bottles, food-garbage, even discarded clothing and pieces of furniture no longer of sufficient value even for the second-hand dealer or the junkman. Under instructions the householder now divides his heavier waste—far too large, all of it, to be disposed of in the drainage pipes—into three major classifications. Food-garbage, which is subject to quick decay, is set aside in separate containers from the two other forms of waste, ashes and rubbish.

Today in the modern city groups of men with tank-wagons make regular visits to the householders, at intervals of once a week or less, and gather up all of this waste from the containers that for their convenience are set out at the street curb. These collections still keep the waste in the two classifications. The more or less imperishable waste is carted to what is generally known as the city dump, where men and women scour it carefully for almost any articles of value that may have been thrown out in the household discard, after which it will be, as far as possible, burned. The food-garbage (swill) is placed automatically in great containers in a mechanical and chemical plant which does strange things with it. From it come valuable commercial products, among them essential

Trickling Filters of One of Rochester's Sewage Disposal Plants.

oils, which eventually may find their way into the making of soaps and of perfumes. We have ceased to be a nation of wasters. No source is too mean, too small, to be worth attention as a possible producer of commercial products.

PARKS

A more fascinating aspect of the American city than its sewage disposal, is its provision for parks. The importance of these to the sizable community may be judged from the fact that more than once have they been referred to as the "lungs of the city." They are its breathing places, where its citizens may go for quiet, for rest, for recreation.

Parks have been among the most recent of the municipal utilities, if indeed one may even call them a utility, to be developed here in America. Foreign cities, coming to their growth much more quickly than ours, long ago found the need of such open spaces. The fact that the cities of old Europe were always far more densely built than ours made some sort of "lungs" an essential to them whole centuries ago. The military scheme of their existence also called for large open places close at hand for reviews and parades. Paris and London have had their parks and squares— at least the smaller ones in the hearts of those metropolitan cities—so long that men almost have lost track of their age. In London, it became the custom to lay out open squares, the deed for which never rested with the community as a whole, but rather with the houses that immediately surrounded them. So it is that, until this day, many of the London squares, with all of their **refreshing greenery**, are surrounded by high iron fences, the gates of which are kept locked, being opened only to permit the entrance or the egress of occupants of the houses who hold the keys to them. Such a square is of little real value save to these. To the community as a whole it is attractive only because of the break that its grass and trees give to the city's monotony of pavements and of brick and stone buildings.

In the United States, our whole scheme of house construction was different. Save in the older towns along the seaboard or close to it, the houses were generally placed in open lawns, and thus we did not come quite so quickly to the necessity of parks, except in those same towns on the seaboard, where early provision was made for them. When William Penn laid out his famous city plan for Philadelphia, he prepared for five open squares, or parks, set at regular intervals in that neat plan. The central one of these, at the precise intersection of the two chief streets of the city, is now completely covered by the City Hall. The others are still used as open breathing spaces for the closely built city. One of them, Washington Square, closely adjoins Independence Hall, while another, Rittenhouse Square, has always been a fashionable center for the community.

Savannah had many similar squares in its early plan, and, after a time, so did New York. Then it was that Washington Square, fashioned from a former cemetery for the poor, Tompkins Square, Stuyvesant Square, Gramercy Square, Union and Madison Squares, were made a distinct part of the city plan of the latter community. These have all played a large part in the history of New York. With the single exception of Gramercy Park, which is held apart in the same fashion

SCENE IN HIGHLAND PARK, ROCHESTER, NEW YORK.

as the London squares, they are all freely open at all times to the public.

Shortly before the Civil War, New York gained its famous Central Park, which originally was looked upon almost as one of the seven wonders of the world. Yet even before that, Philadelphia had her huge Fairmount Park, upon both banks of the lovely Schuylkill, and Baltimore her Druid Hill, while Washington has always been almost a continuous park. Soon after the Civil War, Brooklyn had, upon part of the site of the battle of Long Island in the earlier Revolution, her Prospect Park, justly regarded as one of the most beautiful in the United States. To go further into this would be merely to make a catalogue of the famous city parks of the United States all the way from Revere Beach, near Boston, to Golden Gate Park on the rim of the Pacific at San Francisco.

It is enough here and now to say that parks have become a part of the accepted program of the modern American city. Even cities with as few as ten thousand population have parks, and rejoice in them,—not for fresh air alone but as places for recreation, for hiking, horseback riding, tennis, baseball, golf, hockey, bathing, boating, and all the other manifold athletic diversions of the healthy American race of today. Ofttimes they are used for large public entertainments, such as pageants or carnivals or concerts, either by professional bands of music or by choruses. There is little limit apparently to their possibilities.

While the police, fire and health departments and the public school system of the American city are in a sense utilities, they are not included as such in the purview of this book. The utilities that we have considered in these pages are chiefly those that involve very large physical construction and effort—engineering—both in their building and in their constant upkeep. They constitute the physical city, which the stranger who comes to visit may see in but a few days' time of more or less cursory examination. For the soul of the city, one goes much further. Then it is that he studies the schools—primary, elementary, secondary—which it possesses. He examines its system of specialized training of every sort and, if it is fortunate enough to possess them, its local colleges or universities. He gives attention to its recreations and its amusements. He inquires into the quality of its newspapers. He studies the very fibre of its social, religious and philanthropic life. He notes its many places of worship, its hospitals and similar organizations. If it has art galleries and museums he visits them, not once, but again and again. Then, if he has an opportunity, he goes into, not one, but many of its homes.

The sum total of all these things gives him the first insight into the real life of the community. If in the large majority they are good, the life of the community —its soul, if you please—will be good. Yet without all of these physical utilities that have been set down in these pages, without their constant contribution to the public weal every minute of the twenty-four hours of every day of the year, the soulful endeavor would be hampered at every turn; would come, in the end, to accomplish but little. This is a fact that needs no elaboration.

CHAPTER XVII

SERVICE ORGANIZATION AND POLICY

THROUGHOUT the preceding chapters of this book there have been discussed the historical development of public utilities, the present services afforded the general public by them, and how these services are rendered continuously throughout the twenty-four hours of the day, three hundred and sixty-five days of the year, regardless of the weather or the seasons.

Service in itself requires a more complete explanation for it is not enough merely to supply the transportation of persons or merchandise, or to furnish gas, electric, telephone, telegraph, water, sewer, park and road service. To secure a maximum benefit, the user of such service generally requires some supplementary assistance in its use. Essentially the public utilities supply human needs, some directly, as for example, transportation, where the person who buys service may be himself actually transported bodily from place to place; some semi-directly, as for example, the gas and electric services which are used to secure in turn other services such as the cooking of food or the heating of buildings. Here the gas and the electricity are simply agents, indirectly furnishing means for satisfying human needs. Many other services are quite indirect, as for example, the telephone, where the subscriber simply obtains the right to use facilities of speech communication and must be furnished with such facilities as will enable him to talk with others at a distance.

All these things are best supplied by specialists, for most public utilities are, in essence, engineering enterprises and in general the average purchaser of, or subscriber to public utility service does not himself know enough about the details of the service to use it to best advantage. Consequently it is one of the well recognized obligations of the public utilities to furnish to its patrons, not only service for the commodity but to supply such supplementary advice and assistance as will bring to the user the fullest possible value.

There is also an increasing recognition on the part of public utilities of business ethics and an increasing effort is made to conduct the business operations of the utilities on the basis of fair play, courtesy, and confidence. This is not merely high ethics, it is good business. In the discharge of their obligations to the public which they serve, the utilities are therefore spending great amounts of time and money in the creation of satisfactory working contacts and in the rendering of the supplementary assistance such as has already been described. Reason and experience have long since shown that such a course is not only right but it is good business, not merely for today but for tomorrow. The utilities have learned the value of vision.

In the discharge of these responsibilities, they must therefore necessarily maintain the highest possible type of business organizations. By the very nature of the work they undertake, these organizations must contain craftsmen, skilled and unskilled, in practically every profession and class of labor, including those

PUBLIC UTILITY SERVICE INSPECTOR ON DUTY.

branches of human activities common to all business. There are in the ranks of the utilities, scientists, engineers, chemists, financiers, lawyers and still other professional men, most of whom have come up through the ranks to their positions of importance. The personnel features, which have been described in a general way in this book have made some mention of the inventors, scientists and pioneers, who blazed the way, and of the actual operators in the modern public utility organizations of today. Attention has been directed to some of the romantic experiences through which the utilities have come and to the personal heroism of many of those who have devoted their lives to such service. There are today throughout the length and breadth of the land similar romantic instances not only of the adaptation of science to business, but of the spectacular rise within these far-spread organizations of men of humble beginnings, to positions of national importance. Likewise throughout the rank and file of the employees of the utilities today there are continuous examples of the highest types of heroism, of devotion to one's post in the face of great personal danger, that the public service may not be interrupted and that lives and property may be protected. "On guard" is the eternal slogan of the utilities.

Recognizing their three-fold obligations to stockholders, the public and employees, they make real efforts to build up high-type organizations. This is done primarily by careful selection, proper placement and the education of employees. Their working forces are, naturally, recruited from many walks of life and a large percentage come directly from the various educational institutions of the country. The public utility employees are not only fairly paid and justly treated, provided with safe, sanitary and satisfactory working conditions and environment, but they constantly are encouraged to study, to save their money, to become home owners and to participate in the civic activities of the community in which they live. To this end many of the utility corporations have established day and evening schools. Some of them have made co-operative arrangements with the schools of the local community whereby their employees receive additional instruction. Many have established employees' benefit plans, through which their workers secure sick disability and life insurance benefits; also pension systems to provide for the superannuation of old employees. Home ownership organizations within the utilities are fairly common while almost all of them today provide stock subscription plans under which employees may become in a very real sense part owners of the business. The modern high-type utility takes the position that it is not only the trustee of the money of the stockholder but is to a very real extent the trustee of the employees' welfare.

There are thus today in the service of the utilities many thousands of men and women who have been helped to success by the wide-awake environment in which they labor, the opportunity for education, the development of initiative which is continuously afforded, and the sincere encouragement of their leaders. With the inevitable growth of the country and the corresponding growth of its utility services, these opportunities for development and success will multiply. The utility companies welcome within their organizations young men and women of high personal

OFFICE OF A MODERN UTILITY.

and educational qualifications. For them there is in these public utilities distinct opportunity. Advancement is the rule, not the exception. Moreover, such personal advancement as may come to individuals in the service, will bring a corresponding advantage not merely to the utilities but to the public, because the individual merit which forges ahead will itself all the while invent and perfect further improvements which in turn will carry the utilities on to greater usefulness. The chain is an endless one.

The utilities of today, almost to a man, recognize their obligation to be of real service to the community in which they do business. This often takes the form of the promotion of worthwhile community endeavors for the common good. Their policy, therefore, may be said to consist first, in the supply of their products in adequate quantity and of standard quality—all of this rendered in a satisfactory manner; second, in a recognition of their obligation to develop their employees within the limitations which good business dictates; third, in their responsibility to their stockholders in the trusteeship of the money which has been invested; and fourth, in their participation in and support of such general public service as will promote the good of the city, state or nation, as the case may be. To this end, utility officers and employees today are found everywhere to be active in civic, state and national organizations having to do not only with the promotion of the welfare of the particular industries concerned but in that of the general public as a whole. Public utilities are thus active in the securing of good government, good schools, and all other agencies which are a part of our modern civilization. This is not alone their opportunity. They have come to recognize it as their duty and to fulfill it as their obligation.

The directors and employees of our great public utilities constitute, then, an industrial army, at work not to destroy but to preserve, upbuild, and develop civilization. They are mobilized daily to further our comfort and convenience. They work intelligently and with social outlook to promote the general welfare, and to upbuild not merely the America of today but the America of tomorrow.

CHAPTER XVIII

FINANCING AND REGULATING THE UTILITIES

To build and equip a utility properly, to say nothing of providing for its operation and up-keep, takes money, generally a very great deal of money. Millions of dollars are as nothing when it comes to initial expenditures alone on these huge facilities of communication and transportation, of heating, of lighting and of power. Even at the outset, the bill for the first of these—the railroads—was stupendous. The expenditure since that day has been many, many times the original cost. Today it can be said fairly that the expense of attempting to replace them, together with the other utilities, would be practically prohibitive. Let some unthinkable form of destruction descend upon this nation and wipe out all of its highways and byways, its railroads, steam and electric, its power lighting, telegraph, and telephone companies, and, aside from all the other tragedies of such a sweeping disaster, the cost would mount high—not merely into millions, but into billions of dollars. The cost of beginning anew and replacing them would bankrupt even as rich and as resourceful a nation as our United States of today.

Statisticians, with all of their efforts, can make only rough estimates of what they call the replacement value of these properties. Figures recently published (1927) will serve to give a faint idea of what it would cost to renew some of them. These show that there have been invested already in certain public utilities the following sums of money:

Electric light and power	$8,400,000,000
Electric railways	6,000,000,000
Gas Plants	4,200,000,000
Telephone	3,300,000,000
Telegraph	366,000,000

Here alone is an expenditure of $22,266,000,000 for but five forms of utilities. The steam railroads alone would add at least another twenty-six billions of dollars to this total. More than forty-eight billion dollars are now recorded, to which may be added the great replacement value, far more difficult to ascertain, of the various municipally owned and operated utilities, such as city streets and parks, water and sewage systems, bridges and the like. We should include also the cost of the vast highroads that connect the cities of the union and upon which, in recent years, so many millions of dollars are being expended annually, not alone in paving them in solid and permanent form, but in perfecting their grades and curvatures and in making them in every way far, far better roads upon which to operate the modern motor car and motor truck. When one comes to include these great public improvements one may easily add another forty billion dollars to the total. The grand total of the replacement value of just these utilities mentioned is at least eighty-eight billion, probably much more. One hundred billion dollars, a few years ago an almost unthinkable figure, may possibly represent this nation's total investment in its utilities.

To build this national structure has meant the expenditure of this eighty-seven billions of dollars over a period of many years; otherwise it never could have been built. As the nation has grown, year by year, so has grown its annual bill for utility expenditure, not only on new structures, or plants, but also for the upkeep and operation of existing plants, until the figures of yesterday placed beside those of today seem puny indeed. Only the great and steady growth of the United States could render them possible, and it is that same great growth that in turn rendered necessary the increasing annual expenditures for steadily increasing plant enlargements to the main structure. It is not, as we already have seen, the creation of a day, or a year, or a decade. It is the steady upbuilding of a hundred years, and even more.

Already we have divided the utilities into two great classifications, those that are owned and operated by the government, chiefly city governments, and those that are owned and operated by private investment, or capital. In a few instances, such as some of the New York City subways, government owned utilities are operated by private companies. But these last are so unusual that they will not receive consideration here. We shall give our present thought to the purely privately owned and operated utilities of the American community; later to those that are owned and operated by the cities themselves.

In either case they must be paid for, in hard, ordinary money, that must, sooner or later, be earned, as every man in the community must earn his way. Not only their original cost must be paid for, but also their upkeep, for utilities, like houses and suits of clothes and all mundane things, have a constant tendency to wear out and to go to pieces. Expenditures for property are *investments of capital*, and ordinarily come from without, whereas expenditures for upkeep and operation are *expenses of operation*, and must be paid for out of the revenues received as the result of such operation if the utility is to remain a solvent, going concern. Briefly stated, expenditures for property may, and in large part usually do, come from *without;* expenditures for upkeep and operation *must come from within*. This all is as true of the municipally owned and operated utility as it is of the one privately owned and operated.

It is only at the outset that the method of getting the money shows a difference between the two types of utilities. We shall first consider the privately owned and operated one.

A group of men, let us assume, seeking a fair opening for a new utility, get together and arrange, tentatively, to build it. They organize provisionally what is known as a *company* or corporation, which, upon fulfilling certain rather definite obligations, is recognized by the state, which then legally authorizes it, through *articles of incorporation*. The company acts as a separate, artificial person which comes into being at the behest of the state, and which exists apart from its individual members and has a continuity of its own, distinct from the continuity, or lack of continuity of its owning and operating personnel. Its owners may die, or sell their interests to others, and its directing organization may be rearranged, but the corporation itself is not changed thereby. The state is a rather passive party to the proceeding; its constitution and statutes describe what must be done by the individuals who wish to form a corporation; and when such things have been done and evidence of their having been done has been presented to the proper authorities (usually the Secretary of State) the state certifies that the acts have been done in accordance with the law, and *ipso facto* the corporation comes into being. The individual members of the company hold *shares of capital stock* in it, and they are known as its *stockholders.*

From these, certain men are designated at the outset as its *directors* and usually these directors are formally recognized in the articles of incorporation as issued by the State. Various plans are established for continuing or replacing the directors in office. Other officers, generally the *president* (the chief executive), one or more *vice-presidents*, a *secretary* and a *treasurer* and others, are elected, either from the ranks of directors and stockholders, or from without. The president is always a member of the *board of directors* and generally the presiding head as well. He is also a stockholder. Other important officers may or may not be directors or stockholders.

There is no better parallel for corporate organization than the organization of the state itself. The parallel is a perfect one, from the preamble of the constitution (or charter, in the case of a corporation) to the submission of certain questions to the electorate (or stockholders) and covers the whole ground of legislative, administrative and judicial functions. The corporation is in very fact a little state, supreme in its sphere, and yet subordinate to the sovereign state whose creature it is, just as that sovereign state, supreme in its own sphere, is subordinate to the Federal organization of which it is a part.

THE PRIVATE COMPANY OR CORPORATION

Financing a utility differs in only a few respects from financing other types of corporations. Utility financing is a more or less continuous process, inasmuch as construction usually goes on coincident with the operation of the utility, whereas in an industrial or a mercantile company (factory or large store) after the main facilities are provided the addition of other facilities is infrequent or of minor importance.

The sources from which the average public utility corporation (privately owned) is financed are as follows:

1. Capital stock
2. Bonds
3. Advances on Notes and Open Account from Creditors
4. Reserves and surplus

The first two, viz., capital stock and bonds are the principal sources, and in practice the ratio between them is determined by the dictates of sound business practice.

CAPITAL STOCK

Capital stock represents *proprietorship*, as against *bonds* which represent *creditorship*, but these last frequently are classed with stock in stating the nominal capitalization of a utility. The two securities, however, are distinct and different in their nature from each other.

Typical Stock Certificate and Dividend Check of a Public Utility Corporation.

Certificates of stock are issued to the subscribers to the capital stock as evidence of their investment or ownership in the company. Capital stock, if it is a so-called *par value stock*—such as, for instance, an issue having a nominal value per *share* of $100—is issued in the form of certificates showing the nominal value thereof. In this way a certificate of five shares would be stated as having a nominal value of $500.

If the total outstanding capital stock of the company should be, let us say, 500 shares ($50,000), this 5-share *stock-holder* would then own a one percent interest in the entire business.

Capital stock sometimes is issued as of *no par value*. In this case, the certificates bear only the precise number of shares each represents. Yet, as before, the owner of five shares out of a total of 500, still would have a one percent ownership in the business.

In these days, capital stocks may be of several classes; but almost always they fall into two main divisions: *preferred* and *common stocks*. Preferred stocks are those which, according to the articles of incorporation of the company, entitle their holders to certain rights to which the holders of common stock are not entitled. These rights usually consist of a preference in the distribution of the earnings, in the form of dividends, and a priority in the distribution of assets in case of the dissolution of the business.

Not infrequently there are classifications of the preferred stocks, one taking preference over another and bearing such names as prior preference, first preferred, second preferred, etc. To be effective, a statement of the rights conferred by each must be included in the articles of incorporation of the company.

BONDS

Bonds represent creditorship. They are issued against a property very much in the same manner as the ordinary mortgage is obtained from the savings bank or elsewhere by the man who buys or builds a house or other realty. In all cases, the stockholders (usually by a vote of not less than two-thirds of the capital stock) authorize their officers to mortgage or bond the company to a certain definite amount. This may be done in connection with the initial financing of the business, or afterwards. In the first case, the issuance of bonds would be practically coincident with that of the stock.

Usually it is impracticable to finance a mortgage of such size as the modern utility generally requires by funds from any one source, so here we depart for a moment from the analogy of the house mortgage and show the plan by which, under a mortgage, the sum required is obtained from a large number of bond purchasers.

The mortgage is broken up into units known as bonds, of denominations of $50.00, $100.00, $500.00, $1,000.00 and their multiples. In this way comparatively small denominational bonds can be scattered over a large number of purchasers so that, returning to our analogy, the bond holders collectively stand in the same relation to the Corporation as the Savings Bank, holding the mortgage of the house owner, stands to him.

Inasmuch as bonds are comparatively small units, which are readily negotiable, some central agency representing the bond holders as a whole is necessary. This agency, usually a trust company, is known as a

A PUBLIC UTILITY BOND.

Trustee. The duties of this Trustee are to see that the amount authorized is not over-issued and to act as a'depository for the payment of the interest coupons as they become due, the company placing the necessary funds for that purpose in its hands. A mortgage or deed of trust (which is the equivalent of the mortgage on the house) is executed. This is a contract between the Corporation and the Trustee in which the rights and obligations of the Corporation, the Bond Holders and the Trustee are fully and explicitly set forth.

If the Corporation should default in the payment of interest, or fail to meet its other obligations under the mortgage, the Trustee acts for the bond holders.

The mortgage being broken up into units, or so to speak, into shares, permits many individuals to participate in a loan which by reason of its size could not be undertaken by any single individual or institution. Thus these properties which represent the investment of thousands of millions of dollars, have their ownership distributed directly and indirectly among millions of our citizens. For there are to be counted among the owners of the utilities not only those who themselves own stocks or bonds, or both, but also those thousands of men and women who are indirect owners through life insurance companies, savings banks and trust companies, the funds of which are invested in part in the securities of these utilities.

In this connection there may be mentioned the comparatively recent and very broad-minded policy of many of the utilities, of selling their securities in small units, often on the installment plan, to the public, particularly to their employees and customers. In this way the public not only becomes more interested in the utilities than it would otherwise be, but the periodical saving of the small sums required to pay for the securities develops habits of thrift and self-denial in a large number of individuals, who perhaps could be induced in no other way to save.

By reason of the continuous construction program going on in the utilities, securities are being issued constantly to provide capital for extensions or to reimburse the company's treasury for disbursements which have been made for additions and betterments, so that from time to time bond issues are put out. These may be based upon two dissimilar forms of mortgages, one the so-called closed mortgage and the other, the open-end mortgage.

In the case of the closed mortgage a trust agreement is drawn up containing authority to the corporation to issue, when and as construction is completed to warrant it, a sum not in excess of a certain definite amount, as for instance, $20,000,000. It is contemplated that this amount will be needed in immediately succeeding years. As soon as extensions over a period of years have been made to use up the authorized mortgage (the supposititious $20,000,000) then this closed mortgage is, in fact, closed, and another mortgage agreement must be prepared and issued, provided more money is needed.

In the case of an open-end mortgage, no definite, fixed sum is authorized to begin with. The general mortgage agreement which is drawn up stipulates what the contract shall be between the company and the bondholders, but names no definite, closed amount. As a result, the corporation may issue bonds against this mortgage indefinitely, subject to the limitations which are contained in the trust agreement, such as the relations of property value to bonds outstanding and sufficient earnings to meet interest requirements, et cetera.   Of course, it should be borne in mind that bonds issued under such an agreement must also be supported by adequate fixed capital valuations.

Bonds are classified by their rank.   Those lying closest to the property, that is, those bonds first issued or having no restrictions as to security, are termed *underlying bonds*.   Subsequent issues are *junior* and, in the case of any default or foreclosure, rank after the underlying bonds in the order of payment.

For instance, a company may have a first mortgage issue, which will be the underlying issue, and thereafter may have second, third and fourth issues and even other junior issues, sometimes called general mortgage, refunding mortgage, collateral trust, income bonds, etc.   Bonds usually take their names from the character of the security which is pledged, or mortgaged in support of them.   For instance, *collateral trust bonds* usually have pledged as their security, some stock or other securities as collateral for their issue.   In the case of *income bonds*, the payment of their interest is usually dependent upon its being earned, instead of the usual rule in respect to bond interest, which is that the charge is absolute, whether earned or not and that default in paying it subjects a corporation to the possibility of foreclosure.   *Debentures*, secured by the general credit of the company but not by the specific pledge of any property, are also issued.

Capital stock and bonds may be issued before or after the construction of the facility for which funds are required. If the construction is being built or is already completed before the securities (stock or bonds, or both) are issued, the company doubtless will need temporarily to borrow money from banks to complete or pay for the actual work in hand. After the securities have been sold the money realized from their sale can be used to pay off these notes or to reimburse its treasury for such amounts of cash as have already been advanced for construction.

ADVANCES ON NOTES AND OPEN ACCOUNT FROM CREDITORS

In the natural course of things, a company takes credit from those who sell it goods and materials used in its business and these, on its books, appear as *open account* or as *notes payable*. Or the company may obtain loans through the issuance of notes payable to banks or other creditors. This is another source of capital.

RESERVES AND SURPLUS

Reserves consist of surplus appropriated or set aside for specific purposes other than the payment of dividends, or they may be built up out of income by charges to operating expenses. Sometimes reserves are represented by impounded cash, but the modern practice is to employ the money represented by them as another source of capital which is used in the conduct of the corporation's business, and they are therefore usually found to be invested in the corporation's plant or working capital.

Surplus represents the difference between the assets and the liabilities, capital stock and reserves. Surplus may consist of *earned surplus*, that is the net profit, undistributed and left in the business, or *capital surplus*, which is the capital furnished by stockholders in excess of the par value of their stock; that is to say, if a stockholder pays to the company on an original issue of stock, say $120 for a $100 par value stock, the excess $20 will represent capital surplus, the $100 being credited to capital stock. So surplus furnishes another possible source of capital. This capital is profit left in the business and appears in the assets on the balance sheet.

In this general way have been financed the gas companies, the street railway companies, the steam railroads, the telegraph and telephone, and the electric light and power companies, all the way across this land. The planning of their stable financial structure has hardly been less difficult than that of building their physical structures. Nowadays it is an easy matter to sell the stocks or the bonds of these enterprises; sometimes in the past it was extremely difficult. Public utility companies have to go into the open market to sell both forms of securities in competition with other enterprises which are likewise seeking capital. Sometimes in the early days competition between various companies so reduced earnings as to compel them to sell their securities at prices that were almost ruinous, saddling them with a financial load which retarded the development of the enterprises.

Competition has resulted more than once in the past in placing two or more utility companies, especially electric light, gas, and telephone companies, etc., in a field where there was barely enough business for one.

While the patrons for a time may have revelled in absurdly low prices, nevertheless, the ultimate result was impaired service, the loss of much money, and patrons consequently compelled to pay for at least a part of the mischief that had been done or else lose the service of the utilities entirely. Very few communities are ever willing to do this, and that speaks volumes for the inherent value of the utilities. This, however, does not apply with equal force in the case of steam railroads. Competition generally is regarded as stimulating increased efficiency and communities enjoying the service of competition between two or more railroads for its business are regarded as far more fortunate commercially than those with only one railroad. The railroads, however, have been forced to meet competition through the building of improved highways and the development and construction of natural and artificial waterways.

FRANCHISE RIGHTS

For the more purely civic utilities—such as the companies that sell gas or electric power and heating and lighting service, the street railways and the telephone companies—it has long been customary for the cities to grant a so-called franchise right. In other words, for many years, any group of men could construct a railroad or a telegraph line, or a long-distance telephone or electric power line anywhere across the country, just so long as they could buy or lease the necessary real estate for their producing plants and the lines that carried their product to their customers. For example, a railroad needed nothing more than the faint prospect of traffic to warrant its being plotted, if not actually built. It was, like the building of a factory or the opening of a store, a business risk, nothing more. If a company of men wished to take this risk, and were possessed of the means to carry it through, they were perfectly free to undertake it. If they made money, well and good. If they lost it, also, well and good. The communities that they reached did not particularly care, at least so long as they considered themselves properly served by the railroads and at rates which they were pleased to consider not excessively high. This often happened before a community learned the valuable lesson that the greatest extravagance in which it may indulge is a single superfluous public utility. In the long run it is the community itself that pays for the serious mistake that brings such an unnecessary utility into being. All of this will be explained later.

Today no new railroad, no important extension of any existing railroad, can be constructed without authorization which is the equivalent of a franchise from the federal government.

In other words, a trained and centralized power has been created at Washington in the Interstate Commerce Commission, which has judicial functions, and which with these is permitted to say, after a careful examination and hearing of the facts, whether a new railroad or an extension of a railroad, shall or shall not be built. This is not all. That same commission also passes upon all important financial transactions of these railroads, the issuance of stocks and bonds, even the price at which they are sold. With these things in mind, and with detailed standardized reports of the revenues and expenses of the railroads before it, the commission also regulates, after a careful examination and hearing, the rates that the railroads may charge for hauling passengers and freight.   In this connection, the commission is directed by law to prescribe just and reasonable rates so that under honest, efficient and economical management and reasonable expenditures for maintenance of way, structures and equipment the railroads, as a whole, or groups or territories, as the commission may designate, will earn an aggregate annual net railway operating income equal, as nearly as may be, to a fair return upon the aggregate value of their property held for and used in the service of transportation.   At the present time, the commission has determined that a return of 5¾% upon the investment is a fair one.

This is an important responsibility, and it brings into this narrative the large question of the regulation of utilities in general, which runs hand in hand with the problem of their franchises.   With the advent of the regulatory commissions the utilities began to be protected against ruinous competition.   The Interstate Commerce Commission and the various state commissions stand committed today to this fundamental proposition.

Experience has demonstrated that, whatever may be the merits of competition as a regulator of general business, and as a stimulant toward greater efficiency and better service for the affected communities so far as the railroads are concerned, it is not satisfactory when applied to other utilities.   These last differ, and this is true of the railroads in many respects, from so-called private business in at least two important particulars.

The first difference between the private enterprise and the public utility is the use to which the invested capital is put.   In the private enterprise it usually is chiefly invested in stock of goods, finished and unfinished, and the operation of the business consists of finishing and marketing the product, or merely marketing a product already finished by another.   A large part of the capital is thus invested in what are termed *liquid assets*, so-called because they are readily convertible into cash or its equivalent; in fact the conduct of the business is the process of converting such assets into cash which is then reinvested in other assets, only to convert these into cash again.   This complete cycle of operations is gone through often several times a year.   The volume of annual business may therefore be several times the capital investment.

On the other hand, the capital invested in a utility is almost all in what are known as *fixed assets*—in rights-of-way and rails, in locomotives and in cars, in power-stations, transmission lines and distribution systems, in buildings, switchboards and so on.   The money thus invested must remain so; it scarcely ever can be converted back into cash or its equivalent. In the private enterprise the volume of business in a single year may be easily several times the invested capital; in the utility it requires the aggregate business of a number of years to equal the invested capital.

It is, therefore, the nature of the investment which largely determines that public utilities shall normally be non-competitive in their various territories whereas private enterprises need not be.   A prerequisite of public utility service is a large investment in "fixed" assets (plant) which cannot ordinarily be reconverted into cash except by incurring very substantial losses. The conversion of the assets of private enterprise into cash is, on the contrary, a normal process, and is carried on, normally, with profit, so that even a forced conversion need not be the cause of any very great loss.

Public utilities do not earn profits to the same extent that the ordinary business does. Just as there is the difference between the public utility and the private enterprise in the use to which the invested capital is put, so there is a difference in the profits. In any enterprise the profits are what remain after the expenses of conducting the business have been paid. In the private enterprise the profits may be very large by comparison with the amount of capital invested, because, as has already been mentioned, the volume of business in a single year may be several times the invested capital, and each cycle of conversion (commonly called the "turnover") yields its own profit. These profits are often allowed to remain in the business, and themselves to earn other profits, so that it has happened from time to time that huge enterprises have grown from humble beginnings within the span of the lifetime of a single individual. In public utilities generally, on the contrary, the profits are limited to just enough more than the bare hire of the money used in the business to provide a margin for contingencies. Money for the expansion of the business comes from without; the surplus which could be put back into the business is far too small to keep pace with the ordinary utility's growth. In the case of the railroads, however, the law provides that should any one of them receive in any year a net railway operating income in excess of 6% of the value of its railroad property used in the service of transportation, one half of such excess shall be paid to the Interstate Commerce Commission for the purpose of establishing and maintaining a general railroad contingent fund to be used by the commission in the furtherance of the public interest in railway transportation.

The second difference between the private enterprise and the public utility is in the patronage. The private business may select its customers. If it so choose, it may sell to A, but not to B. The utility may make no such selection. It must serve all who apply; it is, as the technical phrase puts it, "affected with a public interest."

THE PRINCIPLE OF UTILITY REGULATION

Two public utility plants serving the same territory will represent a much greater investment than a single adequate plant, and the necessary charges for service will be much greater in the first instance than in the second.

In order, then, to prevent such useless and utterly wasteful duplication and competition, particularly in the case of electric light, gas and telephone companies, the regulatory commission steps in. It creates virtual unification in the utilities, gives, as it were, exclusive franchises, a protection against ruinous competition, to the existing companies, in which great sums of money have already been expended. This is not only of value to the companies themselves, but is of even greater value to the communities which they serve. The commission also regulates both the rates and the practices of the various utilities that come under its control.

Throughout all the years this is the recognized function of government: to exercise supreme control and regulation over those great forces with which the average citizen comes into contact at almost every turn of the day. Today it is a fully recognized principle, and no one is quicker to acknowledge it than the utilities themselves.

State regulation of railroads began as long ago as 1844. Federal governmental regulation of the railroads began in 1887, with the establishment at Washington of the Interstate Commerce Commission, previously noted, with rather limited powers. Gradually Congress has seen fit to add to these powers and privileges, until today that Commission is one of the most powerful judicial bodies in all the world.

But in one way its powers have always been most circumscribed. Owing to the fundamental plan of our federal system of government, the United States has never been possessed of authority over transactions coming to pass entirely within the limit of any one of the states. These become, in turn, a matter of state authority and regulation. The word, *interstate*, of itself determines the nature of the functions of the Washington Commission. Things which lie entirely within the boundaries of any one state are known as *intrastate*. As a matter of actual fact, however, most of the so-called Common Carriers in the land reach out of one state into another; or if their lines do not actually cross a state boundary, their business relations are almost certain to do so. This still brings them within the control of the Interstate Commerce Commission.

For the exercise of state control within the state boundaries many of the larger states years ago created regulatory commissions. At first these exercised their functions over the railroads alone. But in 1906, Massachusetts, which for the previous twenty years had asserted for herself a certain control over gas and

New York State Utilities are Regulated by the State Government,
State Capitol, Albany, New York.

electric companies, created a full-sized commission with large powers over these. The following year, the states of New York and of Wisconsin followed her example. Since then the idea has spread all the way across the country.

In addition to all of this, it may be added here that even long years before the coming of these state commissions, the average American city held for itself the privilege of granting franchise rights to the utilities, when and where it felt that the public necessity and convenience justified the granting of such rights. This custom also to some extent still continues. The American utility today has not one governmental master, but several. If it chances to be interstate in its functions, it may have many, such as the Interstate Commerce Commission of the federal government at Washington, the regulatory commissions of the various states into which it may enter, and the city councils of the municipalities that it serves. Generally, but not always, these masters agree in their policies and practices toward the individual utilities. It is a complicated sort of thing, but one which under our system of government seems quite unavoidable.

State as against municipal regulation of utilities works out to the greatest advantage for the reason that the various municipalities concerned are limited in their jurisdiction to the territory within their own corporate boundaries, whereas the state can regulate the operations of the corporations as a whole. With a large number of utilities covering a wide range of activities, the State can afford to maintain a staff of experts, which municipal commissions cannot afford to do. This is the reason why the utilities themselves favor regulation by state or national commissions rather than that of the municipalities, particularly the smaller communities.

Moreover, the more progressive of them now favor, instead of blanket franchises—either perpetual (rarely ever granted these days) or for a specified term of years —what are known as indefinite permits, which are issued by the state commissions. This already has become the practice in Indiana, in Wisconsin and in some other states.   It enables the utility companies to plan definitely for steadily continuing business and so to prepare for future development years in advance, instead of being confronted all the while with a possible expiration date of their franchises.

As a matter of fact, the franchise has all but passed out of existence since the advent of the regulatory commissions.   Such commissions have frequently ignored or set aside franchise provisions and their acts have been sustained by the courts.   In other words, when the legislature of a state delegated its powers of regulation to a commission, it thereby abrogated any former delegation of such powers to other agencies, and the courts have held this to be the intent, even when such intent has not been expressly stated.

We have now come close to the whole heart of the regulatory problem.   The commissions can and do exercise a supervision over the practices of the utilities. In the public interest they send experts into the field to supervise rather minutely their operation.   For instance, the Interstate Commerce Commission has a large corps of inspectors who travel up and down the land seeing that the locomotives and other rolling stock of the railroads are maintained in a safe and efficient condition. If a railroad wishes, for instance, to withdraw trains and there is public protest against the withdrawal, the Commission holds hearings and examines into the particular case and decides whether or not these trains may be withdrawn. Similarly the state commissions exercise, within their territorial bounds, their own authority over the railroads, steam and electric, and the other utilities. They inspect the gas and electric meters. Generally speaking, they perform functions similar to those of the Interstate Commerce Commission. All of these bodies also employ expert accountants and auditors who see that the utilities maintain their accounts correctly and in accordance with certain standards, set down for them in much detail.

The present-day service or public utility commission has jurisdiction over the construction, accounting, financing, rates and service of the public utilities. In the different states, the authority and the methods vary. The commissions have broad powers and, generally speaking, no new public utility may lawfully begin operations or construct new plants, nor may an existing utility extend its sphere, nor may two or more utilities consolidate or merge, without first having been given formal consent and approval by the commissions that have authority. On the other hand commissions have the power to require improvements in methods and service, extensions into new territory, the improvement of wire and pole lines, and in the case of the railroads, the addition of new train service, the elimination of grade crossings and other changes from time to time which may call for large expenditures.

No utility may issue any stock, or incur any debt or

obligation running for more than a year, without its first having been authorized by the commission. This has proved to be a very satisfactory provision of the law, and in those states where it is in force, it has had the effect of raising the securities of public utility companies above the general level, because the state has, in effect, put its stamp of approval on them. The state, of course, does not in any sense guarantee the soundness of the investment in such securities; it merely approves the issue as being in compliance with the law, and for the purpose for which it is issued. In practice, however, it is extremely doubtful whether any commission would authorize the issue of any security which was or was likely to become unsound.

Financing necessarily must depend, very largely, upon good accounting, particularly in seeing that capital transactions are kept separate and distinct from those which have to do with operation and maintenance. The regulatory commissions that in various states exercise a certain over-sight over the utilities have laid down general rules, more or less alike, for the keeping of utility corporation accounts. It generally is required that a balance sheet and profit and loss statement be presented annually and an income account monthly or quarterly. The balance sheet is a statement of condition and purports to show the assets owned by the company on the one hand, and on the other its liabilities, capital and surplus. The income account shows the amounts and sources of revenue and the details of operating expenses, and includes also the taxes, rents and interest applicable to the period. The profit and loss account indicates the changes in corporate surplus or deficit, brought about by the operations of the fiscal period and by various adjustments not properly attributable to the period. Dividends may be payable either from income or surplus.

The commissions have power to prescribe, and do prescribe, the form in which the accounting shall be done and there are rapidly coming into all but universal use the various uniform systems of accounts which they have ordered. The public has been prone to believe in the past that utilities have earned huge profits, but by adroit bookkeeping have been able to disguise them. Even if a utility were disposed to use loose methods of accounting, or otherwise to falsify its books, the requirement of uniform systems of accounts, with periodical checking by commission accountants, and the publicity given to the utilities' reports, would make such a course impracticable.

They also require reports—at the least, at yearly intervals—from the utilities, showing not only the financial transactions of each company for the stated period but ofttimes very detailed accounts of their operation, such as car miles, passengers and freight carried, the number of kilowatt hours of electricity generated and sold, the amount of gas manufactured, the number of telephones in service, the number of toll messages and telegrams and so on, together with classifications of employees, number of accidents, amounts of plant added or abandoned and all other pertinent details designed to give the commission a complete picture of the company's operations.

The commissions are, in their very nature, quasi-judicial. They review cases, hear evidence and make decisions, to the end that substantial justice will be done to all concerned. They sometimes handle ex-

tremely important affairs; a single one of their cases
may involve the people of a whole great state and property valued at hundreds of millions of dollars.   Time
and time again their decisions have been reviewed by
the courts and there has grown up around the exercise
of commission powers a long list of higher court decisions defining these powers, and the manner in, and
the extent to which they may be used.   Commissions
may not make decisions which are confiscatory.   The
utilities cannot be deprived of their properties, without
due process of law.   The close supervision exercised by
the commissions is neither management nor analogous
to management.

Because it is the feature of state regulation which
receives the greatest amount of publicity, the supervision exercised by the state commissions over rates of
electric light, gas and telephone companies, etc., is, in
the public mind, the most important function of these
bodies.   As railroad lines seldom are confined to one
state, they are almost entirely under the jurisdiction of
the Interstate Commerce Commission and state commissions exercise little authority in their rate making.

The charges made by a public utility for its product
or service are based on schedules of rates, or unit prices,
which are so designed as to distribute the burden of
operating the utility fairly among its patrons.   It is an
accepted and basic principle of public utility regulation
that all patrons must be accorded the same treatment;
there must be no favoritism or discrimination shown to
any patron or class of patrons.   This does not mean
that all must be charged the same rates, but it does

mean that the charges to all receiving the same kind or class of service under like circumstances and conditions must be based on the same rates.

The charges made by a utility must cover operating expenses, which include the cost of labor employed and materials and supplies consumed in the manufacture of its product or the rendering of its service, the upkeep of its plant, the cost of plant worn out in service, rents, taxes, and the hire of the capital employed in the business.

The use of money must be paid for just as any other commodity must be paid for, but because different terms are used to describe the payments, they are not always recognized as being basically the same.   Thus, payments for personal services are called salaries and wages, payments for the use of real estate are called rents, payments for the use of money are called interest and dividends.   A utility must use money in the conduct of its business.   That money is supplied by those who buy its securities (stocks, bonds, notes, etc.) and those who supply the money expect to be paid for its use.   The charges for money are governed, as are the prices of other commodities, by the supply and demand, but in the case of money, another element, that of security, enters.   Consequently, when a utility enters the market for money, it must be prepared to show not only that it can pay the market price for the use of the money which it needs, but also that that money will be secure, that is, wisely used, and that the utility can and does earn, not merely the bare hire of the money, but enough more to enable it to accumulate a surplus sufficient to safeguard the investor, so that even if there are lean years, when the utility may not earn its way, the hire of the money can still be promptly paid. The charges for money vary, at different times, in different places, and under different circumstances. Consequently, the rate at which a utility must earn, likewise varies. It is the function of regulatory bodies, which have supervision over utility rates, so to fix those rates as to permit the utility to earn at least enough to enable it to pay for the money it uses, and to attract the new money which the growth of its business will require. In the state of New York, where the prevailing rate for money is about 6 percent, earnings of 8 percent have not been regarded as unreasonable. This does not apply in the case of the railroads where the Interstate Commerce Commission has determined that 5¾ percent upon the investment shall be regarded as a fair return. Such earnings, whatever the rate may be in the particular case which is under review, are always based on the value of the property actually used or useful in the rendering of the service. They are not based on the amount or value of the securities which may be outstanding.

Obviously the revenues produced from the rates must exceed the costs of conducting the business. If they do not, the utility cannot remain long in business. It cannot operate indefinitely at a loss.

When rates fall short of producing sufficient revenue, it is the function of management to do one or more of three things,—reduce the expenses of operation, develop the business further, if that can be done without proportionately increasing the expenses, or increase the rates. Only the last mentioned ordinarily comes under the review of a regulatory body.

In case any or all of the foregoing fail to produce

sufficient net earnings, the consequence would probably be that the utility's creditors or its stock-holders would appeal to the courts and a receiver would be appointed whose duty it would be either to sell the property as a going institution to some one who felt that he could make it pay, or else to close it down and dispose of its physical assets in the best possible manner.

The amount of securities outstanding and the rates of interest and dividends paid thereon, while subject to the regulation of the commission, are not determining factors in computing the so-called rate of return which a company is permitted to earn. As already stated, a return is allowable on the value of the fixed assets used or useful in the public service plus a reasonable amount of working capital. Working capital is the sum required by a company to finance its current operations during the interim between the time of furnishing the service and the collection of payment therefor. It consists of cash, accounts receivable, bills receivable, materials and supplies and other current assets less current liabilities, and is usually allowed as part of the value in fixing the so-called invested capital (rate base) of a company for the purpose of determining rates. In the case of the railroads, the Interstate Commerce Commission, acting under the La Follette Act of 1913, has undertaken to make a valuation of the railroads of the country and under the law, when finally determined, this is to be used as a basis for rate making purposes.

Assume, for example, a small utility with a plant and other property valued at $1,000,000.00. Assume there are outstanding against it bonds and notes aggregating $500,000.00, preferred stock, $200,000.00, common stock, $300,000.00.

New income from operation (8% on the property of $1,000,000).....................	$80,000.00
Deduct interest at 6% on bonds and notes of $500,000.............................	30,000.00
Balance.........................	$50,000.00
Deduct dividends on preferred stock at 7% of $200,000.............................	14,000.00
Balance (equal to 12% on common stock of $300,000).............................	$36,000.00

It is seen that the common stock in this illustration has earned at the rate of 12% per annum, and this could lead the average layman to conclude that it was excessive, but it is shown that the property as a whole earned no more than its reasonable 8% as allowed. Thus it is evident that the rate of earnings on securities issued has little bearing on the earnings on the plant and working capital, which together form the true basis on which to calculate a return.

However, in this example it would not be good business judgment to pay out the whole 12% earned on the common stock, but to set aside a portion of it to provide a surplus out of which the dividend rate could be maintained in those years when the earnings might fall short of those shown.

In the United States today we see certain utilities coming more and more to be recognized as the function of privately owned and operated companies, and other utilities regarded solely as the function of municipalities. In this first group may be placed the steam railroads and electric railways, the telegraph and telephone companies, the gas and electric companies supplying heat, light and power. In the second, we find waterworks, sewage disposal plants, parks, streets, subways, police, fire and health protection and the like. There are, nevertheless, some few exceptions. Certain of our cities are operating their street railways or their electric lighting plants.

The community—large town or city—that sets out to provide itself with all the many necessities of the modern municipality, such as streets, parks, schools, water works, sewers and other facilities of today, must have the same recourse to borrowing that the private company has. Before it can issue and sell bonds, it too must have a tangible something to offer as their security, namely, its credit based upon the assessed valuation of its property upon which it may levy taxes. Its rates—in this case, generally called *taxes*—should be sufficient also to provide not only operating cost (labor and materials and fuel) but, as in the case of the private company, a reserve fund against decay, obsolescence and inadequacy, and also the interest upon its issued bonds. It too pays insurance, if not taxes.

Its citizens stand in the dual relation of both customers and stockholders—customers in that they buy with the rates (taxes and charges for services) the services which are afforded, stockholders in that they collectively own the facilities by which these services are rendered.

The financial problem of any great public utility is in itself stupendous. Wages must be adequate, interest and dividends must be sufficient to attract capital, and at the same time charges must not be so high as to limit the use of the utility. In the case of the railroads for example, wages, interest, dividends, taxes and replacement costs must all be forthcoming and yet freight and passenger rates must not be allowed to mount to the point where other means of transportation will be sought. The regulatory commissions such as, in the case of the railroads, the Interstate Commerce Commission and the state public service commissions, are created to realize the extent and the importance of the financial problem and to act as intermediaries to see that public interest is safeguarded and at the same time that the utilities have adequate opportunity for business life and growth.

CHAPTER XIX

THE FUTURE OF THE AMERICAN CITY

WHAT is the future of the American city?

Here is the supreme problem, perhaps the problem of problems, which many and many a community here in the United States is facing at this very moment. It is the problem over which great engineers, of a wide range of experience and of many qualifications, are puzzling their heads more and more all the while.

That these cities will continue to grow, and to grow rapidly, is a foregone conclusion. The experience of the past is sufficient authority for this statement. Engineers and statisticians get together and between them "plot curves," based upon the population totals for any given city for five-year or ten-year periods, back to its very beginnings.

Placed upon a diagram-chart, a line drawn from the tips of these totals usually begins to have the distinct semblance of a curve. The rest is simple. The curve, keeping the same general direction and sweep, is extended down through the years to come; and the point at which it crosses the five-year lines and the ten-year lines is apt to show what should be, approximately, the population of that one city in any one of those years.

Once in a while, this curve is subject to extreme variations. The acquisition or the loss of a single great

357

industry in a city may have a tremendous effect upon its population. Take Detroit, for instance. No curve plotted, as recently as twenty years ago, on the basis of seventy-five years of the earlier growth of that city, would have indicated its size as it actually is today, a community of nearly one and one-half millions of people. The sudden, the absolutely unprecedented growth, of the motor-car industry within her borders, has placed Detroit completely out of line of all scientific predictions or prophecies. Similarly, there are old towns, right here in the United States, just shriveling up and decaying for lack of industries. Some of them are towns for which, a century more or less ago, a brilliant future was predicted; wise plans were laid for a development that never came to pass.

But generally the growth of the American city is reasonably consistent; it has an astounding way of following in an approximate fashion the curve of future development plotted out for it by the city engineers. With this as fact, the rest is easy, or should be easy, in theory at least.

Here is an imaginary city; let us call it Cosmopolis, and say that today it has about 350,000 people living in it. It is just a hundred years old. Last summer, with much ado, it celebrated its first centenary. With reasonable decorum, it has followed, very closely indeed, the growth-curve plotted for it thirty-five years ago, by a shrewd and far-visioned engineer, who based his curve on the sixty-five years of previous growth.

Cosmopolis has always prospered, at some seasons more than others, but in the long run, pretty nearly all of the time. It has a pleasant location, abundant natural resources, varied industries, splendid credit,

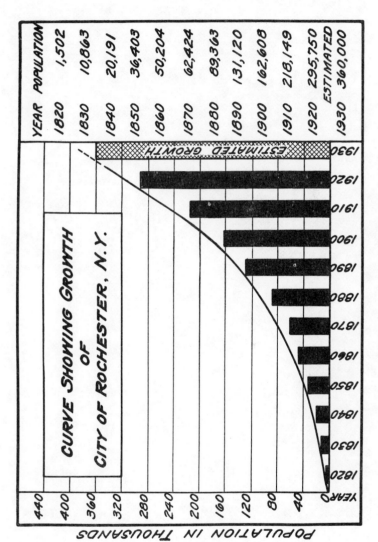

YEAR	POPULATION
1820	1,502
1830	10,863
1840	20,191
1850	36,403
1860	50,204
1870	62,424
1880	89,363
1890	131,120
1900	162,608
1910	218,149
1920	295,750
1930	ESTIMATED 360,000

CURVE SHOWING GROWTH
OF
CITY OF ROCHESTER, N.Y.

ESTIMATED GROWTH

POPULATION IN THOUSANDS

POPULATION GRAPH OF A TYPICAL AMERICAN CITY.

good banks, good schools, a university, churches, parks, hospitals and various recreations and amusements. It is noted for its fine homes, as well as for the attractiveness of its social life. It always has been remarkably free from scandal, either social, business or political. All in all, a most lovely American city, is this Cosmopolis.

Yet, Cosmopolis has problems of its own, and rather grave problems they are. Its pleasant location, on a sharp hillside, or rather a series of parallel hillsides, facing a broad river, is, in itself, a problem. The hills always have been hard to conquer with highways; in winter, when there is plenty of snow and sleet, its streets are particularly difficult, either to climb or to descend, in safety. The broad river is a constant and increasing problem of expensive bridges. The city, rich as it is, has always found it very difficult to obtain sufficient funds for all these bridges and its important hill-climbing highways.

Recently, its problem has been much complicated, by the coming of the motor-car. Its downtown streets, in the narrow level tract between the river and the first of the parallel hills, were laid out, most of them, nearly a hundred years ago. They may have been adequate for the small traffic of the earlier years of the city's history, but for a number of years past, they have become woefully inadequate; they are far too narrow, and, in many instances, far too twisting. In addition to all of this, the business folk of Cosmopolis are insisting that space be found in those downtown streets by the harassed city government for the parking of their cars. This is a great problem in all our American cities today.

The American city attempts to do much, but it does not always succeed in accomplishing it. Cities have been begun in locations that later proved unsuitable to growth, or failing in early visions they have found subsequent efforts blocked by conditions which might have been avoided in the beginning.

No one better understands than the men at the City Hall what Cosmopolis should be doing for itself *today* and for the *future*. The curve-plot shows that, by 1937, it will have 450,000 people. It is high time, therefore, that preparations were being made for them. Private capital will house them and employ them, provide much of their amusement and recreation; the privately-owned and operated utilities will give them gas and electric light and heat, telegraph and telephone service, and transportation of every sort. But the city, itself, will have to give them streets in which to move freely, parks in which to play, schools to which to send their children for well-rounded education, police and fire and health protection, in addition to such humble but highly necessary things as water supply and waste removal.

Here, then, is where the *city-plan* comes back into our picture. Cosmopolis has a city-plan; as a piece of carefully developed and detailed foresight it is a really superb accomplishment. Engineers and architects, educators, bankers, experts of every sort, public-spirited citizens of many types, all have worked together to perfect it.

In that plan, some of the old, narrow, twisting streets of the town are straightened and widened. Here and there, a brand new street is cut through and added. New bridges are provided, over the broad river. High-

THE IMPOSING MUNICIPAL GROUP OF SPRINGFIELD, MASSACHUSETTS.

level bridges they are called, because they start well back from the river bank and bridge some of the downtown streets parallel to and nearest to the river, and so escape some of their provoking traffic. New, broad highways, easily graded, are plotted over the hilltops and grade reductions suggested for the older streets that cross them. In at least two instances long highway tunnels are planned right through the hills, like those in Rome, Italy, or in this country, in Pittsburgh and Los Angeles and San Francisco and Seattle. Parks are a part of the city plan; many, large and small, are to be added for the Cosmopolis of 450,000 folk; existing ones are to be enlarged and improved.

For the city beautiful is not the least of the idealistic hopes of the modern American community. It seeks, always, to make itself an efficient city. So Cosmopolis plans, in the great scheme for its future, to tear down many blocks of obsolete, shabby buildings by its waterfront and to make, along her riverside, a formal open park, such as those which, for many years, have been the joy and pride of European cities. What has been done in Paris, in London, in Zurich, can be done, and already is being done in the United States. Witness two near-by capitals for this, Albany, New York, and Harrisburg, Pennsylvania. See what has been done in a third, Hartford, Connecticut, and in its neighbor, Springfield, Massachusetts, in Boston and in Des Moines, and you will have full proof of what a riverside in an American city can become. In the making of the city plan for the modern community the architect and the landscape gardener join forces with the engineer.

Back of all this, there are other provisions, smaller

only in a comparative sense. We have seen the need for an equally dependable water supply. Additional water-works must be planned and financed and built, before the coming of that extra hundred thousand folk. It may, or it may not, mean seeking out new water sources and building huge aqueducts and reservoirs and pumping-stations, but it will certainly demand the addition of many important mains, or in any event the radical enlargement of existing aqueducts and reservoirs and pumping-stations. Similarly more sewers, trunk and lateral, for the unseen but highly necessary cleansing function of the modern city, will have to be planned and financed and built, all in good time.

Schools—elementary, and junior and senior high schools, and specialized training schools, perhaps a college or a university—cannot be neglected in the growing Cosmopolis. These, too, will have to be provided, fully equipped and staffed with the best teachers that can be secured. There will have to be more fire stations, with a plenitude of modern fire-fighting equipment, police stations, traffic controls and health service bureaus, in addition to the minor municipal endeavors of all kinds. All of these things are to be directly provided by the city.

But the private corporations, supplying it with its great essential utilities, also come into the development of this city plan. New streets, that carry water-mains and sewers, must also carry gas mains, conduits for electric light and telephone wires and other kinds of service. There may be new street railways or, what is far more likely today, provision for highly modern bus transportation, perhaps in correlation with the street railways. Nor are these all the needs; new

VIEW OF HARTFORD, FROM THE CONNECTICUT RIVER

street railway tracks, gas mains,—laterals and trunks,—
electric power lines and telephone cables may, and perhaps will, mean more central stations, gas works or
power stations or additional exchanges. The utility
companies are forever making city plans. They try to
keep the programs for their development at least ten,
or fifteen, or twenty years ahead of the growth of any
individual city. All of this means not only large
engineering expense but a constant problem of finding
funds as such expansion becomes immediately and
physically necessary. With the revenues from their
services as their only real source of income, they must
arrange such issues of new stocks and bonds as will
keep their owners content with the returns on their
securities and still enable them to give the best and
most modern devices and service to their patrons.

Multiply Cosmopolis all the way across the United
States. Say that we have ten thousand such communities, larger or smaller, between the Atlantic and
the Pacific rims of this nation and you will begin to get
but a faint concept of the hugeness of the problem of
its utility companies—not merely the local and civic
ones, but the vast organizations that cover whole states
and groups of states, with their railroads, their electric-
power lines, their telegraphs and their telephones.
The American city has grown fast indeed; but its
utilities have grown even faster. They are neither
blind, nor are they deaf. Not infrequently, they
are its inspiration to idealism. Many times they assume real leadership in bringing this to the modern city.
A single structure, like the pumping station of the
Spring Valley Water Company in San Francisco, may

serve as an architectural inspiration for the entire community.

Side by side and hand in hand go the utilities and the modern American city. The problems of the one are, in large measure, the problems of the other. Neither can stand quite alone.

The problems of the one are the problems of the other; and the hope of the one is the hope of the other. Good friends they are, good neighbors too, at times sharing privations, hardships, perplexities, but in the great today that forever is becoming tomorrow, they are reaping together their own just reward.

INDEX

A

Accounting:
  Balance sheet, 348
  Fixed assets, 341
  Liquid assets, 341
  Profit and loss statement, 348
  System prescribed by Public Service Commission, 347
Agamemnon, British warship carrying first Atlantic cable, 205
Agriculture, effect on location of cities, 3
Albany, N. Y.:
  Early railroad, 35
  Reason for location of, 4
  Terminus of first public railroad in U. S., 26
Alternating current (*see* Electric lighting)
American city (*see also* Cities)
  Beginning of, 3
  Future problems of, 359, 360
    Beautification of, 360, 361
    Plotting curve of growth, 357
      Variations in 357-8
    Providing for growth, in city plan, 360
      Extending municipal utilities, 360
      Extending privately owned utilities, 360
American Express Company, 39
American Telephone and Telegraph Co., 225
American village (*see* Cities)
Ammonium-sulphate, by-product of coal gas manufacture, 137, 138
Ampere, unit of electric current, 182

Amplifiers, vacuum tube in television apparatus, 273
Aniline dyes, derived from coal tar, 134
Army, Industrial, composed of, 324
Ashley, Pa., inclined plane on railroad still in use, 31
Ashokan Reservoir, water supply for New York City, 298
Assets, liquid, fixed, 341
Athens, Greece, evidence of city plan, 276
Atlantic cable (*see* Cable)
Attica, N. Y., early railroad, 35
Auburn, N. Y., early railroad, 35
Auer, Carl (von Welsbach), inventor of Welsbach burner, 126
Augusta, Ga., reason for location of, 5
"Automatic" telephone, 254

B

Baltimore, Md., determines to build railroad, 28-29;
  first commercial gaslight installation in U. S., 122
Baltimore American, comments concerning early use of gas, 119
Baltimore & Ohio R. R., plans for "inclined planes," 30
Baltimore Patriot, first newspaper to publish telegraphic dispatch, 193
Barton, Sir Henry, Lord Mayor of London, introduced street lighting, (1416), 113
Batavia, N. Y., early railroad, 35
Bell, Dr. Alexander Graham, inventor of telephone, 218

365

Bell Telephone Co., predecessor to American Telephone & Telegraph Co., 225

Bell Telephone Laboratories, development of television, 273

Best Friend, first American built locomotive, 29

Binghamton, N. Y., on first Erie Railroad, 33

Binns, Jack, wireless operator on sinking *Republic*, 211

Black Hawk, famous locomotive, 43

Blake, Francis, inventor of telephone transmitter, 228

Blending coal and water gas, 134

"Blow," term used in water gas manufacture, 133

Blue gas, 132

Bonds, 332

"Boosters," gas, 143

Boston, Mass.:
Early railroad, 36
Lack of city plan in early development, 276

Bridge, Bridges:
Arched, concrete, 287
Stone, 286
Brooklyn Bridge, 289
Cabin John, Washington, one of greatest single stone arches in world, 287
Construction of, 284
Covered, 285
Early, 275
First railroad, across Hudson River, 40
Iron, 285–286
Over Niagara River, 40, 289
Over Ohio River at Wheeling, 21, 288
Peace Bridge, 290
Steel, 285–286
Simplest form of, 284
Suspension, 288
Truss type, 284

Bright, Sir Charles, England, one of organizers of Atlantic Telegraph Co., 204

British House of Commons investigates scheme of "electric lighting," 147

Broadway, beginning of Albany Post Road, 19

Bryant, Gridley, builder of first railroad in U. S., 26

Buffalo, N. Y.:
Early railroads, 35
Reason for location of, 5, 14

Bunker Hill Monument, stone transported from Quincy, Mass., 26

Bunsen Burner, invention of, 125

Burr, Theodore, builder of wooden bridge at Trenton, (1804), 46, 285

By-products of coal gas manufacture, 134

C

Cabin, John (*see* Bridges)

Cable, submarine telegraph:
Atlantic, first:
Attempts to lay, 205
Completion of, 205
Failure of, 206
First message over, 206
Atlantic, second, laying of, 207
English Channel to Paris, completion of, 204
Hazards in construction and maintenance, 208
Break in Bay Roberts-Penzance No. 2, 1915, 208
Lines across Atlantic in 1877, 207
Problems, 204
Speed of service, 208

California, long distance high voltage electric transmission, 185

Camden, N. J., early railroad, 46

Canal, Canals (*see also* Navigation):
Building of, 14
Chesapeake & Ohio, 28
Erie
Cities benefited by building of, 28
Completion of, 28
Packet boat lines, 38
In U. S. not considered obsolete, 14–15
New York Barge, 15
Sault Ste. Marie, 14
Welland, 14
first, completed 1827, 5

Candles as street lights, 113
Carburetion of gas, 132
Carburetted blue gas, 132
Casson, Herbert N., historian of
telephone, 221
Centennial Exposition, demon-
stration of first telephone, 220
Gas stove exhibit, 126
Central, telephone, 240
Chappe, Claude, claimed by
French as inventor of tele-
graph (semaphore), 189
Charleston, S. C., early railroad
efforts, 29
Chesapeake & Ohio Canal, (see
Canals)
Chicago, Ill., reason for location
of, 14
Chief operator, telephone, 251
Christiansen, Hans Christopher,
first water supply engineer
in America, 294
Cincinnati, Ohio, reason for loca-
tion of, 14
City, Cities (see also American
City):
Beginnings of, 3
Dependence upon public utili-
ties, 11
Finances:
Capital outlay, 292
Current expenses, 292
Debt service, 292
Restriction of power to levy
taxes and borrow money,
293
Utility expenses, 293
Plan:
Athens, Greece, evidence of,
276
Boston, Mass., lack of, 276
Necessity for, 278
New York City, error in,
277
Paris under Napoleon, 276
Philadelphia, Pa., 276
Savannah, Ga., 276
Use of in U. S., 278
Washington, D. C., 277
Zoning, 279
Reasons for location of, 3
Clermont, first practical steam-
boat, 13

Cleveland, Ohio, reason for loca-
tion of, 14
Clinton, De Witt, first locomotive
on Mohawk & Hudson R. R.,
26
Coal:
Mechanical equipment for
burning, 170
Pulverized, for use in power
plants, 170
Quantity burned in modern
electric generating plants in
America, 169
Storage for power plants, 169
Coal gas (see Gas, manufactured)
Coal tar, by-product of coal gas
manufacture, 134
Derivatives, value of, 134
Cochituate River, water supply
for Boston, 301
Cohen, Jacob J., Baltimore, first
residence lighted by gas in
U. S., 122
Coke, by-product of coal gas
manufacture, 134, 135
Colorado River, water power on,
185
Commissions, federal regulatory,
343
Interstate Commerce, 339–343
State, 344
Communication:
Ancient use of messengers,
187
Early problem of, 187
Method used by Montezuma,
last Aztec king, 187
Communities, beginning of (see
Cities)
Conestoga Wagons, 44
Connecticut River, 12
Contact bed, 313
Corning, N. Y., on first Erie Rail-
road, 33
Cornish, Thomas E., placed tele-
phones in Philadelphia in
opposition to telegraph, 228
Cortez, Enrico, builder of first
important North American
highways, 16
Cost of gas manufacture, 135
Costs, operating, savings in coal
gas manufacture, 137

Croton Reservoir, water supply
for New York City, 296

D

Davenport, builder of first passen-
ger cars on Auburn & Rochester R. R. (N. Y. C. R. R.),
36
Davenport, Thomas, early ex-
perimenter with electric rail-
way motors, 87
Davidson, Robert, Aberdeen,
Scotland, builder of minia-
ture electric locomotive, 87
Davy, Sir Humphrey, English
scientist, interested in electric
telegraph, 191
Debentures, 335
Delaware River, 12
Detroit, Mich., reason for location
of, 14
Dickens, Charles, comments on
Portage R. R., 43
Direct current generator (see
electric lighting)
Douglas, Stephen A., author of
law granting state lands to
Illinois Central R. R., 56
Drake, Col. E. L., discoverer of
petroleum fields of western
Pennsylvania, 123
Drexel, Morgan & Co., early user
of electric light, 152
Drugs, made from coal tar, 134
Dunkirk, N. Y., western terminus
of New York & Erie R. R., 33
Dyes, aniline, derived from coal
tar, 134
Dynamo (see Electric Generators)

E

Edison, Thomas A.:
Inventor of commercially successful electric incandescent
lamp, 147, 148
Inventor of first successful
electric railway in U. S., 88
Plan to light lower section of
New York City, Sept., 1879,
149

Problems of lighting on large
scale, 148
Public demonstration of electric
lighting at Menlo Park, N. J.,
December 31, 1879, 150
Edison Electric Illuminating Co.
of New York, first electric
generating company, 151
Electric, Electrical:
Energy, impossibility of stor-
ing, 159
Generators:
Alternating current, 176
Direct current, 176
Measurements, 182
Power, development of, 167
Power plants (see Power plants)
Transmission from power sta-
tion, 182
Electric lighting:
Alternating current, develop-
ment of, 153
Experimental system at
Great Barrington, Mass.
155
First commercial installation
in U. S., Lawrenceville,
Pa., 155
Founding of Westinghouse
Electric & Mfg. Co., 154
In use at Buffalo, N. Y.,
Christmas, 1886, 155
Opposition to, 154
Electrocution at Auburn,
N. Y., 1887, used as ar-
gument against, 154
Purchase of American rights
to Gaulard and Gibbs
patents by George West-
inghouse, 153, 154
Development of decorative pos-
sibilities with, 156
Direct Current, 152–153
Display at Pan-American Ex-
position, Buffalo, N. Y., 156
Display at World's Columbian
Exposition at Chicago, 1893,
156
Early problems in direct cur-
rent power stations, 152, 153
Edison's plan to light lower sec-
tion of New York City, Sept.,
1879, 149

Electric Lighting—*Continued*
Edison Electric Illuminating
Co. of New York:
Incorporation of, 151
Growth in first four months,
152
Installation of plant, 151
Current turned on for com-
mercial service, Sept. 4,
1882, 151
Flood lighting of capitol dome
at Washington, 156
Growth of, 155
Incandescent lamp invented by
Thomas A. Edison, 147,
148
Investigated by committee of
British House of Commons,
147
Lamp invented by Jablochkoff,
shown at Paris Exposition,
1879, 146
Newspaper comments in 1879
on Edison's invention, 150
Newspaper comments on first
electric lighting, 151, 152
Problems of lighting on large
scale, 148
Details necessary to com-
pete with gas system, 148
Maintaining constant volt-
age, 148
Metering electricity, 148
System of distribution, 148
Public demonstration by Edi-
son at Menlo Park, N. J.,
Dec. 31, 1879, 150
Electric motor, 167
Electric production, increase of,
131
Electric railway (*see also* Street
Railway):
Early experiments with, in
U. S., 87
Early installation at Rochester,
N. Y., 89
Economic and social importance
of, 91, 92
First in U. S., 88
First practical in world, Berlin
Fair, 1879, 84
Interurban, 90
Motor, development of, 103

Origin of in U. S., 1834, 87
Rapid transit in metropolitan
areas, development of, 110
Elevated, 110, 111
Subway, 110, 111
Relation to steam railroad, 91,
92
Richmond, Va., first city in
U. S. to have almost complete
equipment, 89
Street car, modern, 104, 105
Cost of, 105
"One-man cars," 105
Suburban, possibilities of, 89, 90
"Trackless trolley," 112
Trolley car, 9, 89, 99
Electricity:
Household uses of, 164
Introduction of, 9
Uses of, 9–10
Ellsworth, Miss Anne, writer of
first telegraphic message, 193
Erie Canal (*see* Canals)
Exchange, telephone, 249

F

Farmer, Prof. Moses G., builder
of first electric car in U. S. to
carry passengers, 87
Federal regulatory commissions,
343
Field, Cyrus W., New York, one
of organizers of Atlantic Tele-
graph Co., 204
Filter, trickling, 313
Financing private utility compan-
ies:
Loans, 336
Notes payable, 336
Open accounts, 336
Reserves, 336
Surplus, 336
Types of securities, 330
Bonds, 332
Collateral trust, 335
Debentures, 335
Income, 335
Mortgage, 332
Trustee, 333
Capital stock, 330
Fitch, John, builder of early
steamboat, 13

Flambeaux, early method of street lighting in London and Paris, 114

Forbes, Col. W. H., reorganizer of Bell Telephone Co., and first president of National Bell Telephone Co., 228

Franchise rights of utility companies, 338

Freight trains, early size, etc., 37

Fuel, motor, by-product of coal gas manufacture, 135

Fulton, Robert, builder of first practical steamboat, 13

G

Garbage disposal:
  Collection of waste, 314
  Commercial products from, 314
  Early method of, 314
  Plant, 314
Gas:
  "Boosters," 143
  Bunsen burner, 125
  Carburetion of, 132
  Coal, 132
    Blending with water gas, 134
    By-products of, 134
      Value to consumer, 135
    Modern plant for manufacture of, 136
      Coal consumed in, 136
        By-products of, 137, 138
        Coke produced per ton of coal, 137
        Economies of, 137
        Gas produced per ton of coal, 137
        "Producer" gas used in, 137
        Saving in operating cost of, 137
    Process of manufacture of, 135
    Refining of, 140
    Removal of by-products, 138
    "Scrubbing," 140
    "Washing," 139
  Discovery of and early research, 115
  Distribution, 142
    Maintenance of, 143
  Engine motor-fuel, 135

First company in U. S., 122
First company in world, in London, 119
First permanent installation in U. S., 122
First private company in London, 118
First works, 116
Forms manufactured, 132
"Geist," origin of name, 115
Generators, 133
Holders, 140, 142
Illuminating, introduction of, 7
Increase in use of, 127
Manufactured:
  Advantages in use of, 127
  Carburetted blue, 132
  Oil, 132
  Process of production of coal and oil, 132
  "Producer," used in modern coal gas manufacturing plants, 137
  Production, increase in compared with electricity in last five years, 131
  Use of, increase in, 131
  Uses of, 127 ff.
    Home heating, 129
    In ceramic industries, 128
    In foodstuffs industries, 129
    In non-ferrous industries, 128
    In steel industry, 128
    Refrigeration, 130
  Water (or carburetted blue gas), 132
    Blending with coal gas, 134
    Method of manufacture, 132
  Natural, 125
  Pumping stations, 143
  Storage holders for, 140
Gas lighting:
  Covent Gardens Theater, 119
  Demonstration at Lyceum Theatre, London, (1804), 118
  Early gas works in U. S., 124
  Early opposition to, 122
  First commercial installation in U. S., Peale's Museum, Baltimore, (1816), 122
  First commercial, mills of Phillips & Lee, Manchester, England, 116

Gas lighting—*Continued*
First company granted charter, 119
First used in home of Wm. Murdock, (1792), 116
Gas tip, invention of, 117
House of Jacob J. Cohen, Baltimore, first in U. S., 122
In engine building works of Boulton, Watt & Co., Soho, England, 116
In houses, 125
In London, mentioned in Baltimore American (1815), 119
Lantern made by Wm. Murdock, 117
Natural gas, 125
On Westminster Bridge (1813), 119
Used in celebration of Peace of Amiens (1802), 116
Welsbach burner, 126
Gas stove, first shown and demonstrated at Centennial Exposition (1876), 126
Gaulrad, French, experimenter with alternating current in Italy and London, 100, 153
General Electric Co., manufacturers of impulse steam turbines, 162
Generation of electrical energy by steam, 160
Steam turbine, 161
Ancient invention of, 161
Early use near Syracuse, N. Y., 1835, 161
Expansion of steam, 162
Impulse, 162
Reaction, 162
Superiority to water power, 160
Turbo-generator, 162
Generators, electric, 176
Gas, 133
Genesee River, water power on, 185
Genesee Turnpike, early stage-coaches on, 38
Georgetown, Md., reason for location of, 5
Gibbs, English experimenter with alternating current in Italy and London, 100, 153

Gifford, Walter S., President of the American Telephone and Telegraph Co., first to telephone from New York to London, 231, 262
Gilboa Reservoir, water supply for New York City, 300
Gold rush to California, 1849, 197
Goshen, N. Y., on first Erie Railroad, 33
Gray, Dr. Frank, contribution to development of television, 273
Gray, Stephen, England, with Granville, Wheeler, early experimenter with electric telegraph, 190
Great Eastern, English ship used to lay second Atlantic cable, 207
Gwynn, William, editor *Baltimore Gazette* and one of incorporators in first gas company in U. S., 122

H

Haigh, J. H., first paying telephone subscriber in New York City, 226
Halladie, Andrew S., designer of street railway for San Francisco, 1871, 87
Halliday, Ben, operator of "Pony Express," 197
Harbors, effect on location of cities (*see also* Navigation)
Harper's Weekly, comment on Edison's electric lamp invention, 1879, 150
Hartford, Conn., reason for location of, 5
Haussman, Baron, worked out details of city plan for Paris, 276
Hemlock Lake, source of water supply for Rochester, N. Y., 302
Henry, Joseph, Smithsonian Institution, Washington, tested telephone at Philadelphia Centennial, 222

Herald, New York, record of first commercial electric lighting, 152

Hero, inventor of a steam turbine about 120 B.C., 161

Highway, Highways (*see also* Roads):
Description of travel at end of 18th century, 24–25
Development caused by growth of colonies, 16
Early existence of, 15
First important North American, 16
Obstacles to early American, 16
Public, background to public utilities, 23
Relationship to cities, 23

Holders, gas, 140

Hollidaysburg, Pa., early railroad, 43

Holmes, E. T., Boston, owner of first telephone exchange in world, 224

Holyoke, Mass., reason for location of, 6

Honesdale, Pa., terminal Delaware & Hudson Canal Co., 25

Hoover, Herbert, Secretary of Commerce, participated in demonstration of television, April 7, 1927, 233

House, Royal E., inventor of "printing telegraph," 194

Household uses of electricity, 164

Hubbard, Gardiner, father-in-law of Dr. Bell, assisted in putting telephone on market, 220

Hudson River, 4, 12, 13

Hydrolytic tank, 311

I

Illinois River, 12

Illuminating gas (*see* Gas)

Imhoff tank, 312

"Inclined plane," railroad engineering device, 30, 31

"Information," telephone, 253

Interstate Commerce Commission, Washington, 339, 343

"Iron Horse," familiar name for locomotive, 54

Ives, Herbert E., Dr., research in development of television, 273

J

Jablochkoff, inventor of electric lamp shown at Paris Exposition, 1879, 146

Jefferson, Thomas, National Road project of, 20, 21

Jersey City, N. J., on first Erie Railroad, 34

Johnstown, Pa., early railroad, 43

K

Kelvin, Lord, tested telephone at Philadelphia Centennial, 222

Kennebec River, 12

Kerosene lamp, first used, 1865, 123

Kilowatt, unit of electric power, 182

King, James G., second president New York & Erie R. R., 34

L

Lamplighters in New York, 114

Lanterns on outside of houses, first method of street lighting, 114

Lanthorns in London (1416), beginning of street lighting, 113

Lawrence, Mass., reason for location of, 6

Lebon, Phillippe, Paris, early experimenter with gas, 118

Lemond, French scientist, early telegraphic experiments, 190

L'Enfant, Major Charles Pierre, designer of city plan for Washington, 277

Leslie's comment on Edison's electric lamp invention, 1879, 150

Leyden jar used in early telegraph, 190

Lighting (*see* Gas *and* Electric Lighting, *also* Street Lighting)

Lincoln, Abraham, attorney for Rock Island R. R., 58
Connected with formation period of Illinois Central R. R., 56
Link boy, early method of street lighting in London and Paris, 114
Little Falls, N. Y., reason for location of, 6
Locks in Mohawk River, first artificial aid to navigation in America, 5
Locomotive:
Beginnings of in the U. S., 25
"Best Friend," first American built, 29
Called "Iron Horse," 54
George Washington, first to climb "inclined plane" unassisted, 31
Invention of, 24
"Rocket" in England, first successful in world, 25
"Stourbridge Lion," first operated in America, 25
London & Westminster Gas Light & Coke Co., first gas company in world, 119
London, England, reason for location of, 4
Long distance telephone (*see* Telephone)
Louisville, Ky., reason for location of, 6, 14
Lowe method of manufacturing water gas, 132
Lowell, Mass., reason for location of, 6

M

Magnetic telegraph (*see* Telegraph)
Magnetic Telegraph Co., pioneer Morse organization, 193
Mahoning, Pa., "inclined plane" still in use, 31
Manchester, N. H., reason for location of, 6
Manhattan Water-Works, 295
Mauch Chunk, Pa., "inclined plane" still in use, 30–31

Medicines, made from coal tar, 134
Melville, David, early American experimenter with gas, 121
Minckelers, Jean Pierre, Belgium, early experimenter with gas, 117
Mineral resources, effect on location of cities, 3
Minneapolis, Minn., reason for location of, 6
Milwaukee, Wis., reason for location of, 14
Mississippi River, 12
Water power on, 185
Missouri River, 12
Mohawk River, 4, 5
Montezuma, Aztec king, methods of communication, 187
Montreal, Canada, reason for location of, 5
Morse, Professor Samuel F. B., inventor of practical electric telegraph, 191
Appeals to Congress for funds to make commercial use of telegraph, 191
Morse code, telegraphic alphabet, 191
Mortgage bonds, 332
Morton, E. R., contribution to development of television, 274
Motor bus, competition with street railway, 106
Motor, electric, 167
Motor fuel, by-product of coal gas manufacture, 135
Municipal utilities, 275
Murdock, William, father of artificial gas, 115
Murray, Sir G. Evelyn P., Secretary of General Post Office of Great Britain, first to telephone from London to New York, 232
Muscle Shoals, Ala., water power at, 185

N

Napoleon, city plan for development of Paris, 276

Napoleon—*Continued*
Skeptical concerning use of gas, 118
Navigation (*see also* Canals, Harbors, Locks, Rivers)
Effect on location of cities, 4, 14
Neon tubes, used in television receiving apparatus, 271
New York & Mississippi Valley Printing Telegraph Co., original name of Western Union Telegraph Co., 195
New York City, error in city plan, 277
New York Herald, comment on Edison's electric lamp invention, December 21, 1879, 150
New York Stock Exchange, early user of electric light, 152
Niagara, American warship carrying first Atlantic cable, 205
Niagara Falls power development, 156
Extending power transmission lines from, 158, 159
Impossibility of conserving electric energy, 159
Storage batteries, 159
Using electricity at Niagara Falls, 160
Permission from United States and Canadian governments, 157
Plans for use of water power, 157
Power house at Niagara Falls, 1895, 157
Generators of, 157, 158
Improvements, 158
Schemes for transmitting power, 157
Norris, William, builder of first locomotive to climb "inclined planes," 31
North Road, England, early built road in use today, 16

O

Ohio River, 12
Water power on, 185
Oil, uses of in water gas manufacture, 132

Oil gas (*see* Gas, Manufactured)
Oil lamps, used for street lighting, 114
Uses of, 123
Oils, light, by-product of coal gas manufacture, 138
Oneida Lake, 4
Ontario, first steamboat built on open waters, 13
Ontario, Lake, 5
Operating costs, in manufacture of coal gas, 135
Operator, telephone, 250
Oswego, N. Y., reason for location of, 5
Oswego River, 5
"Owl Cars," term for early morning street railway cars, 94

P

Page, Professor, builder of early electric car, 88
Paris, France:
Early street lighting in, 114
Exposition, 1879, electric lamp shown for first time in Europe, 146
One of first great cities to have plan for development, 276
Reason for location of, 4
Parks:
In United States, 315
New York City, 316
Philadelphia, 316
Savannah, 316
London, 315
Necessity for in European cities, 315
Of modern American city, 317
Parsons Co. of England, manufacturers of reaction steam turbines, 162
Passenger cars, luxurious, on Auburn & Rochester R. R., 36–37
Sleeping berths in, middle of "fifties," 39
Paterson, N. J., on first Erie Railroad, 34
Reason for location of, 6
Pavements (*see* Streets)

Peale, Rembrandt, Baltimore, owner of the first commercial gas light installation in the U. S., 119

Pedro de Alcantara, Dom, Emperor of Brazil, first to talk over telephone at Philadelphia Centennial, 222

Penn, William, founder of Philadelphia, Pa., 276, 316

Penobscot River, 12

Petroleum fields, discovery of, 123

Philadelphia, Pa., first American community laid out by a city plan, 276

Philadelphia & Columbia R. R., "George Washington" demonstrated steep grade climbing abilities, 31

Photoelectric cells, used in television sending apparatus, 270

Piermont, N. Y., early eastern terminus of New York & Erie R. R., 33

Pitch bowls, used for street lighting in Paris, 114

Pittsburg, Pa., reason for location of, 6, 14

Pony Express:
Organization and equipment, 198
Reason for, 197
Record trip, 199

Portages, effect on possibilities of river travel, 4, 13

Postal Telegraph Co., 203

Postoffice, not regarded here as a public utility, 8

Potomac River, 12

Power plants, electric:
Early problems in direct current, 152, 153
Switchboard in, 178
Location, 178
Operation of, 179
Operator, 179
Switches, 180
Transforming stations in cities to reduce voltage for domestic use, 183

Power plants, steam (see also Steam Turbines)
At coal mines, 169

Coal burned in, 169
Coal storage, 169
Pulverized coal, 170
Turbo-generators in, 173, 177
Auxiliaries to, 178
Water supply for, 171
Condensers, 172

"Printing Telegraph," early rival of Morse telegraph, 194

Private utilities, 330

"Producer" gas used in modern coal gas manufacturing plants, 137

Public utility (see Utilities)

Pullman, George M., builder of Pullman car, 39

Pumping stations, gas, 143

Q

Quincy, Josiah, description of highway travel, 24-25

Quincy, Mass., quarries furnished stone for Bunker Hill Monument, 26

R

Radio:
Greatest value of, 210
Introduction of, 10
Wonder of, 210

Railroad, Railroads (see also Street Railway):
Advance across middle west, 50
Alleghany Portage, 44
Auburn & Rochester—first cars for, 36-37
"Back shops" of, 82
Baltimore & Ohio, 27
Beginning of, 27
Early struggles of, 46-47
Growth of, 47
Washington branch, 48
Boston & Albany, 29
Bridge over Mississippi at Rock Island cause of contention with steamboat men, 58
Buffalo, Rochester & Pittsburgh, 42
Business of American system of, 68

Railroad, Railroads—*Continued*
Central Pacific, organization of, 61
  Building of, 62, 63
Chicago & Alton, 58
Chicago, Burlington & Quincy, 58
Chicago & Northwesterm system, beginnings of, 58
Chicago & Rock Island, 58
Classes of trains in freight service of, 71
  passenger service of, 72
Cleveland & Pittsburg, 52
Cleveland, Columbus & Cincinnati, 51
Construction in recent years, 65
Delaware & Hudson, 40
Delaware, Lackawanna & Western, 41
Departmental system of organization, 71
Development in Illinois, 53
Divisional system of organization, 71
Early construction of, 30
Early, in United States, 26
Early traffic across central and western portions of New York State, 38
Economic value of electric traction to, 91, 92
Erie, 32
First all-rail route from Boston to Buffalo, 36
First built by Baltimore, 29
First built by Boston, 29
First built by Charleston, S. C., 29
First in United States, 26
First railroad bridge over Mississippi, at Rock Island, 58
First through line from Lake Erie to Ohio River (Mad River & Little Miami), 51
First through route from New York to St. Louis, 48
First trans-continental, 59
Freight service on present American system of, 66, 67
Freight terminals, 80
  Importance to cities, 83
Freight transfer-houses, 81

Freight yards, 81
Galena & Chicago Union, 58
Great Western Railway Co., 55, 56
Handling of freight on, 80
Hannibal & St. Joseph, 59
Hudson River, 39
Illinois Central, 55
  Building of present, 56, 57
  Incorporating of present, 56
  Law granting state lands to, 56
  Today, 57
Illinois legislative appropriation for in 1837, 53
Industrial side tracks of, 80
Lake Shore combining with Michigan Southern, 52
Lehigh Valley, 41
Little Miami, 51
Mad River & Lake Erie, 50
Marietta & Cincinnati, 48
Master time tables for operating trains on, 73
Meeting of Union Pacific and Central Pacific, 60
Michigan Central completed from Buffalo to Chicago, 52
Michigan Southern combining with Lake Shore, 52
Mohawk & Hudson, first public railroad organized in U. S., 26
Movement of trains on, 74
New York & Erie (Erie Railroad), 32
  Building of, 33
  Chartering of, 32
  Freight revenues first six months, 34–35
  Route, 33
New York Central:
  Early development of passenger business, 36
  Early freight trains, 37
  Early passenger cars, 37
  First train on, 26
  Formation of first New York Central, 35
  Incorporation of, 39
  Luxurious passenger cars on Auburn & Rochester line, 36–37

Railroad, Railroads—*Continued*
New York Central—*Continued*
Merger resulting in N. Y. C. & H. R., 40
Roads merged into, 40
N. Y. C. & H. R., 40
Night traffic on, 76
Northern Cross, 54
Northern Pacific, 63
Ohio & Mississippi, 48
Operating extra freight trains on, 73
Extra passenger trains on, 74
Operating organization, 68
Division superintendent, 70
General manager, 70
General superintendent, 70
President, 68
Resident vice-president, 69
Vice-Presidents, 69
Operation of, 71
Trains at passenger stations, 79
Trains on, 71
Oswego Midland, 40
Owners of American system of, 68
Partnership between cities and, 83
Passenger service on present American systems, 66
Passenger stations, 77, 78
Pennsylvania, 35
Chartering of, 45
First route of, 42, 43
First train from Philadelphia to Pittsburgh, 45
Merging of United Railroads of N. J. with, 46
Roads brought into, 46
Pennsylvania system, beginning of, 28
Philadelphia & Columbia, first link of Pennsylvania, 42
Operation of by State of Pennsylvania, 43
Portage, 43
Pullman sleeping cars on, 76
Race of Michigan Southern and Michigan Central to Chicago, 52
Rochester & State line (B. R. & P.), 41

Rome, Watertown & Ogdensburgh, 40
Roundhouses, 82
Route miles of in United States today, 65
Santa Fé, 64
South Carolina, 29
Southern Pacific, 64
Super utility in United States, 66
Tonawanda, 35
Train conductor on, 75
Train despatcher, 74
Union Pacific, building of, 59, 60
Union stations, 77
Use of caboose on freight trains, 75
Use of electric traction by, 91
Use of "inclined plane" on early, 30
Utica & Schenectady, 35
Waybilles for freight, 75
Western New York and Pennsylvania, 42
West Shore, 41
Ramapo, N. Y., on first Erie Railroad, 33
Receiver, telephone, 242
Regulation of utilities:
Advantage of state over municipal, 344
Federal commissions, 343
General principles, 342
Relationship between modern American cities and, 76
State commissions, 343
Supervision by commissions, 345
Accounting, 347 348, 349
Construction, 347
Financing, 347
Inspection, 346, 347
Rates, 350
Richmond, Va., reason for location of, 5
Rivers, first pathways of commerce, 12
Road, Roads (*see also* Highways)
Albany Post, Broadway, beginning of, 18
Route of, 18
Appian Way, Rome, world's first great street, 15

Road, Roads—*Continued*
  Boston Post Road, first con-
    tinuous road from Bos-
    ton to New York, 16, 19
  Main routes, 17–18
  Early American, 16, 17
  Genesee Road, route of, 19
  Lancaster Pike, description of,
    in 1796, 20
    Now Lincoln Highway west
      from Philadelphia, 20
  National Road:
    Cause of early prosperity of
      Wheeling, 22
    Established by Congress, 20
    Legal beginning of, 21
    Original scheme for, 21
    Route of, 21
    Suspension bridge at Wheel-
      ing crossing Ohio river, 21
    Use of, 22
  Pennsylvania roads, called
    turnpikes, 20
Rochester, N. Y.:
  Early railroad, 35
  First headquarters of Western
    Union Telegraph Co., 195
  Reason for location of, 6
  Sewage disposal plants at, 313
Rocket, first successful steam loco-
    motive in the world, 25
Roebling, John A., Trenton, N. J.,
    21, 40
  Expert in suspension bridge con-
    struction, 288
Romans, first road builders, 15
  Rome, N. Y., 4
"Run," term used in water gas
    manufacture, 133

                  S

Salem, Mass., early railroad ef-
    forts, 29, 30
Sanders, Thomas, Haverhill,
    Mass., chief financial backer
    in putting telephone on mar-
    ket, 223
Sault Ste. Marie Canal, 14
Savannah, Ga., laid out on city
    plan, 276
Sawyer-Man, incandescent lamp
    patents, 154

Schenectady, N. Y., 4; terminus
    of first public railroad in U. S.,
    26
Schoharie River, water supply for
    New York City, 299
Scott, Sir Walter, ridiculed gas
    lighting, 118
Scott, Thomas A., president of the
    Pennsylvania R. R. and first
    to have telephone in Phil-
    adelphia, 228
"Scrubbing" coal gas, 140
Sedimentation tank, 311
Selden, Judge Samuel L., Ro-
    chester, N. Y., promoter of
    House telegraph system, 195
Sewage disposal:
  Early methods of, 307
  Into rivers and lakes, 309
  Modern methods of, 310
  Problems of, 308
  Stations (plants), 310
Sewage tanks, 311
Sewers, public:
  Growth of, 308
  Introduction of, 7
  Trunk, 309
Shandaken Tunnel, part of New
    York City water works,
    300
Short, Bob, letter to *Baltimore
    American* concerning first use
    of gas, 120
Sibley, Hiram, contractor for first
    transcontinental telegraph,
    200
  Early supporter of Western
    Union Telegraph Co., 195
Sludge, activated process, 312
Smokeless fuels produced from
    gas manufacture, 144
South Road, England, early built
    road in use today, 15
St. Lawrence River, 12
  Water power on, 185
St. Louis, Mo., reason for loca-
    tion of, 6, 14
St. Paul, Minn., reason for loca-
    tion of, 14
Stagecoach, first dependable in-
    land mode of communication,
    17
Stanford, Leland, 61

Stanley, William, incandescent lamp patents, 154
State regulatory commissions, 343
Steamboat:
  First built on open waters, 13
  First on upper lakes, 13
  First practical, 13
  Increase in use of, 14
  Invention of, 13
  Limitations of, 14
Steam engine, Watt & Murdock, 115, 116
Steam power generating plants, development of in United States, since 1914, 173
  Modern electric, 168
Steam turbines, 161, 175
  Impulse, 162, 175
  Reaction, 162, 175
Steinmetz, Charles P., 167
Stephenson, George, builder of first successful steam locomotive, 25
Stoller, H. M., contribution to development of television, 273
Storage batteries, 159
Storage holders for gas, 140
Stourbridge Lion, first steam locomotive operated in America, 25
Street, the, first public utility, 6
Street lighting:
  Beginning, London, 1416, 113
    Lanthorns, hung out of houses, 113
  Beginning of, 7
  Early attempts in London and Paris, 113, 114
    Flambeaux carried by link boy, 114
    Lanterns on outside of houses, 114
    Pitch bowls in streets, 114
  Electricity applied to, 9
  Gas, 7
  In New York City, 114
    First contract with New York Gas Co., 115
    First systematic form, (1762), 114
    Oil lamps on posts, 114

Use of gas for, 119 ff.
Use of kerosene for, 123
Street railway (see also Electric Railway)
  and the motor bus, 107, 108
    Extension of trolley to suburban country, 108, 109
  at San Francisco, 1871, 87
  Beginning of, 8
  Cable road, 87
  Competition of motor bus with, 106, 107
    Double-deck bus, 108
    "Jitney," 106
    Recognized rights of railway, 107
  Day service of, 95
    Peak loads, 95
  Early, 85
  Electricity motive power of, 98
    Alternating current, 100
    Converter, changing AC current to DC, 102
    Danger in use of alternating current, 101
    Direct current, 100
    Generation, 99
    Present method of using alternating current, 101, 102
    Transforming station, 103
      Portable, 103
  Electrification of, 9
  Flexibility in emergencies, 97
  Mass transportation, ability to take care of, 109
  Necessity for development of, 86
  Night service of, 94
  Time tables, 96
Streets:
  Flags, 280
  Formation of, 6
  Pavements:
    Asphalt, 282
    Brick, 281
    Cobblestones, 280
    Concrete, 283
    Early London and Paris, 280
  Roman, 280
  Vital to growth of city, 275
  Wood-block, 281
Suffern, N. Y., on first Erie Railroad, 34

Sulphur, impurity in coal gas, 140
Sun, New York, record of first
    commercial electric lighting,
    152
Supervisor, telephone, 250
Susquehanna, Pa., Erie Railroad
    shops, 34
Susquehanna River, 12
    Water power on, 185
Switchboard in electric power
    plants, 178
Switchboard telephone, 239, 249
Syracuse, N. Y., early railroad
    center, 35

T

Tanks for treatment of sewage,
    311
Telegraph cable, first across At-
    lantic, 205
Telegraph, device used at opening
    of Erie Canal from Albany to
    Buffalo, 189
    Electric, early discoveries in
        England, 190
    Electro-magnetic:
        Alphabet known as Morse
            code, 191
        American invention as used
            today, 191
        Appropriation of $30,000 by
            Congress to build first line,
            192
        Attempt to build overland
            from San Francisco to Mos-
            cow, Petrograd and Paris,
            201
        Beginning of, 8
        Dependability of, 212
        Extension of, 203
        First line, built along B. & O.
            R. R. from Washington to
            Baltimore 1843, 192
        First message, 193
        First printed newspaper de-
            spatch, 193
        First transcontinental, 199
        Growth of system, 193
        Handling emergencies, 213
        Invented by Professor Sam-
            uel F. B. Morse, 1832, 191
        Limitations of, 217

Machines of modern office,
    214
Magnetic Telegraph Co. pio-
    neer organization, 193
Multiplex system of printing
    telegraphy, 215, 216
Opening of first line, May 24,
    1844, 192
Opposition to telephone, 224,
    227
Process of sending messages,
    212
Rivals of Morse's original
    company, 194
    Printing Telegraph in-
        vented by Royal E.
        House, 194
    Safeguarding privacy of mes-
        sage, 212
    Value during Civil War, 202
        Record at Rochester, 202
    Visual signal system invented
        by Claude Chappe, 189
        Use of signal lights, 188
Telephone:
    Advertising circular of early,
        223
    Agreement between Bell Com-
        pany and Western Union, 229
    American, taken to France by
        A. E. F., 234
    Automatic, 254
    Beginning of, 9
    Busy signal, 243
    Call entering Central, 240
    Central, 240
    Chief operator, 251
    Chinese exchanges in San Fran-
        cisco, 238
    Development in New York
        City:
        First directory, 226
        First pay station established,
            226
        First paying subscriber, 1877,
            226
        System in 1893, 226
    Development of Trans-Atlan-
        tic, 231
        Calls first day of service, 233
        Ceremonies in connection with
            opening of service, 232
    Directory, 253

Telephone—*Continued*
Disconnecting calls, 245
Exchange, terminal room, 251-2
Experiments of Dr. Bell, 218
Financial struggles of Bell interests, 227
First commercial use of, 224
First exchange, 224
First exhibited at Philadelphia Centennial, 220
First machines leased for use in Charleston, 223
First, March, 1876, 219
Human element necessary in intercommunication, 240
"Information," 253
Instruments, 236
    Number in New York City, 238, 239
    Number in U. S. today, 237
Interior of an exchange, 249
Invented as mechanical organ of speech and hearing, 218
Invention of, 219
Keeping record of message-rate telephones, 248
Legal battle between Bell Co. and Western Union Telegraph Co., 229
Long distance:
    A-board operation, 257
    B-board, 262
    Call entering exchange, 256
    Central, 257
    Clock for recording time of calls, 257
    Development of, 230
    Entering call, 257
    Exchange, 257
    First call on record, 223
    Handling incoming calls, 262
    Handling outgoing calls, 257
    Locating number of party desired, 258
    Problems hindering development, 230
    Recording time required for call, 259
    Use with radio broadcasting, 264, 265
Making connection, 243
Multiple exchanges:
    "A-board," 246

"B-board," 246
    Connection between, 246
    Connections with, in one exchange, 247
    Necessity for, 245
Name under which patent was obtained, 220
Necessity for central point in inter-communication, 239
Operators, 250
Operators' apparatus, 242
Opposition of telegraph companies, 224, 227
Party wires, 247
Pay stations, 247
Popularity of American in France during and after World War, 235
Possibilities of, 236
Problems in meeting demands of growth, 266
Rapid increase in volume of business, 224, 225
Receiver, 242
Reception at Philadelphia Centennial, 220
Reserve power equipment, 253
Ringing subscribers' telephones, 244, 253
Sanders, Thomas, chief financial backer in putting on market, 223
Strategy used to establish first lines in Philadelphia, 228
Supervisors, 250
Switchboard, 239, 249
    Jack, 240
    Multiple, 241
Territory reached by, 237, 238
Trans-Atlantic:
    Developing privacy of radio transmission, 265, 266
    Handling calls, 262
    Alternate short wave channel for transmission from N. Y. to London, 264
    Radio receiving stations, 262, 263
    Radio transmission stations, 263
    Selecting radio wave length, 263

Telephone—*Continued*
  Produced by Thomas A. Edison for Western Union, 227
  Transmitter invented by Francis Blake, Boston, 228
  Universal use in U. S., 238
  Vail, Theodore N., organizer of present system, 225
  Value in World War, 234
  Wire chief, 251
Television:
  Apparatus for, 268
  Demonstration of at Washington and New York, April 7, 1927, 233
  General theory, 268
  Operation of receiving apparatus, 270
    sending apparatus, 269
  Points in common with transmission of pictures by wire or radio, 268
Tennessee River, water power on, 185
Tesla, Nikola, inventor of induction motor, 154
Thomson, Sir William, electrical expert, tested telephone at Philadelphia Centennial, 222
Times, New York, record of first commercial electric lighting, 152
Transportation (*see* Highways, Navigation, Railroads, *and* Street Railways)
  Early importance of, 5
  Situation in west prior to 60's, 59
Travis tank, 311
Tribune, New York, record of first commercial electric lighting, 151
Trolley car (*see* Electric Railway)
Trustee, mortgage, 332, 333
Turbo-generators, 162, 173
Turnpikes, roads in Pennsylvania, 20
Tyndall, scientist, 147

U

Utica, N. Y., early railroad, 35
Utilities:
  Beginning of, 6

  Business policy of, 323, 324
  Classifications of, 327
  Compared with private business, 340
  Cost of building and equipping, 325
  Definition of, 10–11
  Development caused by growth of communities, 8
  Disadvantages of competition, 337
  Employees, qualifications and training of, 321, 322
  Ethics of business, 320
  Importance of, to present American city, 11
  National investment in, 326
  Obligations of, 320
  Personnel, qualifications of, 320
  Profits limited, 342
  Replacement value of, 325, 326
  Responsibilities of municipal, 275, 291
  Service, elements of, 319
Utility Companies:
  Employees' welfare, 322
  Financing private, 330
  Franchise rights of, 338
  Growth of, 327
  Organization of, 328

V

Vacuum tubes used as amplifiers in television, 273
Vail, Alfred, New Jersey, assisted in perfecting machine for Morse telegraph, 191
Vail Theodore N., organizer of present telephone system, 225
Van Helmont, John Baptist, early experiments with marsh gas, 115
Village, American (*see* Cities)
Volt, unit of electric potential, 182
von Bunsen, Robert Wilhelm, inventor of blue flame gas burner, 125

W

Wachusett Reservoir, water supply for Boston, 301

Walk-on-the-Water, first steamboat on upper lakes, 13

"Washing" coal gas, 139

Washington Bridge, Harlem River, New York, example of steel bridge, 286

Washington, D. C., efforts to secure railroad, 28

Washington, George, conceived possibilities of National Road, 20

Washington, George, first locomotive to climb "inclined plane" unassisted, 31

World model in city planning, 277

Water gas, 132
  Method of manufacture, 132

Water necessary for production of electric energy in steam stations, 171

Water power:
  Effect on location of cities, 3, 6
  Possibilities in America, 184
  Rivers in process of development, 185

"Water Seal," use of in gas manufacture, 142

Water Supply:
  Anticipating growth of city, 323
  Early, 7
  First engineer in America, 294
  For power plants, 171
  Reason for separate charge by cities, 291
  Selection of source, 304

Water Works:
  Aqueducts built by Romans, 294
  In Mexico City built by Spaniards, 294
  Baltimore, 1804, 295
  Beginning of in U. S., 294
  Blackstone River, purification of water from, 305
  Boston, Cochituate River, 301
    Wachusett Reservoir, 301
  Chlorination of water, 305
  Early systems:
    Bethlehem, Pa., 294
    Boston, Mass., 294
    Schaefferstown, Pa., 294
  First pumps used at Bethlehem, Pa., 294

In U. S. in 1800, 295
  Today (1926), 295

New York City:
  Reservoirs:
    Ashokan, 298
      Aqueduct connecting with city, 298, 299
      Esopus Creek, 298
    Croton, 296
      Aqueduct to Central Park, 296
      Completion of, 1842, 297
      Distributing reservoirs, 296
      Second aqueduct from Croton Lake, 1885, 297
      Storage reservoir in Bronx, 297
    Gilboa, 300
    Old, 295
      Between Prince and White Streets, 1774, 295
      In Chambers Street, built by Manhattan Water Works, 295

Philadelphia, 1822, 295

Pumping stations, 306

Purification of water, 304
  Chemical aid to, 305
  Filters, mechanical, 305
  Sand, 305

Rochester, N. Y.:
  Aqueduct from Hemlock Lake, 302
  Reservoirs, 302*n*.
  Use of Genesee River for fire protection, 303

Steel conduit first used by Newark, N. J., 1892, 303
  Laid by Los Angeles for water supply, 303

"Waterless" gas holder, 142

Watling St. Road, England, famous Roman built road, 15

Watson, Thomas A., assistant to Dr. Bell in invention of telephone, 219

Watt, James, associated with Wm. Murdock, father of artificial gas, 116

Waybills, railroad, 75

Webster, Daniel, guest on first Erie R. R. train, 34

Welland Canal (*see* Canals)

Wells, Fargo & Co., "Pony Express," 197

Welsbach burner, invention of, 126

Western Union Telegraph Co.:
Agreement with Bell Telephone Company, 229
Consolidation with rival companies resulting in name, 196
First dividend, 1857, 196
First headquarters, 195
Growth in first fifteen years, 203
Legal battle with Bell Telephone Company, 229
Opposition to telephone, 224, 227
Original name of, 195
Present magnitude, 203
Rights acquired to Morse patents, 196
Telephone transmitter produced by Thos. A. Edison for, 227

Westinghouse, George, development of A.C. system of electric generation and transmission, 153

Westinghouse Electric & Mfg. Co., manufacturers of reaction steam turbines, 162

Wheeling, early prosperity of, 22

Wheeler, Granville, England, with Stephen Gray, early experimenter with electric telegraph, 190

Wilson, President, American telephone headquarters in Paris, 235

Winsor, Frederick Albert, early experimenter with gas, 118

Wire chief, telephone, 251

Wireless (*see* Radio)

Worcester, Mass., early railroad, 36

World's Columbian Exposition at Chicago, 1893, electric lighting at, 155

Z

Zoning of Cities, 279

TECHNOLOGY AND SOCIETY

An Arno Press Collection

Ardrey, R[obert] L. **American Agricultural Implements.** In two parts. 1894

Arnold, Horace Lucien and Fay Leone Faurote. **Ford Methods and the Ford Shops.** 1915

Baron, Stanley [Wade]. **Brewed in America:** A History of Beer and Ale in the United States. 1962

Bathe, Greville and Dorothy. **Oliver Evans:** A Chronicle of Early American Engineering. 1935

Bendure, Zelma and Gladys Pfeiffer. **America's Fabrics:** Origin and History, Manufacture, Characteristics and Uses. 1946

Bichowsky, F. Russell. **Industrial Research.** 1942

Bigelow, Jacob. **The Useful Arts:** Considered in Connexion with the Applications of Science. 1840. Two volumes in one

Birkmire, William H. **Skeleton Construction in Buildings.** 1894

Boyd, T[homas] A[lvin]. **Professional Amateur:** The Biography of Charles Franklin Kettering. 1957

Bright, Arthur A[aron], Jr. **The Electric-Lamp Industry:** Technological Change and Economic Development from 1800 to 1947. 1949

Bruce, Alfred and Harold Sandbank. **The History of Prefabrication.** 1943

Carr, Charles C[arl]. **Alcoa, An American Enterprise.** 1952

Cooley, Mortimer E. **Scientific Blacksmith.** 1947

Davis, Charles Thomas. **The Manufacture of Paper.** 1886

Deane, Samuel. **The New-England Farmer,** or Georgical Dictionary. 1822

Dyer, Henry. **The Evolution of Industry.** 1895

Epstein, Ralph C. **The Automobile Industry:** Its Economic and Commercial Development. 1928

Ericsson, Henry. **Sixty Years a Builder:** The Autobiography of Henry Ericsson. 1942

Evans, Oliver. **The Young Mill-Wright and Miller's Guide.** 1850

Ewbank, Thomas. **A Descriptive and Historical Account of Hydraulic and Other Machines for Raising Water,** Ancient and Modern. 1842

Field, Henry M. **The Story of the Atlantic Telegraph.** 1893

Fleming, A. P. M. **Industrial Research in the United States of America.** 1917

Van Gelder, Arthur Pine and Hugo Schlatter. **History of the Explosives Industry in America.** 1927

Hall, Courtney Robert. **History of American Industrial Science.** 1954

Hungerford, Edward. **The Story of Public Utilities.** 1928

Hungerford, Edward. **The Story of the Baltimore and Ohio Railroad, 1827-1927.** 1928

Husband, Joseph. **The Story of the Pullman Car.** 1917

Ingels, Margaret. **Willis Haviland Carrier, Father of Air Conditioning.** 1952

Kingsbury, J[ohn] E. **The Telephone and Telephone Exchanges:** Their Invention and Development. 1915

Labatut, Jean and Wheaton J. Lane, eds. **Highways in Our National Life:** A Symposium. 1950

Lathrop, William G[ilbert]. **The Brass Industry in the United States.** 1926

Lesley, Robert W., John B. Lober and George S. Bartlett. **History of the Portland Cement Industry in the United States.** 1924

Marcosson, Isaac F. **Wherever Men Trade:** The Romance of the Cash Register. 1945

Miles, Henry A[dolphus]. **Lowell, As It Was, and As It Is.** 1845

Morison, George S. **The New Epoch:** As Developed by the Manufacture of Power. 1903

Olmsted, Denison. **Memoir of Eli Whitney, Esq.** 1846

Passer, Harold C. **The Electrical Manufacturers, 1875-1900.** 1953

Prescott, George B[artlett]. **Bell's Electric Speaking Telephone.** 1884

Prout, Henry G. **A Life of George Westinghouse.** 1921

Randall, Frank A. **History of the Development of Building Construction in Chicago.** 1949

Riley, John J. **A History of the American Soft Drink Industry:** Bottled Carbonated Beverages, 1807-1957. 1958

Salem, F[rederick] W[illiam]. **Beer, Its History and Its Economic Value as a National Beverage.** 1880

Smith, Edgar F. **Chemistry in America.** 1914

Steinman, D[avid] B[arnard]. **The Builders of the Bridge:** The Story of John Roebling and His Son. 1950

Taylor, F[rank] Sherwood. **A History of Industrial Chemistry.** 1957

Technological Trends and National Policy, Including the Social Implications of New Inventions. Report of the Subcommittee on Technology to the National Resources Committee. 1937

Thompson, John S. **History of Composing Machines.** 1904

Thompson, Robert Luther. **Wiring a Continent:** The History of the Telegraph Industry in the United States, 1832-1866. 1947

Tilley, Nannie May. **The Bright-Tobacco Industry, 1860-1929.** 1948

Tooker, Elva. **Nathan Trotter:** Philadelphia Merchant, 1787-1853. 1955

Turck, J. A. V. **Origin of Modern Calculating Machines.** 1921

Tyler, David Budlong. **Steam Conquers the Atlantic.** 1939

Wheeler, Gervase. **Homes for the People,** In Suburb and Country. 1855